Transmitting Mishnah

Departing from the conventional view of mishnaic transmission as mindless rote memorization, *Transmitting Mishnah* reveals how multifaceted the process of passing on oral tradition was in antiquity. Taking advantage of the recently burgeoning field of orality studies, Elizabeth Shanks Alexander develops a model of transmission that is both active and constructive. Proceeding by means of intensive readings of passages from tractate Shevuot and its talmudic commentaries, Alexander alerts us to the fact that transmitters and handlers of mishnaic text crafted both the vagaries of expression and its received meanings. She illustrates how the authority of the Mishnah grew as the result of the sustained attention of a devoted community of readers and students. She also identifies the study practices and habits of analysis that were cultivated by oral performance and shows how they were passed on in tandem with the verbal contents of the Mishnah, thereby influencing how the text was received and understood.

Elizabeth Shanks Alexander received her Ph.D. from Yale University in 1998. She has taught at Haverford College and Smith College, and she is currently an assistant professor at the University of Virginia. She received an NEH summer grant to work on this book.

Transmitting Mishnah

The Shaping Influence of Oral Tradition

Elizabeth Shanks Alexander
University of Virginia

CAMBRIDGE
UNIVERSITY PRESS

CAMBRIDGE UNIVERSITY PRESS
Cambridge, New York, Melbourne, Madrid, Cape Town, Singapore, São Paulo, Delhi

Cambridge University Press
The Edinburgh Building, Cambridge CB2 8RU, UK

Published in the United States of America by Cambridge University Press, New York

www.cambridge.org
Information on this title: www.cambridge.org/9780521104623

First published 2006
This digitally printed version 2009

A catalogue record for this publication is available from the British Library

Library of Congress Cataloguing in Publication data

Alexander, Elizabeth Shanks, 1967–
Transmitting Mishnah : the shaping influence of oral tradition /
Elizabeth Shanks Alexander.
p. cm.
Includes bibliographical references.
ISBN-10: 0-521-85750-3 (hardcover)
ISBN-13: 978-0-521-85750-5
1. Mishnah – Criticism, interpretation, etc. 2. Tradition (Judaism) 3. Oral communication – Religious aspects – Judaism. 4. Jewish law – Interpretation and construction – History – To 1500. 5. Mishnah. Shevu'ot – Criticism, interpretation, etc. I. Title.
BM497.85.A44 2006
296.1′2306–dc22 2005026195

ISBN 978-0-521-85750-5 hardback
ISBN 978-0-521-10462-3 paperback

For Avraham Dov Baer ben Avraham

Contents

Acknowledgments

This book is based on research I did for my doctoral dissertation at Yale University. A huge debt of gratitude goes to my two mentors there whose intellectual gifts make their mark on my work in countless ways every day. Steven Fraade introduced me to the idea of reading texts for their performative effect, an approach that is fundamental to my work in this book. Christine Hayes gave me a vocabulary and set of descriptive categories for discussing rabbinic hermeneutics, thereby enriching my understanding of how rabbinic intellectual culture was generated. Both were generous teachers, making my years at Yale a rich and rewarding experience. Both inspire me with the rigorous approach they take in their own scholarship; they remain powerful role models for me.

I must also thank Martin Jaffee, without whom this book simply would not have come about. When I was a doctoral student just starting to work on my dissertation, a conference on midrash brought Professor Jaffee to New Haven. I took the opportunity to make an appointment with him to share ideas about my project. The feedback he gave me has been fundamental to everything I have done since. I recall sitting with him in Claire's Kosher Cafe, as he told me that my thinking about the relationship between the Mishnah and the Tosephta was all wrong. He suggested I do a little reading in the area of orality studies, and he gave me a bibliography. From that simple redirection has come all that follows. This book, simply stated, is an exploration of how the insights of orality studies open up new ways of thinking about the relationship not only between the Mishnah and the Tosephta but also between the Mishnah and the Talmuds, and about what the Mishnah is at its core. Ever since that auspicious moment, Professor Jaffee has been generous with his time in support of my learning. I am extraordinarily grateful for his kind assistance and willingness to engage me so extensively, and even more important, for my good fortune that he invested so much energy mastering a field that has proved so fruitful to my work. I recently had the opportunity to reread his book *Torah in the Mouth* while working on an article, and I was impressed by how many new things I saw in what was, at least, my tenth complete reading of the book. Through conversations and his writings he has opened up avenues of insight that would otherwise be unavailable. I thank him.

Today, as in antiquity, the discussion of rabbinic wisdom and tradition often becomes an occasion to form social bonds. I would like to thank Hindy Najman and Jonathan Schofer, whose intellectual companionship has infinitely broadened my horizons. Both read significant parts of the manuscript and offered valuable feedback, but equally (and maybe even more) importantly, both were conversation partners in whose presence the ideas discussed here (and others!) came to life so that they could be interrogated and invigorated. I must also thank my dear friend and long-term study partner Rachel Cousineau. Together we read and studied more than a third of the Mishnah, between pregnancies and babies. Throughout the course of our study I tested many of the hypotheses in this book, and I thank Rachel for allowing our study to open up to the world of scholarship. Daniel Schreiber and Alena Nye-Knutson were also valuable study partners for assorted tractates of the Mishnah.

At various points in the writing I received valuable feedback from readers who generously gave of their time. I would like to thank Shaye

Cohen and the anonymous reader from the Brown Judaic Studies Series who read a very early version of this book. They offered insightful and intelligent suggestions, which ultimately led to a complete restructuring. Jessica Feldman, Harry Gamble, Peter Ochs, Robert Wilken, and the anonymous readers from Cambridge University Press all read the manuscript in its entirety and made comments that led to substantive improvement. Reader B deserves a special note of thanks for reading the manuscript with painstaking care and attention, not once but twice! I, of course, accept full responsibility for any errors or weaknesses that remain. I am grateful that they caught as many problems as they did and directed me to elegant solutions.

The Department of Religious Studies at the University of Virginia has proved a very collegial environment in which to work. My colleagues create an atmosphere of stimulating and respectful conversation in which I have flourished. I thank everyone – faculty, students, and staff – for providing an environment conducive to productive work. I would especially like to thank the students of my seminar in the spring of 2002, entitled "Orality, Tradition and Religion," who shared in the intellectual development of many of the ideas in this book. The larger university has also proved very supportive. I would like to thank the Dean's Office for generous grants that enabled me to work on this book during the summers of 2000, 2001, 2003, and 2004. The National Endowment for the Humanities provided generous support during the summer of 2002. A grant from the Yad HaNadiv/Beracha Foundation enabled me to do the final revisions in Jerusalem in the fall of 2004.

Thanks also for the support of Andy Beck, Phyllis Berk, Janis Bolster, and others at Cambridge University Press whose interest and faith in the project, as well as hard work on its behalf, helped to provide a publishing venue.

Chapter 3 began its life as an article entitled "Casuistic Elements in Mishnaic Law: Examples from M. Shevu'ot." I extend my gratitude to the *Jewish Studies Quarterly* for permission to reprint substantial portions of that article in this context.

Finally, I would like to thank my family. Their abundant love anchors me in all that I do. I thank my father, Hershel Shanks, whose embrace of vigorous debate and hard work inspires me and who taught me from a very young age not to be afraid of criticism. I thank my mother, Judith Shanks, for being a constant presence in the life of my young family. She has offered extraordinary physical and emotional support as we navigate the complexities and challenges of daily life. I thank my sister, Julia Shanks, for her companionship and friendship. My husband, Drew Alexander, has been a source of constant and unfailing support. He has had faith in the value of this project since its inception and in my ability to bring it to fruition. He has generously given of his time as a reader and talked with me about how to resolve various challenges that arose in the process of writing. Whenever I reached an impasse, I could always count on his insight to help me find a way through. His intellectual and emotional companionship grounds me to such an extent that I cannot imagine tackling a project like this without it. Finally, I would like to thank my children, Charlie and Nancy, who as of yet understand nothing of the Mishnah and Talmud but whose eager faces reveal a glimpse of the next generation of Torah learning.

For each of these blessings, I thank the Creator.

Elizabeth Shanks Alexander
Jerusalem, Israel
17 Tevet 5765
December 29, 2004

Abbreviations

b.	Bavli
BB	Baba Batra
Bekh.	Bekhorot
Bik.	Bikkurim
BK	Baba Kamma
BM	Baba Metzia
Dem.	Demai
Deut.	Deuteronomy
Dt.	Deuteronomy
Eruv.	Eruvin
Ex.	Exodus
Ez.	Ezekiel
Gen.	Genesis
Git.	Gittin
Hal.	Hallah
HJP	*Hellenism in Jewish Palestine*
Hor.	Horayot
IRSG	*Iggeret Rav Sherira Gaon*
ITL	*Introduction to Tannaitic Literature*
ITM	*Introduction to the Text of the Mishnah*

Ker.	Keritot
Ket.	Ketubot
Kid.	Kiddushin
Lev.	Leviticus
Mak.	Makkot
Maas.	Maaserot
m.	Mishnah
Meg.	Megillah
Ned.	Nedarim
San.	Sanhedrin
Shab.	Shabbat
Shev.	Shevuot
Shevi.	Shevi`it
Shevu.	Shevuot
Sif.	Sifre
t.	Tosephta
Ter.	Terumot
y.	Yerushalmi
YBC	Yale Babylonian Collection
Yeb.	Yebamot
Zev.	Zevahim

Introduction

The Mishnah is an ancient book of case law[1] (c. 200 C.E.) that provides a set of norms that have defined Jewish communal life in the ritual, civil, and criminal domains for centuries.[2] Though many of its

[1] The issue of whether the Mishnah was intended to function as a law code or academic handbook for young rabbinic scholars has long been contested among academic scholars of rabbinics. Arguing on behalf of the Mishnah as law code are: Zacharias Frankel, *Methods of the Mishnah* (Hebrew) (Tel Aviv: Sinai, 1959 [repr.]), 224–27; J. N. Epstein, *Introduction to Tannaitic Literature: Mishnah, Tosephta, and Halakhic Midrashim* (Hebrew), ed. E. Z. Melamed (Jerusalem: Magnes Press, 1957), 225–26; Alexander Guttman, *Rabbinic Judaism in the Making* (Detroit: Wayne State University Press, 1970), 240–44; and Menachem Elon, *Jewish Law: History, Sources, Principles* (Ha-Mishpat Ha-Ivri), vol. 3, trans. Bernard Auerbach and Melvin J. Sykes (Philadelphia: Jewish Publication Society, 1994), 1057–78. Arguing in favor of Mishnah as pedagogical handbook are Abraham Goldberg, "The Mishnah – A Study Book of Halakha," in *The Literature of the Sages*, ed. Shmuel Safrai (Philadelphia: Fortress Press, 1987), 211–51; and Robert Goldenberg, "The Talmud," in *Back to the Sources: Reading the Classic Jewish Texts*, ed. Barry Holtz (New York: Simon and Schuster, 1984), 133–34. An intermediate view of the Mishnah as a compiled collection of opinions can be found in Chanoch Albeck, *Introduction to the Mishnah* (Hebrew) (Jerusalem, Tel Aviv: Dvir, 1959), 105–7.

[2] As discussed in n. 1, different views exist as to whether the Mishnah was compiled for the purposes of serving as a law code. What cannot be disputed is that the Mishnah did eventually come to be used as a law code. See an interesting discussion of the amoraic seeds of the activity of using the Mishnah as a code by crafting rules for

prescriptions build on and presume biblical law, it goes far beyond the Bible in its scope, depth, and detail. Its appearance marked a new achievement in the history of systematizing Jewish law, creating a paradigm and model for the other important codes of Jewish law that would follow in the Middle Ages. In the years following its compilation (traditionally attributed to R. Judah the Patriarch),[3] the Mishnah became the central text in the rabbinic curriculum of sacred study, occupying a place of honor alongside the Hebrew Bible. Sages in both Palestine and Babylonia engaged in extensive conversations about the Mishnah's meanings and intentions that often ended with tangents in related and not-so-related directions. These discussions centered on the Mishnah eventually produced a literary manifestation. The two Talmuds (Palestinian, c. 370–425 C.E., and Babylonian, c. 600 C.E.), which record the accumulated wisdom of the rabbinic

negotiating among the diverse rulings in Dov Zlotnick, *The Iron Pillar – Mishnah: Redaction, Form, and Intent* (Jerusalem: KTAV Publishing House, 1988), 194–217. The prescriptions, norms and legal categories outlined in the Mishnah are the basis for all later codes.

[3] The traditional attribution is based on the honorific title "Rabbi" (taken to refer to R. Judah the Patriach) used within the Mishnah itself and a cryptic statement in the Babylonian Talmud that links R. Judah (along with R. Natan) with the end of mishnaic teaching: "Rabbi and R. Natan represent the end of mishnaic teaching; Rav Ashi and Ravina represent the end of amoraic teaching" (b. BM 86a). The statement has been interpreted as linking R. Judah with the redaction of the Mishnah and R. Ashi and Ravina with the redaction of the *gemara* (the portion of the Talmuds that comments on the mishnaic text). The second half of this statement (the attribution of talmudic redaction) was refuted already in the 1930s. See Julius Kaplan, *The Redaction of the Babylonian Talmud* (New York: Bloch Publishing Company, 1933). It has always seemed somewhat remarkable to me that the traditional attribution of the mishnaic composition has been maintained by the majority of scholars, while they have rejected the historical value of the other half of this obviously parallel statement. I generally agree with the skepticism expressed by Stemberger: "Nevertheless, M in its present shape cannot possibly come from Rabbi himself" (H. L. Strack and G. Stemberger, *Introduction to the Talmud and Midrash,* trans. Markus Bockmuehl [Minneapolis: Fortress Press, 1992], 149). Stemberger bases his skepticism on many of the same criteria that were central to Kaplan's dismantling of the traditional attribution of the Bavli to Rav Ashi and Ravina. Jacob Neusner laments the strong impact of the traditional perspective on modern scholarship on the Mishnah. See Jacob Neusner, *The Modern Study of the Mishnah* (Leiden: E. J. Brill, 1973), xii–xx.

movement (c. 80–600 C.E.), were organized as commentaries around the skeletal structure of the Mishnah. Judaism as we know it today is essentially a product of the talmudic world, from which its fundamental beliefs and rituals derive. The influence of the Mishnah, then, has been profound. One might well ask what it was about this document, which on the face of it appears to be a dry collection of arcane legal materials, that warranted its place of privilege as the foundational document of rabbinic Judaism. While the answer to that question depends in part on the document's content, this book seeks an understanding of how the circumstances of being transmitted and studied orally helped establish the centrality and importance of the Mishnah. Central to the investigation is the view that the ancient handlers, students, and transmitters of mishnaic tradition were not passive agents conveying an established or already authoritative tradition; rather, they were active shapers of what the Mishnah was in the process of becoming.

My interest in mishnaic transmission derives from the Mishnah's traditional association with orality. Within a hundred years or so of the Mishnah's appearance, the ever-growing corpus of rabbinic teachings (of which the Mishnah was but one, albeit significant, part) came to be known as "Oral Torah." The appellation "Torah" indicated that this body of teachings was taken to be divine instruction, and the specification "Oral" distinguished it from the other main body of divine instruction, namely, "Written Torah." Whereas the Written Torah was etched in stone and fixed for eternity in the text of the Hebrew Bible, the Oral Torah of the rabbis was unfolded in an ongoing manner through debate, dialogue, and argumentation.[4] In another way of thinking about the relationship between the two, the Oral Torah provided a much-needed and valuable interpretation of the cryptic but weighty words of the Written Torah. The designation of the two Torahs

[4] A valuable elaboration of the distinctive qualities evoked by the appellation "Oral Torah" can be found in Shmuel Safrai, "Oral Tora," in *The Literature of the Sages*, ed. Shmuel Safrai (Philadelphia: Fortress Press, 1987), 35–120.

as "oral" and "written" was also meant to indicate something about the medium of their initial revelation. Whereas the words of the Written Torah were inscribed on the tablets, the words of the Oral Torah were conveyed from God to Moses by word of mouth. Furthermore, the respective designations "oral" and "written" were taken to be directives as to how the two bodies of material should be transmitted.[5] In the words of R. Yehudah b. Nahmani: "Words that have been received in writing, one is not permitted to recite by word of mouth; words that have been received by word of mouth, one is not permited to recite from a written exemplar" (b. Git. 60b, b. Tem. 14b; see also p. Meg. 4:1, 76d). In other words, Oral Torah should be transmitted orally, Written Torah from a written exemplar.

The prescription that texts of Oral Torah be transmitted using exclusively oral techniques has generated much scholarly interest among those who study the Mishnah, which stands out within the rabbinic corpus as a document particularly well suited to oral transmission. Talmudic texts describe a functionary of the rabbinic academy known as the "tanna," whose job it was to recite mishnaic traditions from memory.[6] In addition, the ubiquitous presence of parallelism and

[5] Scholars have long debated the question of whether the traditional materials that eventually came to be known as Oral Torah were in fact transmitted using exclusively oral techniques or if scribal techniques were also involved. See my article "The Orality of Rabbinic Writing," in *Cambridge Companion to Rabbinic Literature,* ed. Martin S. Jaffee and Charlotte E. Fonrobert (New York: Cambridge University Press, forthcoming). In my own work I follow the conclusions of Martin S. Jaffee, who suggests that although the rabbis used scribal techniques to record their teachings, they placed a high premium upon the social setting in which the texts were brought to life in an oral exchange between sage and disciple. See Martin S. Jaffee, *Torah in the Mouth: Writing and Oral Tradition in Palestinian Judaism, 200* BCE–400 CE (New York: Oxford University Press, 2001).

[6] J. N. Epstein provides a thoroughgoing review of the ancient evidence (both Jewish and non-Jewish) for how the tanna performed his job. See J. N. Epstein, *Introduction to the Text of the Mishnah* (Hebrew), 3d ed. (Jerusalem and Tel Aviv: Magnes Press and Dvir, 2000), 673–91 (hereafter referred to as *ITM*). See also the discussion in Saul Lieberman, "The Publication of the *Mishnah,*" in *Hellenism in Jewish Palestine* (New York: Jewish Theological Seminary of America, 1994), 88–90 (hereafter referred to as *HJP*).

repeating phrases that facilitate oral recitation provide further evidence for the fact that the Mishnah was, at some point, transmitted orally. It is ironic that although rabbinic tradition ascribes great importance to *orality* as the Mishnah's mode, scholars have most often used *literary* paradigms to understand the transmission of Mishnah in antiquity. Most significantly, scholars have assumed that transmission of Mishnah involved verbatim reproduction of a fixed text. When reconstructing ancient practices of oral mishnaic transmission, scholars commonly emphasize how the short, pithy style of the Mishnah facilitates rote memorization.[7] Implicit in the conventional view of oral performance of mishnaic materials is the notion that they were formulated with great precision, that they consisted of fixed verbal content, and that they were reproduced in a verbatim fashion from one performance to another. Recent scholarship on oral tradition in diverse cultures, however, calls into question the reflexive acceptance of these assumptions. Scholars have shown that oral transmission does not necessarily start with a fixed text, nor does oral performance necessarily aim for verbatim reproduction. Notably, the work of Albert Lord has shown that the view of oral transmission as verbatim reproduction of a fixed text is only possible in the world of print, where literary copies make such a result possible.[8] Lord argues that in orally based societies, there exist different ways of viewing textuality and transmission that do not depend on the notion of "text as fixed exemplar."

Inspired by Lord's perspectival shift toward a so-called oral view of textuality, this book seeks to expose visions of mishnaic textuality and transmission that have long been ignored by the dominant literary

[7] See, e.g., David Weiss Halivni, *Midrash, Mishnah and Gemara: The Jewish Predilection for Justifed Law* (Cambridge, MA: Harvard University Press, 1986), 38–65, esp. 52–54; Jacob Neusner, *Oral Tradition in Judaism: The Case of the Mishnah* (New York: Garland Publishing, Inc., 1987); Birger Gerhardsson, *Memory and Manuscript: Oral Tradition and Written Transmission in Rabbinic Judaism and Early Christianity* (Grand Rapids, MI: William B. Eerdmans Publishing Co., 1961, repr. 1998), 136–47; and Elon, *Jewish Law*, 1078.

[8] Generally, see Albert B. Lord, *The Singer of Tales*, 2d ed., ed. Stephen Mitchell and Gregory Nagy (Cambridge, MA, and London: Harvard University Press, 2000).

lens. The so-called oral view of textuality, which will be discussed at length in the next section, is characterized by an appreciation of the multiplicity and fluidity of textual forms. Rather than seeing texts as fixed and stable and labeling variants as deviants from an original, the oral view recognizes the inherent fluidity of texts in oral settings. It notes the importance of the performer in bringing the text to life, and it finds coherence and continuity in structural frameworks rather than in linear sequences of words.

I have found that the so-called oral conceptual lens leads us to two important insights about mishnaic textuality and transmission. The first concerns the Mishnah's authority. Traditional accounts suggest that the authority of the mishnaic text is a function of its literary form. The elegance of its precise formulation led to the Mishnah's immediate acceptance and widespread authority.[9] Other accounts point to particular features of the mishnaic text (like its suppression of the implicit biblical bases of the law or its straightforward, commanding voice) that boster its authority, additionally linking the Mishnah's authority to its literary form.[10] Attention to the oral conceptual lens, however, alerts us to the constructed character of the Mishnah's authority. Attending to more fluid views of textuality exposes the likelihood that the Mishnah's earliest transmitters did not understand mishnaic textuality to be fixed. The absence of fixity in the earliest stages of its transmission undermines the idea that the Mishnah achieved an immediate authoritative status based on its fixed literary form. The oral conceptual lens helps

9 See the traditional account of rabbinic historian R. Sherira Gaon (eleventh century): B. M. Lewin, ed., *Iggeret Rav Sherira Gaon: The Spanish Text and the French Text* (Haifa: Itzokofsky, 1921), 28–30 (hereafter referred to as *IRSG*).

10 Neusner argues that Mishnaic authority emerges in conjunction with the suppression of the implicit biblical bases of its norms. By asserting the commands in a straightforward sense, without reference to biblical scripture, the Mishnah co-opts the authority of scripture. See Jacob Neusner, *Judaism: The Evidence of the Mishnah* (Atlanta: Scholars Press, 1988), 217–23. While noting the Mishnah's reticence about its biblical origins, Halivni also stresses that the Mishnah's authority is a function of its apodictic form, which he defines as "categorical pronouncements" (7). Halivni, *Midrash, Mishnah and Gemara,* 40, 54–59, 64–65.

us appreciate the role that the receiving audience or readership played in constructing the view of mishnaic authority as rooted in its textual fixity. Rather than seeing mishnaic authority as an intrinsic feature of the Mishnah's literary form, we can see it as the result of a devoted community's reading and interpretive practices. Returning to a central curricular text over and over again, a devoted community of students and readers came to *attribute significance to a perceived fixity and precision.* The oral conceptual lens helps us appreciate that the Mishnah's authoritative status is not the de facto effect of its literary form but the constructed work of its transmitters (not necessarily even conscious), over the course of several generations.

The second major insight that follows from relaxing our notions of textual fixity in ancient mishnaic transmission concerns the analytic aspect of tranmission. Traditional accounts suggest that oral performance of mishnaic materials consisted primarily of rote memorization and *excluded the possibility of intense analytic engagement* of the materials.[11] Lord's insight that oral texts are not fixed, however, suggests that the process of reproducing a text from one performance

11 See, e.g., Goldberg, "The Mishnah," 212–13. See also the discussion of Saul Lieberman, *Hellenism in Jewish Palestine,* 88. Zlotnick, *The Iron Pillar,* 14–15, draws on Lieberman's characterization. The perceived mutual exclusivity between rote memorization and discursive analysis is fundamental to views that describe mishnaic form as a succinct distillation of wide-ranging analytic discussions, arguments, and debates. See, e.g., Halivni, *Midrash, Mishnah and Gemara,* 2–3, and Gerhardsson, *Memory and Manuscript,* 136–48. Scholars have presumed that a similar mutual exclusivity between rote memorization and discursive analysis is useful in distinguishing between the transmissional life of *halakhah* and *aggadah.* Whereas halakhah necessitates precise formulation, aggadah can be more discursive and free-form. On this idea, see Gerhardsson, *Memory and Manuscript,* 96, 146–47; Jose Faur, *Golden Doves with Silver Dots: Semiotics and Textuality in Rabbinic Tradition* (Bloomington: Indiana University Press, 1986), 87; and Jacob Z. Lauterbach, "Midrash and Mishnah," in *Rabbinic Essays* (Cincinnati, OH: Hebrew Union College Press, 1915, repr. 1951), 182 ff. The dichotomy between rote memorization and discursive analysis also proves useful in characterizing tradition in the amoraic period. See Kaplan, *Redaction of the Babylonian Talmud,* 196–97, 220, 234; Hyman Klein, "Gemara and Sebara," *Jewish Quarterly Review* 38 (1947): 69, esp. n. 7, and 90; Halivni, *Midrash, Mishnah and Gemara,* 62–93; and David Kraemer, *The Mind of the Talmud: An Intellectual History of the Bavli* (New York and Oxford: Oxford University Press, 1990), 26–98.

to another is not an entirely passive one. Without a fixed exemplar, passive rote memorization is simply not possible. Instead, active intellectual engagement is required in order to reconstruct the text in each new performative context.[12] This insight proves central to the current study of ancient processes of transmitting Mishnah, which argues that transmission of mishnaic materials *did* include an analytic component. Transmission of Mishnah involved not only the conveyance of the verbal contents of the legal traditions but also, and equally as important, the cultivation of certain analytic habits with which to regard the legal cases recorded therein. Alongside the textual materials was a set of study practices that was as much a part of the mishnaic tradition as its content of legal prescriptions. The value of adopting the so-called oral conceptual lens, then, is that it allows us to see how much more active the transmissional process was than we generally have imagined. Transmitting mishnaic materials involved not only the conveyance of textual materials but also the crafting of their authority and the cultivation of intellectual habits through which to analyze and interpret them.

The basis for this book is a series of close readings from a single mishnaic tractate (tractate Shevuot, "Oaths"). Each reading is designed to illustrate a limited point or claim, but together they form a collage of evidence that supports the general description of mishnaic transmission provided earlier. The analysis does not claim to account for mishnaic texts in general; the conclusions pertain only to the texts examined. It is, however, my hope that the insights garnered from these close readings will prove useful in the study of other mishnaic texts. For myself, I have found that the conclusions reached here can

[12] In the epic oral poetry that Lord examines, the active intellectual engagement takes the form of recomposition each time the materials are performed. Lord, *The Singer of Tales*, 4–5, 13–29. My stress on the active analytic component of oral performance also reflects deep engagement with the work of Mary Carruthers. See Mary Carruthers, *The Book of Memory: A Study of Memory in Medieval Culture* (New York: Cambridge University Press, 1990), and Mary Carruthers, *The Craft of Thought: Meditation, Rhetoric and the Making of Images, 400–1200* (New York: Cambridge University Press, 1998), esp. 8–9.

be profitably transfered to other mishnaic texts. Although I often use the general term "Mishnah" in the course of my discussions, this usage is intended to refer only to the materials discussed from tractate Shevuot. This book also includes extensive discussions of the talmudic commentaries to m. Shevuot. The two talmudim (= y. and b. Shevuot, the Palestinian and Babylonian commentaries to the mishnaic tractate of Shevuot) contain extensive interpretive comments by subsequent generations of sages (c. 200–600) that were eventually woven into a complex interpretive and argumentational superstructure around the mishnaic text. I have found that the talmudic commentaries offer some of the best evidence available for how the mishnaic text was received, handled, and studied by subsequent generations after its consolidation and formalization. Though at times I refer to the "Talmud" or the "talmudic commentaries" or "talmudic sages," the reference should be understood as a reference to b. and y. Shevuot and the sages cited therein. My hope is that in recording the results of my close readings, others will find here an analytic tool that, while subjected to somewhat limited testing, nonetheless sheds light on other mishnaic texts and their related talmudic commentaries.

The Oral Conceptual Lens

The central insights informing this study come from the newly emerging field of orality studies.[13] Perhaps most seminal in opening up the

[13] For a variety of works attentive to the *medium* of textuality, see Milman Parry, *The Making of Homeric Verse: The Collected Papers of Milman Parry*, ed. Adam Parry (New York and Oxford: Oxford University Press, 1987); Lord, *The Singer of Tales*; Walter J. Ong, *Orality and Literacy: The Technologizing of the Word* (London and New York: Methuen & Co., 1982); Ruth Finnegan, *Oral Poetry: Its Nature, Significance and Social Context* (Bloomington: Indiana University Press, 1977); Ruth Finnegan, *Literacy and Orality: Studies in the Technology of Communication* (Oxford: Basil Blackwell, 1988); Brian Stock, *The Implications of Literacy: Written Language and Models of Interpretation in the Eleventh and Twelfth Centuries* (Princeton, NJ: Princeton University Press, 1983); John Miles Foley, *Immanent Art: From

scholarly community to an awareness of nonfixed conceptions of textuality has been the work of Albert Lord and his mentor, Milman Parry. Working at the intersection of classics and folklore, Lord devoted his great intellectual energy and creativity to completing the project begun by his teacher, Parry, and to drawing out its full implications. Parry, who was a classicist by training, submitted Homer's two great epic poems, the *Iliad* and the *Odyssey*, to detailed textual analysis with the goal of resolving long-standing questions concerning the compositional process that produced the great works.[14] His work confirmed the prevalence of repeated phrases, each of which he designated a "formula," concluding that they were "traditional" in nature, that is, generated and perpetuated by communally shared manipulative processes. He noted that different formulas had the same metrical values, which allowed them to be plugged interchangeably into the poems' hexametrical lines. These literary observations led him to a strikingly innovative theory about the compositional process underlying the Homeric epics: An oral poet had shuffled traditional formulas into the appropriate positions and thereby produced a classic age-old narrative in a traditional manner.[15] Such a method of poetic creation did not necessarily require innovation, but rather fluency in the corpus of traditional elements. In justifying this method of poetic creation as a valid artistic process, he explained, "one oral poet is better than another *not because* he has by himself found a striking new way of expressing his own thought, but because he has been better able to make use of the tradition. . . . The good singer wins his fame by his ease and versatility in handling a tradition which he knows more thoroughly than anyone

Structure to Meaning in Traditional Oral Epic (Bloomington: Indiana University Press, 1991); John Miles Foley, *The Singer of Tales in Performance* (Bloomington: Indiana University Press, 1995); and Marshall McLuhan, *The Gutenberg Galaxy: The Making of Typographic Man* (London: Routledge and Kegan Paul, 1962). Also very formative has been the work of Mary Carruthers. See her *Book of Memory* and *Craft of Thought*.

14 See the useful summary of these issues in Lord, *The Singer of Tales*, 3–12.

15 See Parry's collected works in Parry, *The Making of Homeric Verse*, esp. 1–191, 266–364.

else."[16] As his career progressed, Parry identified other traditional elements (thematic units and overarching narrative structure) that the oral poets behind the Homeric poems would have used in their composition. In its most developed form, Parry's model of Homeric composition suggested that illiterate poets composed by means of established phraseology (formulas), which they worked into traditional thematic units (themes) to construct a full-form replica of a traditional narrative. The idea that oral composition manipulates fixed formula into established superstructures offers a way to view textual continuity that is neither linear nor literal.[17]

Parry's model of oral composition in Homer was partly creative conjecture, though it did draw on folklorists' accounts of living poetic traditions. Ultimately, however, Parry found it necessary to analyze a living tradition of oral poetic performance himself. Between 1933 and 1935, he made two trips to Yugoslavia to record and analyze the living tradition of illiterate storytellers (*guslari*) who performed a tradition of epic poetry that closely resembled the Homeric epics. Parry's student and co-worker Albert Lord accompanied him on the second and longer of the two trips.

When Parry died in 1935 as the result of a tragic accident, Lord took it upon himself to bring to fruition the scholarly agenda charted out by his mentor. Whereas Parry's scholarship had begun with the classical epic and turned toward contemporary oral performers, Lord's movement was in the opposite direction. His guiding insights came from analysis of the live tradition of storytelling for which he had extensive documentation in the form of the recordings he and Parry had made together. With Lord's analyses of the live oral tradition, Parry's intuitions about the role of formula and theme in epic composition in a strictly oral context were confirmed.

16 Parry, *The Making of Homeric Verse*, 334–35.

17 Mary Carruthers also has a very useful discussion of medieval memory, which presumes that text production results from the manipulation of bits of data. Only in the context of performance are the raw bits of data rendered into usable form as knowledge. See Carruthers, *Book of Memory*, 16–45.

Lord's masterful analysis of the tradition of oral performance that he found in rural Yugoslavia included two components. On one hand, he executed detailed textual analysis of the transcripts of the oral performances, identifying the formulas and themes used in that particular tradition of oral performance. On the other hand, he studied extensive interviews with the poets for evidence of how *they* conceptualized their poetry and the act of performance. The interviews enabled Lord to get into the minds of the illiterate poets who performed without the aid of written notes and to gain insight into how they understood what they were doing. He could confirm the theoretical assumptions Parry had made about the process of oral composition by illiterates, assumptions which he himself had further developed on the basis of textual analyses of the transcripts. Lord's dual perspective (considering both the "objective" textual evidence and the "subjective" point of view of the performer) helped him draw out arguments that had merely been implicit in Parry's work.

Lord's most important insights derive from his ability to think outside the framework of his own literate culture. From his detailed analysis, he came to believe that most literates improperly understand oral phenomena, for they intuitively absorb many conceptual biases associated with a literate society and apply them unconsciously to the oral phenomena. In trying to expose how this bias affects one's understanding of textual transmission, he writes the following:

> It is true that the oral epic is transmitted by word of mouth from one singer to another, but if we understand thereby the transmission of a *fixed text* [emphasis added] . . . with all the natural errors of lapse of memory and exaggeration and distortion, then we do not fully comprehend what oral transmission of oral epic is. [In] oral poetry . . . oral learning, oral composition and oral transmission almost merge; they seem to be different facets of the same process.[18]

[18] Lord, *The Singer of Tales*, 5.

Two fundamental and complementary moves emerge in his argument here. First, Lord exposes the conceptual bias involved in thinking of oral transmission in terms of reproducing a fixed exemplar. Only someone from a literate society where exact reproduction is technologically possible and confirmable would assume that oral transmission preserves text in a verbatim fashion. Elsewhere, Lord demonstrates that singers speak of "word for word" similitude even when transcripts reveal diverse kinds of variations among performances.[19] He suggests that the notion of verbatim reproduction as a measure of faithful transmission is only possible when access to a written exemplar is available.[20] In his second important move, Lord seeks to correct this literary bias by offering an alternate way to think of reproducing text from performance to performance and from singer to singer. He proposes that oral transmission be understood in terms of *serial events of renewed composition.*[21] Building on Parry's isolation of the role of formula and theme in Homeric composition, Lord identifies the technology that makes possible rapid-fire composition in the context of performance. Traditional elements (or formulas) function as compositional building blocks; these are in turn worked into traditional thematic units to narrate traditional narrative structures.[22] The oral performer does not need original insight to compose anew. Instead, his success depends on his *fluidity* in the repertoire of tradition.[23] Reproduction of the text from one performance to the next is an engaging, rather than passive, process; it requires the performer's active understanding and mastery of his subject matter.

19 See Lord, *The Singer of Tales,* 27–29.

20 For example, he notes that the presence of the storybooks among literate storytellers changes the way the song is learned. Lord, *The Singer of Tales,* 20–23.

21 As when he writes, for example, "for the oral poet, the moment of composition is the performance" (13).

22 Lord, *The Singer of Tales,* 22–27.

23 See also Mary Carruthers, who notes that oral performance is best accomplished when certain basic building blocks of a speech have already been almagamated. Like Lord, she notes that the skilled performer is one who can effortlessly work predetermined elements into meaningful configurations, rather than the one who recites a fixed exemplar by rote memorization. See Carruthers, *Craft of Thought,* 8–12.

These two insights – that oral transmission need not presume a fixed exemplar and that oral transmission involves an active mastery of the subject matter – are fundamental to the reconstruction of mishnaic transmission attempted in this book. They provide a conceptual orientation that allows us to imagine the transmissional life of the mishnaic text within rabbinic academic circles in profound new ways. Before we turn our attention back to the Mishnah, however, it is important to consider some of the caveats that have been raised with respect to the Parry-Lord theory of oral composition, as it has come to be known.

Caveats to the Theory of Oral Composition

Parry and Lord's scholarly genius consisted in being able to imagine a world of oral tradition that lay far beyond their experience in literate society. Lord especially did much to mitigate against the conceptual biases that interfere with accurate apprehension of oral phenomena. He posited a conceptual orientation associated with orality that parallels the conceptual bias he recognized as implicit in literate society. In the conceptual orientation of orality, texts have an inherent multiformity, with no single version holding a privileged position over the others as an "original" or "authentic" version. Furthermore, in the conceptual orientation of orality, texts are not distinct from performance. Textual transmission requires and is constituted by renewed events of textual creation. Lord's corrections, however, were based on a stark analytical distinction between "orality" and "literacy," and between texts produced by literary, as opposed to oral, compositional processes. In considering the question of whether or not there is such a thing as a "transitional text," Lord answered emphatically in the negative. He wrote that "the two techniques [oral and written composition] are, I submit, contradictory and mutually exclusive."[24] He likewise conjectured

[24] Lord, *The Singer of Tales*, 129.

that oral and literate societies conditioned altogether different ways of conceptualizing text. In ascribing the notion of a fixed exemplar to literate society and the notion of textual multiformity to oral society, he believed that he had identified with certainty "the difference between the oral way of thought and the written way."[25]

While the paradigm shift that Parry and Lord proposed by offering a new conceptual model for the theorization of oral phenomena has left an indelible mark on the study of oral tradtion, the so-called Great Divide between orality and literacy,[26] which they presumed, has been called into question by a number of scholars.[27] While it is useful to be able to adopt a nonliterary conceptual paradigm, it must be recognized that the "oral" and the "literary" interact in all kinds of ways.

Ruth Finnegan has made many important strides in nuancing the stark polarization of orality and literacy that characterized the Parry-Lord theory of oral composition.[28] She argues strongly against

[25] Lord, *The Singer of Tales,* 125.

[26] Ruth Finnegan, an articulate critic of the view that orality and literacy are mutually exclusive, has coined this useful phrase to describe the point of view she rejects. See Ruth Finnegan, "Literacy vs. Non–Literacy: The Great Divide?" in *Modes of Thought: Essays on Thinking in Western and Non-Western Societies,* ed. Robin Horton and Ruth Finnegan (London: Faber and Faber, 1973), 112–44.

[27] John Miles Foley has contributed a number of terminological distinctions that have helped move the scholarly discussion away from stark polarization in the treatment of oral and literary phenomena. Foley suggests that one speak of oral and literary *registers* as a way of minimizing absolutism in the description of oral and literary qualities. This vocabulary greatly aids in developing models of interpenetration. It becomes possible to speak of an "oral register" even when a text appears in written format. In a similar vein, he distinguishes between *actual* oral texts, i.e., those performed in live settings, and *oral-derived* texts, which display many traits of oral composition, but which reach their current audiences in written form. Such a designation allows us "to maintain the perspectives initiated by Parry and Lord" (163) concerning the role of oral compositional techniques in the genesis of texts, while still "allowing the possibility that writing played a role in the transmission or even in the creation of the [texts] as we know them" (163). See John Miles Foley, "Oral Tradition and Its Implications," in *A New Companion to Homer,* ed. Ian Morris and Barry Powell (New York: Brill, 1997), 146–73.

[28] See generally Finnegan, *Oral Poetry,* esp. 52–87, for her discussion of the theory of oral composition, and Finnegan, *Literacy and Orality.* A comparable critique can be

"a clear-cut differentiation between oral and written literature,"[29] and suggests instead "that the oral/written distinction, so far as it exists, is more like a continuum (or perhaps a complex set of continuums) than a sharp break between two separate categories."[30] Her conclusions follow from a consideration of diverse manifestations of oral poetry. While finding that the Parry-Lord model of multiformity adequately describes some traditions of oral poetry, it by no means accounts for all, as Lord seems to have implied that it could.[31] Finnegan demonstrates that in some traditions of oral poetry, the oral performers *do* think in terms of memorizing a fixed exemplar.[32] Such instances of oral poetry display features of both "oral" and "literary" traditions. In a further breakdown of the polarity, she documents instances in which written and oral media are used in various combinations in the distribution and transmission of "oral" poetry.[33] Finnegan's moderation of the polarity between "orality" and "literacy" aids in the interpretation of mishnaic texts, which display signs of *both* the oral and the literary ends of the continuum.[34] While the high density of formulaic language and dominant presence of mnemonic patterns provide evidence of an

found in Rosalind Thomas, *Literacy and Orality in Ancient Greece,* Key Themes in Ancient History (Cambridge: Cambridge University Press, 1992), 29–51.

29 Finnegan, *Oral Poetry,* 272.

30 Finnegan, *Oral Poetry,* 272.

31 See his essay on "Oral Poetry" in the *Encyclopedia of Poetry and Poetics,* 591, cited in Finnegan, *Oral Poetry,* 7.

32 See Finnegan, *Oral Poetry,* 75–84. Especially compelling for this reader was the discussion of composition and performance as distinct processes among Eskimo poets (81–83).

33 See Finnegan, *Oral Poetry,* 134–69. Especially compelling to this reader was her discussion of the use of oral and written media in the distribution of the broadside ballads (162–68).

34 Steven Fraade notes that rabbinic scholars have tended to presume a linear relationship between orality and writtenness in rabbinic texts. Whereas oral materials were understood to be popular and early, written materials were taken to be later and more elite. Following the work of Finnegan and others, Fraade critiques the notion of linear progression from orality to writtenness and suggests a more complex process of cycling between written texts and oral performance. See Steven D. Fraade, "Literary Composition and Oral Performance in Early Midrashim," *Oral Tradition* 14, no. 1 (March 1999): 33–36.

active oral life for the texts, the fact that the texts reach their current audiences in written form mitigates against a purist model of exclusive orality. As has already been argued by Martin Jaffee, a model of interpenetration between written and oral means of distribution and transmission along the lines described by Finnegan best accounts for the rabbinic evidence.[35]

Another important moderation of the Great Divide between orality and literacy has come from the work of Brian Stock. His analysis of the rise of literacy in medieval Europe demonstrates the complexity of interactions between orality and literacy in structuring human consciousness. Although he upholds Lord's basic insight that the shifts from orality to literacy affect "a fundamental process of categorization"[36] in the mind, he presents a more nuanced picture of the *interpenetration* of oral and written modalities. For example, he writes that "the type of orality for which the Middle Ages furnishes the most abundant evidence is verbal discourse which exists in *interdependence* with texts [emphasis added]."[37] Stock's work repeatedly emphasizes the fact that "the two [orality and literacy] *worked together* [emphasis added]."[38] Rather than suggesting that orality and literacy produce pure ways of thinking that operate in mutually exclusive societal settings, he focuses on the gray areas of overlap between oral and literary tendencies of conceptualization. Oral modes of conceptualization can be maintained even when writing is used, and literary or textualized modes of conceptualization can function even when the information is conveyed by word of mouth.[39] When we turn to mishnaic texts, it will likewise be important to allow for the fact that these texts did not necessarily circulate in purely oral or strictly literary academic settings.

35 See Martin S. Jaffee, "Writing and Rabbinic Oral Tradition: On Mishnaic Narrative, Lists and Mnemonics," *Journal of Jewish Philosophy and Thought* 4 (1994): 123–46, and more generally, see Martin S. Jaffee, *Torah in the Mouth.*

36 Stock, *The Implications of Literacy,* 4.

37 Stock, *The Implications of Literacy,* 8.

38 Stock, *The Implications of Literacy,* 12.

39 Stock, *The Implications of Literacy,* 12–87.

It is important to consider the possibility that the two modalities of engaging texts operated simultaneously and mutually impacted each other.

Keeping these considerations in mind, we are now in a position to return to the Mishnah. On the one hand, we want to bring the best of Parry and Lord to our inquiry and refrain from understanding oral phenomena according to strictly literary paradigms. On the other hand, we want to heed the qualifications of Finnegan, Stock, and others[40] and avoid overgeneralized claims about orality, recognizing that the "oral" and the "literary" interact and mutually impact each other. In short, we need to ask what vision of mishnaic textuality and transmission can best account for evidence from *both* the literary and the oral ends of the continuum.

The Literary and the Oral in Mishnah

Any attempt to reconstruct the transmissional life of m. Shevuot, or indeed any rabbinic text, must wrestle with the complexity of the evidence. The rabbinic "'conceit' of orality"[41] must be reconciled with the fact that the texts have been transmitted in written form since at least the thirteenth or fourteenth century (from which our earliest complete manuscripts derive), with the strong likelihood that written notes circulated even during the rabbinic period.[42] On one hand, the texts

40 Notably Thomas, *Literacy and Orality;* Foley, "Oral Tradition"; and Matei Calinescu, "Orality in Literacy: Some Historical Paradoxes of Reading," *Yale Journal of Criticism* 6, no. 2 (1993): 175–90.

41 This turn of phrase comes from Fraade, "Literary Composition and Oral Performance," 46.

42 See the discussion of the role that written notes played in the rabbinic academies in Lieberman, *HJP,* 87–88, and Epstein, *ITM,* 700–706. See also a commonly cited tradition that notes that R. Yohanan and R. Shimon b. Lakish used to study aggadah from a written text in spite of the official rabbinic position prohibiting the use of written texts in the study of Oral Torah (b. Git. 60a; b. Tem. 14b).

contain a high density of formulaic language and a number of recurring syntactical patterns that display sure evidence of oral recitation.[43] On the other hand, the fact that the Mishnah was eventually transmitted in written format means that at some point, oral learning interfaced with written media.[44] How are we to make sense of diverse evidence that leads to conflicting conclusions concerning the "orality" of m. Shevuot?

The prevailing tendency among scholars has been to assume that mishnaic orality looked very much like the texts that were later produced. While written notes might have existed during this early period, only the oral version would have been authoritative. Scholars have speculated that oral transmission of the Mishnah strove to achieve a verbatim accuracy so that the eventual transcription into manuscript form represented only a shift in medium, not a conceptual reorientation. In a much-quoted article, Saul Lieberman suggests that the Mishnah underwent a publication process analogous to that of a book in antiquity. He cites contemporary Greco-Roman publishing practices, which involved depositing an original authentic copy in a temple or library or in archives. He explains that "such an act guarded the book against possible forgeries. In case of doubt or controversies regarding readings in a certain book, the copy placed in the archives

[43] Jacob Neusner has made a very valuable contribution in noting and discussing these features of the text. See especially Jacob Neusner, *Oral Tradition in Judaism* and Jacob Neusner, *A History of the Mishnaic Law of Purities: The Redaction and Formulation of the Order of Purities in Mishnah and Tosefta,* Studies in Judaism in Late Antiquity (Leiden: E. J. Brill, 1977). For a very refined discussion of oral traces and their literary manifestations, see Martin S. Jaffee, *Torah in the Mouth,* 100–125. Hayim Lapin, *Early Rabbinic Civil Law and the Social History of Roman Galilee: A Study of Mishnah Tractate Baba' Mesi'a'* (Atlanta: Scholars Press, 1995), 35–118, is also very sensitive to these matters.

[44] Similar questions have been asked with respect to Homeric epic. Granting that it was composed orally, scholars must also account for its current written form. Lord discusses the complexities of the transition from oral to written form in *The Singer of Tales,* 125–28. Thomas, *Literacy and Orality,* 45–50, sees less of a sharp transition and more interpenetration, conjecturing that "the poet of the *Iliad* could have used writing to record his poetry" (50).

would be decisive."[45] When trying to imagine the nature of oral performance of the Mishnah, Lieberman posits an analogous function for oral recitation of the Mishnah.

> A regular *ekdosis,* edition, of the *Mishnah* was in existence, a fixed text recited by the *Tannaim* of the college. The *Tanna* ("repeater", reciter) committed to memory the text of certain portions of the *Mishnah* which he subsequently recited in the college in the presence of the great masters. . . . The authority of the college-*Tanna* was that of a published book. In case of doubt, he was consulted as to the sequence or the arrangement of the several clauses in the *Mishnah.*[46]

Just as the book in the archives was consulted when a question arose concerning the authoritative version of the text, so too the college memorizer was consulted among the rabbis. The extent to which Lieberman uses a literary conceptual model to interpret the phenomena of orality is clear. For him, the oral Mishnah is literally and figuratively just like a book; it differs only in the medium of its preservation. While the book ensures authenticity by the words fixed on its pages, the college reciter ensures authenticity with words etched into his memory.

Implicit within Lieberman's paradigm of oral performer as "living book"[47] is the assumption that oral performance consists of rote memorization. Citing a rabbinic tradition that compares the tannaitic reciter to a magician who mumbles without understanding what he says, Lieberman explains:

> Those *Tannaim* were pupils chosen for their extraordinary memory, although they were not always endowed with intelligence. . . . The

[45] Lieberman, *HJP,* 85. Lieberman draws very heavily on Greek analogues. Thomas, however, alerts us to the fact that archival copies in Greek settings may not have been used in such a straightforward manner. Information was not always easily retrievable, even when stored in archives. Archival sources may have served other more symbolic functions. Thomas, *Literacy and Orality,* 132–44, 93–100.

[46] Lieberman, *HJP,* 88–89.

[47] Lieberman, *HJP,* 90.

stupider the *Tanna,* the more reliable his text; he was not suspected of "doctoring" it.[48]

Lieberman assumes here that rote memorization and analytic comprehension of the materials are mutually opposed to each other.[49] Understanding was not important for the tanna because he was responsible only for verbatim reproduction of the fixed exemplar. In Lieberman's view, oral performance of mishnaic text served only one purpose: to provide a means for reliably retrieving the text.

Jacob Neusner provides further evidence for the fact that the college reciter could reproduce the mishnaic text at will. He analyzes the internal evidence of the Mishnah – that is, the mnemonic features encoded within the text – and proposes that they facilitated the rote memorization that Lieberman attributes to the reciters (tannaim). He writes emphatically: "There is no reason to doubt that if we asked the tradental-redactional authorities behind the Mishnah the immediate purpose of their formalization, their answer would be, to facilitate memorization.... Much in its character can be seen as mnemonic."[50] In Neusner's view, then, the mnemonic features of the mishnaic text are best understood as aids to memorization. Neusner's work complements Lieberman's.[51] While Lieberman cites anecdotal evidence about how the Mishnah was performed orally, Neusner analyzes the text for traces of that activity. Both proceed from the same assumption that oral recitation of Mishnah would have striven to achieve verbatim reproduction of a fixed exemplar.

48 Lieberman, *HJP,* 88. See discussion of similar issues in Zlotnick, *The Iron Pillar,* 14–15.

49 Traditionally, scholarship has drawn a sharp distinction between two different types of intellectual work that took place in the rabbinic academies: textual transmission and analytic analysis. In this scheme, the work of textual transmission is understood to place an emphasis on precision, whereas the work of analytic analysis is understood to be more free-form. Lieberman reflects this conventional dichotomy where he implies that rote memorization and analytic comprehension are mutually exclusive. See fuller discussion of relevant bibliography in n. 11.

50 Jacob Neusner, *Oral Tradition in Judaism,* 102.

51 See Neusner's own acknowledgment of the formative place of Lieberman's model in Jacob Neusner, *Oral Tradition in Judaism,* 102–103.

The difficulty with Lieberman's account of oral recitation and performance of mishnaic materials and Neusner's explanation of the purpose served by the mnemonic features within the mishnaic text is that they give conceptual priority to the literary paradigm. Rabbinic orality is figured in terms of a book. This study comes to correct the tendency exemplified here by Lieberman and Neusner, and implicit in the work of many others, which portrays the oral life of Mishnah solely in terms of rote memorization. Although rote memorization may account for *part* of the oral performative exercises to which the Mishnah was subject, it is by no means an exhaustive representation of the many possibilities suggested by oral performance. This study seeks to reinstate an oral conceptual orientation in the analysis of rabbinic orality and thereby recover a more variegated picture of how the mishnaic text would have been performed and recited as Oral Torah.

Recently, several scholars have begun to develop new models for imagining the oral performative life of rabbinic texts in conjunction with written texts. In their attention to the conceptual orientation of orality, these new models can yield a more satisfying account of the transmissional life of m. Shevuot.

Steven Fraade's analysis of the early midrashic commentary to Deuteronomy offers a useful model for considering how the extant written texts connect to and derive from the oral performance of text that took place in rabbinic circles. He suggests that written transcriptions of Oral Torah be viewed as "the literary face of an otherwise oral circulatory system of study and teaching."[52] Elsewhere, Fraade elaborates on how the oral circulatory system works. He explains that "the performative orality of a text lies as much *before* [emphasis added] its literary face as behind it."[53] As I understand the oral circulatory metaphor, it posits that a series of performative events lie behind the text, and that the text before us represents a literary crystallization of

[52] Steven D. Fraade, *From Tradition to Commentary: Torah and Its Interpretation in the Midrash Sifre to Deuteronomy* (Albany: State University of New York, 1991), 19.

[53] Fraade, "Literary Composition and Oral Performance," 36.

those events. The key point, however, is that the written text remains engaged with oral performance *even after* it is transcribed. The text is more than a record of past performative events; it is also a provisional script for *future* performative events.[54] While Fraade attends to *literary* evidence, he makes use of an *oral* conceptual orientation in that he imagines the written text to have functioned in a *fluid* manner.[55] For him, written records of text do not necessarily imply fixity. For our project, Fraade's work provides an alternate framework for interpreting the oral traces encoded in the mishnaic text. Rather than thinking of them as aids to rote memorization, we might think of them as the provisional *script* for an oral performative event.

Martin Jaffee builds on Fraade's work and clarifies at what point in the texts' development the oral circulatory metaphor is most apt. In his view, the current documentary compilation can be thought of as a "kind of freeze frame of . . . tradition, temporarily stilled by the redactional activity."[56] For him, the text before us is one of many possible texts, each having no more and no less intrinsic authority than the others. According to Jaffee, the text only becomes "fixed" when there is a *shift in perspective* with regard to the text. It achieves a different status when those engaging it regard it differently, that is, when "its transmitters and users began to define the compilation as representing 'tradition' itself."[57] This view assumes that over time, the rabbinic community of disciples will encounter the *same* written

54 The recognition that orality plays a role in the text's performative life both before and after composition distinguishes the current study from the work of Neusner, who focuses on the role of oral performance only *after* composition is already complete. See Jacob Neusner, *Oral Tradition in Judaism*, 133–47.

55 Fraade's description of the interplay between written text and oral performance has much in common with Finnegan's analysis of the oral performance of broadside ballads in nineteenth-century America. Both scholars assume that the existence of a fixed written version does not inhibit the improvisation that infuses oral performance. See Finnegan, *Oral Poetry*, 162–65.

56 Martin S. Jaffee, "Oral Tradition in the Writings of Rabbinic Oral Torah: On Theorizing Rabbinic Orality," *Oral Tradition* 14, no. 1 (March 1999): 23.

57 Jaffee, "Oral Tradition," 23.

records in *different* ways. Whereas for one generation of sages a given text is one of many equally authentic statements, several generations later the same text is regarded as a single, authoritative version.

In this way of thinking, there is a short window of time when written texts are best understood as what Fraade calls "'orally' fluid";[58] this is the short window of time before the perception of them shifts. While Lieberman's model of oral recitation as rote memorization may be correct with regard to the later phases of the "oral circulatory system," it is probably less applicable to the earlier phases. It is to this window of time, then, that I want to direct our attention. In these early phases, what would have been entailed in oral performance of mishnaic materials? What kind of performance did the provisional script of the Mishnah engender? What kind of active intellectual engagement was required to compose the legal cases of the Mishnah? By what processes did the mishnaic text eventually come to be viewed as fixed? And finally, what became of the active component of mishnaic performance once the materials came to be viewed as fixed?

The Theory of Textual Corruption

One reflection of how deeply entrenched is the literary conceptual lens can be seen in the emergence of theories of textual corruption. These theories assume that transmission begins with a fixed text and strives for verbatim reproduction.[59] As in the children's game of telephone, verbatim reproduction is never completely achieved. As the text is transmitted, various corruptions are introduced. In the children's game, of course, the thrill is to see how distorted the "original" message becomes. By way of contrast, scholars using the theory of textual corruption as a basis for understanding mishnaic transmission

[58] Fraade, "Literary Composition and Oral Performance," 46.

[59] Theories of textual corruption are hardly unique to rabbinic studies. Finnegan notes the difficulties in other studies of oral tradition that stress the degenerative element due to failure of memorization. See Finnegan, *Oral Poetry*, 141–42.

invariably see the losses and corruption in a negative light. When one assumes that the transmissional process begins with a fixed, authoritative examplar, any alterations to the pristine original are seen as compromised distortions.

One version of the the theory of textual corruption can be found in the work of J. N. Epstein, who wrote extensively on the shifting permutations of the mishnaic text in the course of transmission.[60] Generally, Epstein is quite sensitive to the fluid character of the mishnaic text. He stresses that almost as soon as R. Judah the Patriarch compiled the official version of the Mishnah, it absorbed a number of textual emendations.[61] Some changes reflected alternative readings from "nonofficial" Mishnah compilations that were still circulating.[62] Other changes entered the text on account of various questions that arose concerning the interpretation of the text.[63] Still other changes were introduced to fill in apparent lacunae in the text.[64] The localized settings in which Mishnah was performed and taught made for yet more fluidity in the text. Each academy or scholar had its or his own official reciter, and in their mouths, the text was adapted, changed, and revised to reflect local teachings or sensibilities.[65]

Given the extent to which Epstein grasps the inherent difficulty in thinking of the Mishnah as a fixed and stable text, it comes as a surprise

60 See Epstein's monumental work, *Introduction to the Text of the Mishnah* (Hebrew). Setting out to write a critical edition of the Mishnah, Epstein began with an "introduction" to the topic (which ended up being well over 1,300 pages long!) in which he catalogued the various methodological challenges that confront the scholar who wishes to establish the "correct" text of the Mishnah. See also Bokser's summary of Epstein's work. As Bokser sees it, Epstein's implicit thesis, though nowhere stated outright, is: "There is no such thing as a *Mishnah text* with a capital M" (14). Baruch Bokser, "Jacob N. Epstein's *Introduction to the Text of the Mishnah*," in *The Modern Study of the Mishnah*, ed. Jacob Neusner (Leiden: E. J. Brill, 1973), 13–36.

61 On the early part of the amoraic period, when few changes were made, see Epstein, *ITM*, 146–352. On the different types of changes introduced into the body of the mishnaic text after the third generation of amoraim, see Epstein, *ITM*, 353–672.

62 Epstein, *ITM*, 429–38.

63 Epstein, *ITM*, 404–23.

64 Epstein, *ITM*, 592–692.

65 Epstein, *ITM*, 677–81.

to find certain elements in his analysis that imply an original fixity.[66] At times, Epstein seems to assume that it is possible to talk about an "original, authentic" version of the text. For example, even though he concludes that during the tannaitic period different versions of the Mishnah were disseminated by different teachers, he nonetheless states that "the Mishnah, 'our Mishnah,' was the same in its essence in Babylonia and the land of Israel."[67] Apparently, R. Judah the Patriarch's act of editing the Mishnah produced a work that, at least in a certain point in its history, was pristine and whose textual boundaries could be identified with certainty. His implicit assumption of the existence of an authentic, original version impacts how he understands the later reception of the text. He states that "to the extent that geographical and chronological distance from the Mishnah's origins increases, preservation of the [original] text version becomes less good and evaluation of its language more subject to doubt. So too, textual corrections

[66] I would argue that this contradiction arises in Epstein's work because he makes room for some kinds of textual fluidity, but not others. Whereas he has a sophisticated understanding of how the *verbal contents* of the Mishnah were in flux throughout the course of their transmission, he is less sensitive to the ways in which the *status* of the Mishnah was also in flux. Though he documents a wealth of textual variants that circulated during the tannaitic period, he sees each variant as deriving from a textual version that is *in and of itself* fixed and stable. For him, each variant testifies to a discrete document edited according to a different teaching style and halakhic perspective in a different school by a different sage. (See discussion in Epstein, *ITM,* 18–74.) Thus, while "our Mishnah" did not achieve the stability of a widely accepted text in antiquity, apparently the Mishnah collections in each individual school did function as fixed, stable, and authoritative texts in their own circles. Shamma Friedman offers a similar analysis and critique of Epstein. He writes: "What may appear as alternate forms of the Mishnah's text are perceived as deriving from independent, parallel works." Shamma Friedman, "Uncovering Literary Dependencies in the Talmudic Corpus," in *The Synoptic Problem in Rabbinic Literature,* ed. Shaye J. D. Cohen (Providence RI: Brown Judaic Studies, 2000), 37, esp. n. 6.

[67] Epstein, *ITM,* 165. Epstein's use of quotation marks around the expression "our Mishnah" reflects his subtle understanding of how fluid the text was in the ancient context. The quotation marks suggest that during the rabbinic period, no clear priority would have been given to this version of the Mishnah. Only from the vantage point of hindsight can we determine that one single version became "our Mishnah."

increase and cross new boundaries."[68] As Epstein sees it, the greater the remove from the original setting in which the Mishnah was formulated, the greater the distortions. In this classic version of the theory of textual corruption, processes of transmission lead from a pristine original to a corrupt derivative. Variant versions result because of a *breakdown* in the transmissional process that distance and time cannot overcome.

A more complex version of the theory of textual corruption tries to account for the unusual character of later interpretations of the Mishnah. According to this version of the theory, *both* the mishnaic text *and* its interpretive tradition were vulnerable to minor textual corruptions in the course of their transmission.[69] The theory suggests that the interpretive tradition was especially vulnerable to corruption since it never achieved a fixed form.[70] Accordingly, successive generations of sages received the sources in varying states of repair and disrepair. In a number of cases, where the relationship between the interpretive tradition and the text had become so distorted as to render the original interpretive insight incomprehensible, later sages had to reconstruct the relationship between the mishnaic text and its interpretive traditions.

68 Epstein, *ITM*, 353.

69 Fundamental to this version of the theory is the idea that mishnaic materials and their analytic interpretation have specific verbal content in the earliest stages of transmission and that the analytic interpretative tradition is transmitted in tandem with the mishnaic materials. On the complementarity between succinct mishnaic sources and their more verbose analytic interpretations, see Halivni, *Midrash, Mishnah and Gemara*, 2, and Gerhardsson, *Memory and Manuscript*, 145–46, 176.

70 See Halivni, *Midrash, Mishnah and Gemara*, 82–83: "Even a cursory examination will show that the apodictic [i.e., short, prescriptive] materials of the Talmud were better preserved than the 'give and take,' the argumentational, the discursive.... One has only to compare the parallel sources to realize that the apodictic remained more or less the same throughout the literature, whereas the argumentational material is almost always radically different in the parallel sources." See also Gerhardsson, *Memory and Manuscript*, 93–112. Lauterbach assumes a similar kind of complementarity between halakhic and aggadic texts. Whereas halakhic texts were to be memorized by rote, aggadic sources were not fixed and were subsequently subject to greater flux in the course of transmission. Lauterbach, "Midrash and Mishnah."

Though it may have been apparent to the later sages that their sources were in a state of disrepair, the sources as they received them were nonetheless authoritative. Working with flawed sources that they felt they had no right to correct, the later sages offered "forced interpretations" that were a good-faith effort to make the most of imperfect sources.[71] Again the literary conceptual bias in this reconstruction of the transmissional process is apparent. The theory distinguishes between the pristine, original sources, which made sense, and the corrupt versions at the end of a long change of transmission, which did not. Furthermore, oral transmission is idealized as verbatim reproduction of a fixed exemplar. Had the transmissional process not broken down, the original, clear relationship between the mishnaic text and its interpretive traditions would have been preserved.

While I am not disputing the claim that both the mishnaic text and its interpretive tradition were in flux during the course of their transmission, the theory of textual corruption provides an incomplete account of why later interpretations of the Mishnah seem so counterintuitive to our eyes today. By assuming that *the only important shift from the early to the later period involves corruption of sources,* the theory of textual corruption fails to take other transmissional factors into account. The oral conceptual lens helps us see that transmission of the mishnaic text involved more than the mere conveyance of verbal contents. Throughout the processes of transmission, the ancient handlers of the mishnaic text were actively shaping their conception of the text. They were developing an ideology concerning the scriptural status of the text based on a perceived fixity, and they were cultivating a set of

[71] Halivni lays out the reconstruction of the transmissional process in *Sources and Traditions: A Source Critical Commentary on Seder Nashim* (Hebrew) (Tel Aviv: Dvir Publishing House, 1968), 7–19. He also reviews it for an English-speaking audience in *Midrash, Mishnah and Gemara,* 76–92. Moshe Benovitz's critical commentary to tractate Shevuot, chap. 3, similarly adopts a theory of textual corruption to explain and account for counterintuitive interpretations of the Mishnah. See the review and analysis of Benovitz, "A Critical Commentary on Chapter III of Tractate Shevuot in the Babylonian Talmud" (Hebrew)(Ph.D. diss., Jewish Theological Seminary of America, 1993), 482–87, in Chapter 4 of this work.

analytic habits through which to study and understand the text. The value of the oral conceptual lens, then, is that it attunes us to the multiplicity of factors that influenced later interpretations of the mishnaic text to take the form and pursue the line of interpretation that they did. Central to this study is an interest in exposing the active component of the later interpreters as readers of the mishnaic text. Rather than seeing them as passive recipients of a sometimes corrupt, sometimes well-preserved, set of sources, I would like to explore how the active work of transmission contributes to the emerging construction of mishnaic meaning.

The Present Study

Through close textual analysis of a small selection of materials, this study shows how attention to the oral conceptual lens provides insight into the nature of mishnaic textuality and transmission. Chapters 1 and 2 suggest that the idea that mishnaic materials are fixed and authoritative is formed quite late, much later than is generally assumed. Chapter 1 indicates that in the earliest stages of the Mishnah's transmission, there existed notions of textual continuity that did not depend on literal and linear textual fixity. Identifying a more fluid notion of textual continuity serves as an important point of contrast when observing how later students, handlers, and transmitters of the text viewed it. Chapter 2 documents the attention that was eventually paid to the text's precise wording and the increasing investment in the idea that the Mishnah be conceived as a fixed text. This discussion is important to rabbinic studies because it reverses long-standing conventions in the field that assume that the Mishnah was authoritative at the time of its promulgation. It also has relevance for other fields, notably biblical studies, that are concerned with the process by which traditional texts become authoritative and scripturalized. It offers one model for thinking about how loosely configured traditions are transformed in the hands of a devoted community of students and readers.

Chapter 3 argues that the transmission of the mishnaic text entails propagation and cultivation of an analytic thought process, in addition to relaying textual artifacts. Analysis and text are not as distinct as they are generally taken to be. These results are significant because they again challenge long-standing conventions in the field of rabbinics that assume that the mishnaic text and the analytic tradition were two distinct textual entities, each subject to its own transmissional process. By way of contrast, the work of Chapter 3 indicates how integral analytic tasks were to the transmission of the textual tradition. Reproducing the legal cases that make up m. Shevuot necessarily involved practitioners in certain analytic practices.

Chapter 4 documents the enduring character of the analytic habits cultivated through mishnaic performance by showing how later students of the Mishnah employed the very same analytic practices. These findings are important because they establish a continuity in the intellectual character of rabbinic culture during its earlier tannaitic and later amoraic and post-amoraic manifestations. Generally, discontinuity has been assumed. Dominant scholarly paradigms suggest that early rabbinic literary production was intimately linked with rote memorization, whereas later literary production was dominated by discursive analysis and argumentation. By showing the continuity of analytic habits from the earlier to the later period, Chapter 4 exposes this characterization as resting on a false dichotomy. Chapter 4 additionally explores how the inherited set of analytic study practices contributed to the creation of a distinctive, if not somewhat counterintuitive, interpretation of the mishnaic text. These conclusions offer a new view of how the conditions of oral transmission impacted talmudic interpretation of the Mishnah. Whereas the dominant scholarly model ascribes the counterintuitivity of many talmudic interpretations to losses, breakdowns, and corruption in the transmissional process, Chapter 4 proposes that the distinctive interpretive style of the Babylonian Talmud results from the use of inherited analytic practices at a time when the mishnaic text was increasingly seen as scriptural in character.

A Brief Introduction to the Tractate of Oaths and Other Technical Terminology

This book offers a series of close readings from the tractate on Oaths, in Hebrew called Shevuot.[72] The mishnaic tractate outlines three general categories of oaths: 1) the **declarative oath** (שבועת ביטוי), in which the oathtaker declares his or her intent to take on a certain obligation or refrain from a certain action; 2) the **testimonial oath** (שבועת העדות), in which the litigant in a civil dispute has the power to force witnesses to testify concerning any information they have that might pertain to the case in question; and 3) the **oath of deposit** (שבועת פקדון), which concerns disputed fines, fees, or goods. The last category encompasses many situations, but the defining feature is that a sum of money or a piece of property belonging to one litigant has at some point passed into the possession of the other litigant, and the court imposes an oath to resolve the dispute. The tractate, then, discusses both personal oaths, dealing with an individual's private behaviors, and those administered by the court.

Though certain features of the mishnaic tractate will be discussed at length in the course of the book, a few general comments may be helpful at the outset. As in most other mishnaic tractates, the material in

[72] Tractate Shevuot treats two entirely distinct topics. Chapters 1–2 deal with transferring impurity through touch, and Chapters 3–8 deal with a variety of different kinds of oaths. According to Jacob Neusner, the unifying element of the tractate derives from the context of scriptural derivation. Lev. 5 treats both transfer of impurity and oaths within a single framework. Jacob Neusner, *A History of the Mishnaic Law of Damages, Part 5: The Mishnaic System of Damages,* Studies in Judaism in Late Antiquity (Leiden: E. J. Brill, 1985), 120. Milgrom suggests that the unifying element in the biblical context is that sins in each of these areas are performed unconsciously or unwittingly and recognized as the result of some negative circumstance that occurs and would otherwise be unexplained. Lev. 5 comes to provide a legal mechanism for righting the unconscious or forgotten sin against God. See Jacob Milgrom, *Leviticus 1–16: A New Translation with Introduction and Commentary,* The Anchor Bible (New York: Doubleday, 1991), 339–64. In order to lend topical, as well as textual, unity to this book, I will treat only those chapters that discuss oaths, that is, Chapters 3–8.

tractate Shevuot is organized topically. Each of the chapters is devoted to discussing a particular kind of oath, defining it, and exploring issues related to its implementation. The last three chapters are devoted to various aspects of the oath of deposit. The individual pericopes (in Hebrew *mishnah* [singular] or *mishnayot* [plural]) generally consist of a short legal prescription or two. Sometimes an alternative view is also offered. Sometimes the traditions are attributed; sometimes they appear anonymously. Irrespective of whether the traditions are attributed or not, the traditions recorded therein are assumed to reflect the cultural world of the **tannaim,** sages who lived and worked from approximately 50 to 200 C.E. Edited and compiled at the close of the tannaitic period, the Mishnah is generally described as a tannaitic document.

Many of the traditions contained in the mishnaic tractate of Shevuot (m. Shevuot) have parallels in other documents from roughly the same period. The **Tosephta** (literally, "the addendum" or "the addition") is organized topically like the Mishnah. T. Shevuot (the tosephtan tractate on Oaths) follows roughly the same structural outline of topics as m. Shevuot, though it does contain discussions without mishnaic parallels and does not touch on every issue mentioned in the Mishnah. The traditions recorded in the Tosephta are attributed to the same set of sages whose work is recorded in the Mishnah, and like the Mishnah, it is considered a tannaitic document. Scholars generally assume, however, that the Tosephta was edited about a hundred years after the Mishnah was compiled.[73] Since the mishnaic material on oaths

[73] For a scholarly overview on the Tosephta, see Strack and Stemberger, *Introduction to the Talmud and Midrash,* 167–82, and Abraham Goldberg, "The Tosefta: Companion to the Mishna," in *The Literature of the Sages,* ed. Shmuel Safrai (Philadelphia: Fortress Press, 1987), 283–301. Other important works that discuss the provenance of tosephtan materials and the dating of the final document include Shamma Friedman, *Tosefta Atiqta. Pesah Rishon: Synoptic Paralles of Mishna and Tosefta Analyzed with a Methodological Introduction* (Hebrew) (Ramat-Gan: Bar Ilan University Press, 2002); and Yaakov Elman, *Authority and Tradition: Toseftan Baraitot in Talmudic Babylonia* (Hoboken, NJ: Ktav Publishing House, 1994). See also David Weiss Halivni,

has roots in certain biblical passages (primarily Lev. 5 and Ex. 22:6–14), tannaitic parallels to m. Shevuot can also be found in midrashic texts that comment on the relevant biblical passages. Though the research for the book included extensive study of the midrashic parallels, the final version of the work does not discuss them since the tannaitic parallels from the Tosephta illustrate the same claims and allow for a more streamlined presentation.[74]

The traditions recorded in m. Shevuot are discussed in two commentaries: y. Shevuot (the **Yerushalmi** or Palestinian Talmud to the tractate on Oaths, c. 425 C.E.) and b. Shevuot (the **Bavli,** or the Babylonian Talmud to the tractate of Oaths, c. 600 C.E.). Each of the two Talmuds is organized around the base text of m. Shevuot and offers a series of comments, reflections, digressions, and arguments on each mishnaic pericope. The portion of the Talmuds that comments on the mishnaic text can also be refered to as the **gemara**. In this work, I will use the terms Talmud and gemara interchangeably to indicate the later rabbinic commentary to m. Shevuot. The gemaras consist of both attributed and unattributed materials. The attributed materials are associated with generations of sages collectively known as **amoraim**. The amoraim are said to have lived from approximately 200 to 450 C.E. Scholars have determined that a large portion of the later Talmud, the Bavli, was composed by an anonymous group of

"The Reception Accorded to Rabbi Judah's Mishnah," in *Jewish and Christian Self-Definition, Volume Two, Aspects of Judasim in the Graeco-Roman Period,* ed. E. P. Sanders with A. I. Baumgarten and Alan Mendelson (London: SCM Press, 1981), 204–12; Alberdina Houtman, *Mishnah and Tosefta: A Synoptic Comparison of the Tractates Berakhot and Shebiit,* Texte und Studien Zum Antiken Judentum (Tubingen: J. C. B. Mohr (Paul Siebeck), 1996); and the seeds of Judith Hauptman's forthcoming book on the relationship between the Tosephta and the Mishnah: Judith Hauptman, "Mishnah as a Response to 'Tosefta,'" in *The Synoptic Problem in Rabbinic Literature,* ed. Shaye J. D. Cohen (Providence, RI: Brown Judaic Studies, 2000).

74 For a discussion of diverse passages in the midrashei halakhah, see my Ph.D. dissertation, whose research forms the basis for this book. Elizabeth Shanks Alexander, "Study Practices That Made the Mishnah: Evolution of a Tradition of Exegesis" (Yale University, 1999), 35–36, 37–38, 88–98.

sages who lived after the amoraim.[75] The major contribution of the post-amoraic generations of sages (c. 450–600 C.E.), was the working of received tannaitic and amoraic traditions into a complex superstructure of discussion, debate, and argumentation.[76] Though the two Talmuds generally do not have punctation marks to indicate when they are beginning and finishing the discussion of a particular issue, the term **sugya** is generally used to refer to a "complete discussion." The determination of the beginning and end of the sugya is admittedly a subjective enterprise,[77] but nonetheless it is useful in demarcating units of talmudic discussion.

[75] See the following seminal works: David Weiss Halivni, *Sources and Traditions: A Source Critical Commentary on Seder Moed* (New York: Jewish Theological Seminary, 1975); 1–12; David Weiss Halivni, *Sources and Traditions: A Source Critical Commentary on Tractate Baba Kamma* (Hebrew) (Jerusalem: Magnus Press, 1993), 7–21; and Shamma Friedman, "A Critical Study of Yevamot X with a Methodological Introduction" (Hebrew), *Texts and Studies: Analecta Judaica,* vol. 1, ed. H. Z. Dimitrovsky (New York, 1977), 275–441. See also the discussion in Richard Kalmin, *The Redaction of the Babylonian Talmud: Amoraic or Saboraic?* Monographs of the Hebrew Union College (Cincinnati, OH: Hebrew Union College Press, 1989).

[76] For an insightful study of the dominant cultural traits of this group of sages, see Jeffrey L. Rubenstein, *Talmudic Stories: Narrative Art, Composition, and Culture* (Baltimore and London: The Johns Hopkins University Press, 1999), and *The Culture of the Babylonian Talmud:* (Baltimore and London: The Johns Hopkins University Press, 2003).

[77] For an interesting discussion of the literary aspects of determining the boundaries of a sugya, see Aryeh Cohen, *Rereading Talmud: Gender, Law and the Poetics of* Sugyot (Atlanta: Scholars Press, 1998).

1

Mishnaic Textuality

In the Introduction, I observed that one of the chief accomplishments of Lord and Parry's work was to alert scholars to the possibility of conceiving textuality in diverse ways. The dominant literary conception understands texts to be fixed, linear sequences of words; variants among parallel versions are understood as deviations from an authentic original. By way of contrast, Lord and Parry's work points to an alternate conception in which variants reflect a text's natural diversity. In this so-called oral conception of textuality, no single version is more authentic or original than any other. Texts are by nature multiform.

In this chapter, I would like to explore the ways in which adopting an oral conception of textuality helps us see m. Shevuot differently. The inquiry focuses on analysis of the relationship between m. Shevuot and its tannaitic parallels. I argue that the gains of adopting the oral conceptual lens when examining this body of materials are twofold. First, by putting aside literary notions of textuality, we open ourselves to the possibility of recognizing *nonlinear* forms of continuity among the parallel traditions. While it is certainly true that parallel versions reproduce linear sequences of words in a verbatim fashion, too much attention to the literal correspondences between parallel traditions can blind us to the presence of other, equally compelling, but *nonliteral* correspondences. The second gain of this exercise is intimately connected with the first. Once we identify nonlinear, nonliteral forms of continuity among the parallel traditions, we can better appreciate how differently conceptions of mishnaic textuality emerge over time. If attention to the nonlinear, nonliteral points of continuity indicates a so-called oral or fluid conception of mishnaic textuality, then attention to other matters likely indicates a shift in perspective. Identifying what is at stake for those invested in one conception of mishnaic textuality raises the possibility that sensibilities will change when this conception gives way to others over time.

Martin Jaffee's work has already alerted scholars to the value of the oral conceptual lens when evaluating the relationship between mishnaic traditions and their parallels. When considering the question of how to account for the variants among parallel versions, Jaffee bypasses the question of priority that occupies so many scholars evaluating parallel traditions.[1] Instead of trying to resolve the question of which version

[1] The classic paradigm in scholarship views the Tosephta as a later response to and commentary on the Mishnah. In this model, tosephtan deviations from the mishnaic text, which are often more drawn out and extensive than the Mishnah's more condensed version, are understood to reflect the Tosephta's function as commentary on the Mishnah. See e.g., Goldberg, "The Tosefta," and Jacob Neusner, *The Tosefta: An Introduction* (Atlanta: Scholars Press, 1992). More recently, the classic chronology has been called into question by scholars noting the *antiquity* of tosephtan traditions relative to their mishnaic counterparts. See Shamma Friedman, "The Primacy of Tosefta to Mishna in Synoptic Parallels," in *Introducing Tosefta: Textual, Intratexual, and Intertextual Studies*, ed. Tirzah Meacham, Harry Fox, and Diane Kriger (Ktav Publishing House, 1999), 99–121; Friedman, "An Ancient Tosefta: On the Relationship of Parallels in the Mishnah and Tosefta (1): All Holy Writings (Shabbat 16:1)" (Hebrew), *Tarbiz* 62, no. 3 (1993): 313–38; Friedman, "An Ancient Tosefta: On the Relationship of Parallels in the Mishnah and Tosefta (2): The Story of Rabban Gamaliel and the Elders" (Hebrew), *Bar Ilan Sefer Ha-Shanah* 26–27 (1995): 277–88; Friedman, "Uncovering Literary Dependencies"; and Hauptman, "Mishnah as a Response to 'Tosefta.'" Stemberger reflects the work of Friedman and Hauptman when cataloguing the differences between T and M. He writes: "T [as opposed to M] often seems

came first, Jaffee illustrates how oral performance can produce just the kind of variety exhibited by the parallels.[2] For him, parallels are best understood as different performative versions. The variants emerge as part of the natural diversity of texts exhibited when an "orally fluid"[3] conception prevails. Having established that the context of oral performance is a valuable one for reflecting on the phenomenon of tannaitic parallels, Jaffee's work lays the groundwork for further inquiries. If an oral conception of textuality produces *variants* in certain patterns,

to have the more original arrangement [of material] as well as the more primitive form of the halakhah itself"; Strack and Stemberger, *Introduction to the Talmud and Midrash*, 171.

2 See Martin S. Jaffee, *Torah in the Mouth*, 101–24. In his discussion, Jaffee carefully attends to the different ways in which the written artifacts of rabbinic scribal culture interact with oral performance. He astutely notes that the active oral performative life of the texts does not mitigate against the possibility of a scribal transcriptional process. In introducing his vision of how the "oral" and the "written" interact, he writes the following: "The readings that follow treat the material inscribed in the Mishnah as the foundation of a scripted performance.... The script or score is produced with the assumption that its meanings will be activated primarily in performance before an audience. Nevertheless, the performance is unalterably reflective of the prior labor of conception, compositional experimentation and editing which produces a script or score. This labor, in my view, was to a significant degree scribal; that is, even to the degree that it rendered material memorized from oral-performative settings, the literary compilation involved tasks such as copying and revising texts transmitted in written form. The results of such editorial activity, such as the Mishnah itself, is neither the 'original script' nor any of its performative versions" (101). At the end of his chapter, he concludes that parallel traditions in Mishnah and Tosephta represent "different performative version[s] of a narrative tradition that circulated in rabbinic communities prior to the redaction of either the Mishnah or the Tosefta" (124).

3 As noted previously (see Introduction, n. 58), this phrase is drawn from Fraade, "Literary Composition and Oral Performance," 36. It is intended to highlight the fact that it may be written texts that are being manipulated. An "orally fluid" conception of textuality does not require that the texts be preserved in oral form exclusively. For a valuable depiction of how the interpenetration between oral and written modalities functions in the tranmissional life of Mishnah, see Jaffee, *Torah in the Mouth*, 100–125. As Ruth Finnegan has vividly illustrated, oral conceptions of text can operate in settings where written texts are used, and literary conceptions of textuality can operate in settings where the texts are handled orally. See Finnegan, *Oral Poetry*; Finnegan, *Literacy and Orality*; and Calinescu, "Orality in Literacy."

what patterns of *continuity* does it facilitate? Are there *features of commonality* among parallel versions that scholars have overlooked because they are conditioned to recognize parallels only when linear sequences of words are reproduced?

The Parry-Lord theory of oral composition offers us a valuable model for imagining how nonlinear, nonliteral points of continuity exist among parallel versions. As we noted, the theory proposes that oral poets and composers rely on a store of stock elements that can be manipulated and arranged into various combinations. According to the theory, familiarity with and fluidity in the stock elements is what allows for rapid composition in the pressured context of performance. The more acquainted the performer is with the stock elements and the various ways in which they can be arranged, the more gracefully he can produce a felicitous and compelling narrative. The identification of the stock elements, which are interchangeably manipulated into various configurations, helps us see the form that nonlinear, nonliteral continuity can take. The foundation of the Lord-Parry theory of oral composition involved the identification of "formula," or fixed phrases of certain metrical lengths that could be slotted into various positions in the hexametrical lines of lyric poetry.[4] In addition to noting the presence of a set of fixed formula interspersed throughout the poets' material, Lord also identified a set of fixed "themes."[5] The themes are stock scenes structured around "a grouping of ideas"[6] that the performer

[4] See Milman Parry, "L'epithète traditionelle dans Homère," in *The Making of Homeric Verse: The Collected Papers of Milman Parry*, ed. Adam Parry (Oxford: Clarendon Press, 1928 repr. 1971), 1–190. See Lord's development of the concept in *The Singer of Tales*, 30–67. Evaluation and critique of the Lord-Parry theory of oral composition can be found in Finnegan, *Oral Poetry*, 52–87, and Thomas, *Literacy and Orality*, 29–51. On the widespread applicability of the theory and its subsequent influence on the study of other oral and oral-derived bodies of literature, see also John Miles Foley, *The Theory of Oral Composition: History and Methodology* (Bloomington and Indianapolis: Indiana University Press, 1988).

[5] See Lord, *The Singer of Tales*, 68–98.

[6] Lord, *The Singer of Tales*, 69.

can use in diverse contexts: banquet scenes, sending off a messenger, writing a letter or decree, summoning the wedding party, and so on. Finally, throughout his work, Lord also seems to imply that the poet-composers are familiar with an overarching narrative into which the themes are combined.[7] John Miles Foley suggests that though no single performer will ever perform the entire narrative, an idealized version lives in the performers' collective imaginations – a whole constructed from the various segments that never has been, and never will be, performed in its entirety.[8] The reason the performer is able to compose so fluently in performance is because, rather than composing anew, he shuffles these traditional elements into their appropriate slots. His training familiarizes him with a set of precisely worded, small units of discourse (formula) and larger structures into which they are manipulated (themes and narrative whole).

When attempting to use the theory of oral composition to illuminate the legal materials of m. Shevuot, it is important not to try to import the categories of the theory wholesale into the rabbinic milieu. Foley has warned scholars of oral tradition to attend to the diversity of oral traditions by making allowances for differences in genre, cultural tradition, and performative context.[9] In my study of

[7] Consider the following: "Before [the singer] actually begins to sing, he is, consciously or unconsciously, laying the foundation. He is learning the stories and becoming acquainted with the heroes and their names, the faraway places and the habits of long ago"; Lord, *The Singer of Tales*, 21. Though Lord never submits the "stories" to the same analysis that "themes" and "formula" undergo, he seems here to assume that a standard set of stories exist. A similar view is represented in a comment of Lord's cited by Foley from an unpublished manuscript: "We have learned that a tradition is made up not of discrete songs but of songs, or, preferrably, stories about a limited number of heroes, tales that overlap and intertwine, in such a way that in the experience of both the singer and his traditional audience any one traditional song can evoke subconsciously a large group of other songs, or stories, in the tradition." Foley suggests that the various stories stand in as a metonymic "part" of an idealized whole. See Foley, *Immanent Art*, 11.

[8] Foley, *Immanent Art*, 9–13.

[9] See Foley, "Oral Tradition," 160, and Foley, *The Theory of Oral Composition*, 109–10.

the legal traditions of m. Shevuot, I have observed three different manifestations of nonliteral, nonlinear continuity: overarching structural frameworks, fixed phrases, and underlying conceptual concerns.[10] These elements are similar to, but not identical with, the formula and themes of Parry and Lord. Because of the ways in which these textual features complement one another in the context of complete legal traditions, I think of them as compositional building blocks. When manipulated in conjunction with one another, they produce the legal traditions of m. Shevuot and its tannaitic parallels. As with the formulae, themes, and idealized narrative whole of the Parry-Lord theory of oral composition, these compositional building blocks contain literal fixity on the micro level (fixed phrases), structural fixity on the macro level (overarching structural frameworks), and abstract fixity (underlying conceptual concerns). In the textual examples that follow, I will illustrate how these compositional building blocks provide for a continuity among the parallel versions, even if the continuity is not immediately recognizable in linear and literal forms. As in Lord's work, it is important to note how the different compositional building blocks work in conjunction with one another. Taken separately, they illustrate limited points of contact, but seen as parts of a whole working together, they provide for a fairly high degree of continuity. The more the parallel sources use the same building blocks in conjunction with one another, the higher the degree of continuity exhibited among them.

I consider each of the three compositional building blocks (overarching structural framework, fixed phrases, and underlying conceptual concerns) in turn. In each case, I indicate ways in which the highlighted textual feature provides for nonlinear, nonliteral points of continuity. Although the textual sample examined here is admittedly small, I hope the depth and detail of the textual work will succeed in convincing readers that much can be gained when we open ourselves to diverse ways of conceiving mishnaic textuality.

10 See Alexander, "Study Practices That Made the Mishnah," 29–39.

Sharing an Overarching Structural Framework: M. Shev. 5:4–5 and T. Shev. 2:16

In the following pair of sources, we see that a common structural framework plays as much of a role in establishing continuity between the two sources as does the linear sequence of words that they have in common. Synoptic comparison of the two sources reveals a common structural framework that each source alternately expands and contracts. While the two sources begin with a verbatim parallel, the mishnaic version soon supplements where the tosephtan source does not. The roles are then reversed, and the tosephtan version supplements where the mishnaic source does not.[11] In spite of the variations, the presence of a common structural framework makes for a strong affinity between the two sources.

משנה שבועות פרק ה' הלכות ד'-ה'	תוספתא שבועות פרק ב' הלכה ט''ז
אנסת ופתית את בתי,	אנסת ופתית את בתי,
והוא אומר: לא אנסתי ולא פתיתי	והוא אומר: לא אנסתי ולא פתיתי
משביעך אני	משביעך אני
ואמר: אמן – חייב.	ואמר: אמן – חייב.
רבי שמעון פוטר,שאינו משלם קנס על פי עצמו.	רבי שמעון פוטר ,שאינו משלם קנס על פי עצמו.

[11] The fact that each source supplements where the other does not suggests that both sources are independently expanding the same structural framework and mitigates against thinking that the common elements resulted when one source cited the other. The model of textual citation is often effective in accounting for instances in which one parallel is more expansive than the other. Shamma Friedman and Judith Hauptman independently argue that in many cases where the tosephtan parallel is more expansive, the mishnaic version represents a condensation of the tosephtan version. The fact that in this example each of the parallel versions expands where the other does not makes a model of textual citation less attractive as a means of explaining how the common elements came to be present in both sources. See Friedman, "The Primacy of Tosefta to Mishna"; Friedman, "An Ancient Tosefta (1)"; Friedman, "An Ancient Tosefta (2)"; Hauptman, "Mishnah as a Response to 'Tosefta.'"

אמרו לו: אף על פי שאינו משלם קנס על פי
עצמו, משלם בשת ופגם על פי עצמו.
. . .
זה הכלל:
כל המשלם על פי עצמו
– חייב,
ושאינו משלם על פי עצמו
– פטור.

זה הכלל:
כל שהוא קנס,
ומשלם על פי עצמו
משביעך אני, ואמר: אמן – חייב.
וכל שאינו קנס,
ומשלם על פי עצמו
משביעך אני, ואמר: אמן – חייב.
וכל שאינו קנס,
אין משלם על פי עצמו
משביעך אני, ואמר: אמן – פטור.[12]

m. Shevuot 5:4–5

I.A. [If a man said to his fellow:]
You raped or seduced my daughter
And he replies: I did not rape or seduce [her]
[If the first wishes to have this confirmed under oath, and says:]
I submit you to an oath
And the [second] says: Amen [signifying acceptance of the conditions of the oath]
[And it turns out he swore falsely] – he is liable.
I.B. R. Shimon exempts him [from liability], since a man does not pay a fixed fine when he admits

t. Shevuot 2:16

I.A. [If a man said to his fellow:]
You raped or seduced my daughter
And he replies: I did not rape or seduce [her]
[If the first wishes to have this confirmed under oath, and says:]
I submit you to an oath
And the [second] says: Amen [signifying acceptance of the conditions of the oath]
[And it turns out he swore falsely] – he is liable.
I.B. R. Shimon exempts him [from liability], since a man does not pay a fixed fine when he admits

[12] Text according to MS Vienna, following Lieberman's preference for its readings.

[to his crime][13]
[and therefore he avers that the monies due for rape and seduction, which include a fixed fine, are not a legitimate subject for the oath of deposit].
I.C. The [sages] said to him: Even though he does not pay a fixed fine when he admits [to his crime], he pays for the [victim's] shame and diminished value when he admits [to his crime]. . . .
II. This is the general rule:

[to his crime][14]
[and therefore he avers that the monies due for rape and seduction, which include a fixed fine, are not a legitimate subject for the oath of deposit].
No I.C.

II. This is the general rule:

[13] R. Shimon here makes reference to a principle that distinguishes between fixed fines, which one pays as punishment for a violation, and "monies" due, which one pays to compensate for damages. See Adin Steinsaltz, *The Talmud: The Steinsaltz Edition, a Reference Guide* (New York: Random House, 1989), 254, for a description of the differences between fines and other compensatory monies due. The principle (found in m. Ket. 3:9) stipulates that if one admits to a crime for which both compensatory damages and a fixed fine are due, one is released from having to pay the fixed fine. The fixed fine is only imposed when the defendant does not admit to his crime and he is subsequently shown to be guilty by an independent procedure of the court. The case discussed here concerns a man accused of rape or seduction, for which both a fixed fine is established and compensatory monies are due for damages. The question that this mishnah considers is whether an oath may be imposed on the defendant accused of rape or seduction in order to procure the monies due to the victim and her family. R. Shimon believes that this is not a legitimate oath because were the accused man to have duly acknowledged his guilt, he would not owe the victim the fixed fine. Oaths of deposit, of which this oath is taken to be an example, may only be imposed over a disputed sum of money. Since the possibility exists that the accused could have acknowledged his guilt, R. Shimon believes that there exists no definite "disputed sum" over which to administer the oath. The sages, whose view is cited previously and whose rationale is given in the following, believe that an oath *can* be administered in such a situation. They reason that even though the fixed fine does not stand up as a "disputed sum," the accused is in any event liable for compensatory damages paid for shame and loss of her value. They see these monies as a standing "disputed sum" between the two parties, irrespective of whether the accused admits to his crime or not.

[14] See previous note.

	A.1. Every [claim] which concerns a fixed fine, and **monies which are paid if he admits** [to wrongdoing]
	[If the first said:] I submit you to an oath [concerning the disputed sum],
	[And the second] replied: Amen [indicating acceptance of the terms of the oath]
	[if he swore falsely], **he is liable.**
A. Every [claim which concerns **monies which] are paid if he admits** [to wrongdoing]	**A.2. Every** [claim] which does not concern a fixed fine,
	[but does concern **monies which] are paid if he admits** [to wrongdoing]
	[If the first said:] I submit you to an oath [concerning the disputed sum],
	[And the second] replied: Amen [indicating acceptance of the terms of the oath]
[if he swore falsely], **he is liable.**	[if he swore falsely], **he is liable.**
	No B.1.
B. Every [claim which concerns **monies which] are not paid if he admits** [to wrongdoing]	**B.2. Every** [claim] which does not concern a fixed fine, but does concern **monies which are not paid if he admits** [to wrongdoing]
	[If the first said:] I submit you to an oath [concerning the disputed sum],
	[And the second] replied: Amen [indicating acceptance of the terms of the oath]
[if he swore falsely], **he is exempt.**	[if he swore falsely], **he is exempt.**

The case discussed here concerns the reparation payments owed by a rapist or seducer to his victim and her family. Mishnaic law stipulates that the violator owes two different kinds of payment. On one hand, he pays a biblically stipulated fixed fine (קנס), and on the other hand, he pays reparation money (ממון) for several different kinds of damage (for shame to the woman and her family, loss of her value since she is no longer a virgin, and in the case of rape, for pain, as well).[15] Chapter 5 of Shevuot stipulates that under certain conditions, an oath may be imposed on a recalcitrant debtor in order to establish the validity of the claim against him and force him to pay what he owes. In the pair of sources presented here, the sages and R. Shimon debate as to whether or not this type of oath, known as the oath of deposit,[16] can legitimately be imposed on the violator in order to extract the aforementioned payments from him in the event that he denies having commited the act. Their debate turns on the fact that the two different kinds of payment alluded to here are subject to different rules if the offender *admits* to having committed the act.[17] If the offender admits his wrongdoing, then he is released from having to pay the fixed fine. In all circumstances, however, he is required to pay the other two (or three) payments compensating for shame, lost value, and pain.[18] As a result of this difference, claims concerning a fixed fine and claims concerning

[15] See m. Ket. 3:4, which states that the rapist must pay the fixed fine, plus three different kinds of damage money (shame, loss of value, and pain) and the seducer must pay the fixed fine, plus two different kinds of damage money (shame and loss of value). M. Ket. 3:9, however, groups these payments into two broader categories: fixed fines, which the perpetrator need not pay if he admits to his crime, and damage payments (for shame, loss of value, and pain), which the perpetrator pays in all cases.

[16] The oath of deposit gets its name from the fact that monies owed by one party to another are considered like a "deposit" that the one party has left in the hands of the other. In the cases listed, it is assumed that the court has the authority to impose an oath on the indebted party in order to get him to return what rightfully belongs to the other. See m. Shev. 5:2 for a basic definition of the oath of deposit.

[17] See m. Ket. 3:9.

[18] Steinsaltz explains that the fixed fine serves as a kind of punishment, from which the offender frees himself when he admits to his crime. He nonetheless remains liable for the other payments, which function as reparation payments for damage done. See Steinsaltz, *Reference Guide*, 254 (entry on קנס).

other kinds of reparation payments function differently with respect to the oath of deposit. The oath of deposit may be imposed only on a *presumptive* debtor, that is, someone of whom a debt can reasonably be assumed. In the case of a claim concerning a fixed fine, however, were the alleged violator to *admit* to wrongdoing, he would *not* have to pay the fine, and he would no longer be a presumptive debtor. Since one never knows how an alleged offender will respond to the accusation, one cannot impose the oath of deposit on claims concerning fixed fines because of the possibility that he might admit to the claims, with the result that there would be no disputed sum between the two parties. When the oath is administered illegitimately, the offender is not liable for violating the oath, *even if* he swears falsely.[19]

In this set of sources, the sages and R. Shimon disagree as to whether one may legitimately impose the oath of deposit on the seducer and rapist. Whereas part of the monies owed to the victim and her family are a fixed fine, over which the oath of deposit cannot be legitimately administered, the other part of the monies owed are an appropriate and legitimate subject for the oath of deposit.[20] The two parties debate which component of the monies owed is definitive in establishing whether or not the oath of deposit may be administered. On one side of the issue stands R. Shimon, who says that it is inappropriate to administer such an oath and that the violator should not be held liable for swearing falsely. In his way of thinking, since the claim against the

19 Menahem b. Shlomo (HaMeiri) (1249–1316), in his commentary to m. Shevuot, makes clear, however, that such a person would be culpable for making a false declaration under oath; i.e., he is liable for what is known as the declaratory oath (שבועת ביטוי). Menahem ben Shlomo (HaMeiri), *Perushei HaMishnah l'HaMeiri*, vol. 5, ed. Menachem Mendel Meshi Zahar (Jerusalem: Dvar, 1974), 120 (ק"כ).

20 This case presents an interesting example of what Neusner calls an "excluded middle, that is, that creature or substance [and here I would add circumstance] which seems to fall between two distinct and definitive categories" because it partakes of both of them. This case deals with a claim that both is and is not a legitimate subject for the oath of deposit. See Jacob Neusner, *Judaism: Evidence of the Mishnah*, 259. See also discussion of borderline and ambiguous cases in Elizabeth Shanks Alexander, "Casuistic Elements in Mishnaic Law: Examples from Tractate Shevuot," *Jewish Studies Quarterly* 10, no. 3 (November 2003): 197–99, 222–31.

violator *includes* a fixed fine (which his confession would cancel), there is no clear disputed sum between the two parties. On the other side of the issue stand the sages. They acknowledge that the claim includes a fixed fine, which could be canceled if the violator confesses, but note that the claim additionally includes other reparation payments, which would remain active even were the alleged offender to confess to his wrongdoing.

A common structural framework undergirds the presentation of issues in the two sources. Both sources have a first part (I.) focused on the debate between R. Shimon and the sages and a second part (II.) elaborating the principle assumed by the sages in their ruling.[21] Within the first part, however, the mishnaic source includes an expansion of the debate that is missing from the tosephtan source. While both sources rehearse the basic positions of the sages and R. Shimon (I.A. and I.B.), the mishnaic version includes a refrain from the sages that develops the legal reasoning underlying their position (I.C.).[22] That is, in addition

21 On the basis of the excerpted portion of the text, one might be tempted to read the general principle at the end of the mishnaic version as representing *neither* the view of the sages *nor* the view of R. Shimon. The principle seems to be worded generally enough to accommodate both points of view. In that way of reading, the principle would be cited because *its interpretation* is at stake in the debate. The sages and R. Shimon would represent two different interpretations of the general principle. In the complete mishnaic context, however, the general principle does not follow immediately after the debate. There, it follows after three intervening pairs of cases that further illustrate the principle. The same issue at stake in the debate between the sages and R. Shimon arises in the first set of cases, and the Mishnah rules according to the sages. No mention is made of R. Shimon's position. Since it makes most sense that the principle would account for the cases it most immediately follows upon, I would argue that the principle elaborates on the sages' point of view alone. See Pinchas Kehati, *Seder Nezikin, Pt. 2*, vol. 8 of *Mishnah with Commentary* (Jerusalem: Hekhal Shlomo, 1977), 106 (קו), intro. to mishnah 5. Other commentators seem to take for granted this interpretation and do not articulate it explicitly.

22 See discussion in Alexander, "Casuistic Elements," 197–99, 222–31, concerning the role of ambiguous cases that can be plausibly resolved according to two different rationales within mishnaic discourse. There, it is observed that it is equally common for disputes to appear in condensed form, with a mere statement of the two positions, or in expanded form, with the rationale for each position drawn out explicitly. The Tosephta here appears to tend toward one stylistic manifestation and the Mishnah toward the other. Ironically, the fact that the Mishnah is more expansive here than the

to an initial presentation that each side is afforded, the mishnaic version grants the sages an opportunity to rebut R. Shimon and explain the inadequacy of his reasoning. This addition by the Mishnah, however, does not add a new structural element. We must assume that the reasoning, which is explicitly spelled out in the sages' rebuttal, is assumed in the initial presentation of their position (I.A.). To borrow a term that Lord uses with respect to the *guslari* (Yogoslavian oral poets), we might think of this addition as a kind of "ornamentation" of the basic presentation.[23] While the ornamentation makes the expression more vivid, and some might argue more clear, it does not supply information or a perspective that has not already been taken for granted. Rather, it states explicitly what is already implied in the basic presentation.[24]

Tosephta contradicts a traditional commonplace assumption about the relationship between the two. It is usually assumed that the Tosephta is the more expansive of the two sources. See for example, Jacob Neusner, *The Tosefta*, xvii–xxi, and Goldberg, "The Tosefta," 289–92.

23 For Lord's discussion of ornamentation, see *The Singer of Tales*, 16–17, 25–26, 88–89.

24 Martin Jaffee makes a similar point with respect to the relationship between a condensed mishnaic text and its more expansive parallels: "One must ask: is this expansion 'exegetical' in the sense that it supplies information needed by a textual exegete to interpret the Mishnah? Or does it simply give textual expression to knowledge the Mishnaic tradent already assumed on the part of students? I suggest the latter"; *Torah in the Mouth*, 138. John Miles Foley explains that in oral and oral-derived texts, the text does not generate meaning in isolation from the larger body of tradition. He explains that in systems of "traditional referentiality," the larger backdrop of tradition is always impinging. He describes the relationship between the explicitly stated terms and implicitly invoked meanings as a type of traditional "metonymy . . . wherein the part stands for the whole" (*Immanent Art*, 7). In our example, the partial presentation of the debate between the sages and R. Shimon found in the tosephtan source stands in for the more drawn out "whole" in the mishnaic source. The "part" draws its meaning from and is sustained by the meanings implicit in the "whole." Even though the tosephtan version of the debate is only partial, the full presentation as reflected in the mishnaic source is assumed and impinges on the reader's or listener's understanding of the partial presentation. See Foley, *Immanent Art*, 2–60. Traditionally, scholars of rabbinics have assumed that the more drawn-out source serves as "commentary" for the more condensed source, especially when the more drawn-out source is the Tosephta. The later redactional date of the Tosephta suggests to scholars that it was compiled as a kind of commentary to the cryptic and condensed Mishnah. The current proposal differs insofar as I do not impute to the more expansive version the *self-conscious* function of commentary. I suggest instead that these meanings were

A similar phenomenon appears in the second part of the two sources, but here the roles are reversed. Here the mishnaic source offers a more compact and condensed presentation and the tosephtan version a more expansive one.[25] The tosephtan version does not introduce new elements to the basic structure; it merely makes more vivid the information conveyed in the Mishnah's basic presentation. Specifically, it unpacks distinctions that the Mishnah assumes but fails to spell out. At first glance, the mishnaic presentation of the rule seems more straightforward and easier to grasp than the tosephtan version. The mishnaic version differentiates between two different kinds of claims that might be subject to the oath of deposit (A. and B.), and it describes them quite simply (claims concerning monies that *are* paid when the offender admits to his wrongdoing and claims concerning monies that *are not* paid when the offender admits). By way of contrast, the tosephtan version differentiates among three different kinds of claims and it describes them with far greater complexity. As I hope to show, however, all of the complexity in the tosephtan presentation is in fact *implied* in the mishnaic presentation.

The first half of the mishnaic rule (II.A.) stipulates that claims concerning monies that are paid irrespective of whether the offender

current and assumed *at the time* that the more condensed text was formulated. Foley's theory of traditional referentiality explains how a condensed and cryptic text can be meaningful in traditional settings: because the listening/reading audience imports a full spectrum of legal concepts, definitions, principles, and norms from the larger tradition and brings them to bear whenever it encounters any single teaching.

25 The fact that the tosephtan version is generally more expansive than its mishnaic parallel has often been interpreted as evidence for the lateness of the tosephtan source relative to its mishnaic parallel. It is reasoned that the tosephtan source serves as an early proto-commentary to the mishnaic source, which explains why the tosephtan expands on the cryptic mishnah. E.g., see Jacob Neusner, *The Tosefta*, xvii–xxi, and Goldberg, "The Tosefta," 289–92. See discussion and rejection of this view of the Tosephta-Mishnah relations in Jaffee, *Torah in the Mouth*, 202, n. 6. Recently, a new trend is developing in scholarship on Tosephta-Mishnah relations that interprets the tosephtan expansiveness as evidence of its chronological *priority* to the Mishnah. In this point of view, the Mishnah intentionally condenses the less focused and more discursive raw tannaitic materials attested in today's Tosephta. See Hauptman, "Mishnah as a Response to 'Tosefta'"; Friedman, "An Ancient Tosefta (1)"; Friedman, "An Ancient Tosefta (2)"; and Friedman, "The Primacy of Tosefta to Mishna."

admits to wrongdoing are legitimate subjects for the oath of deposit, and therefore, the one who swears falsely concerning them is held liable for his false oath. Stating the rule in this manner, however, fails to take into account the complexity of our case, which concerns *both* a fixed fine *and* other kinds of reparation payments. Our case is what Jacob Neusner would call a "mixture," simultaneously exhibiting features of two distinct legal categories.[26] To use the language of the mishnaic rule, the claim concerns monies both *paid and not paid* if the offender admits to his wrongdoing. As formulated, the rule would seem to provide little guidance for our case. Mishnaic commentator Pinchas Kehati explains that the mishnaic rule needs to be read as implying more than it actually states. He states that the first part of the rule (II.A.) is intended to deal with claims concerning *both* fixed fines and other reparation payments.[27] In this reading, the single generalized formulation of the Mishnah could more precisely be expressed by two specific formulations – one dealing with claims concerning fixed fines and other reparation payments and the other dealing with claims consisting solely of other reparation payments. Whereas the mishnaic presentation takes for granted the duality of possibilities contained within its single formulation (and considers *both* subject to the same rule), the tosephtan version spells out both possibilities explicitly. At II.A.1., the Tosephta considers claims concerning *both* a fixed fine and other damage payments, and at II.A.2., it considers claims that *do not* concern a fixed fine but that *do* concern other damage payments. Whereas the Mishnah only assumes as much, the Tosephta explicitly states that both kinds of claims are legitimate subjects for the oath of deposit (and therefore, the offender who swears falsely about either kind of claim is liable for his false oath). The two different sources, then, seem to be making exactly the same point. The difference between them lies in the extent to which the Tosephta's more drawn-out presentation leaves less ambiguity in the interpretation.

[26] See Neusner, *Judaism: Evidence of the Mishnah*, 256–70.

[27] See Kehati, *Mishnah*, 106, (קו), intro. to mishnah 5.

The astute reader will note that the Tosephta does not unpack the second part of the rule with the same thoroughness that it unpacks the first part. I would argue, however, that the second part of the rule implies a two-part structure, even if it does not fully articulate it. The reader will notice that II.B.2. is not complemented by II.B.1. Where II.B.2. in the Tosephta considers "the claim that does *not* concern a fixed fine, but *does* concern monies that are not paid if he admits to wrongdoing," one would expect to find a corresponding II.B.1., which would fill out the four-part structure suggested by A.1., A.2., and B.2. The hypothetical B.1. would address the final constellation of variables; namely, it would consider "the claim that concerns a fixed fine and monies that are not paid if he admits to wrongdoing." This formulation, however, is slightly redundant, as fixed fines are the very monies that are not paid when the offender admits to his wrongdoing. The ruling in this case should be fairly self-evident by this point in the exercise, as it has been assumed throughout the pericope: Claims concerning fixed fines *alone* are not a legitimate subject for the oath of deposit. Indeed, the entire exercise of this pericope has been to investigate how this fact impacts claims that include both fixed fines and other kinds of reparation payments. Thus, I would argue that the Tosephta does not complete its symmetrical presentation in the second part of the rule because it seems redundant and unnecessary.[28]

[28] I have explained the rule according to its presentation in MS Vienna, following Lieberman's preference for its readings. MS Erfurt, however, has a different presentation, which is more difficult to make sense of. Rather than considering three out of four theoretical possibilities (A.1., A.2., and B.2.), it only treats two of the four possible combinations of variables (A.1. and B.2.). Its version of the rule reads:

זה הכלל: כל שהוא קנס, ומשלם על פי עצמו, משביעך אני, ואמר: אמן – חייב.
וכל שאינו קנס, אין משלם על פי עצמו משביעך אני, ואמר: אמן – פטור

As it stands, it seems to suggest in its second clause that instances in which one does pay monies on the force of one's own testimony are the same as instances in which one is *not* paying a fixed fine. This formulation would seem to contradict the rule implied throughout both M and T, which is that those who *are* subject to a fixed fine do *not* have to pay monies owed on the force of their own testimony. It is possible that the Erfurt version has edited out one of the three clauses in MS Vienna to reflect the mishaic version, which only has two clauses. MS Erfurt seems not to have perceived the

The tosephtan version of the rule expands in yet another way that the mishnaic version does not. As before, so too here the expansion does not introduce a new element into the treatment of the issues but simply makes explicit certain assumptions that the mishnaic version takes for granted. In A.1., A.2., and B.2. after the Tosephta describes the different kinds of claims subject to the oath of deposit, it briefly rehearses the conditions under which the oath is imposed. In each instance it follows the description with a brief dialogue: "If the first one said: 'I submit you to an oath' and the second one replied: 'Amen.'" This brief dialogue is a formulaic way of indicating that the oath of deposit is imposed.[29] Unlike the expansion discussed previously, this expansion does not necessarily make the legal issues at hand more clear. What the Tosephta's elaboration does, however, is remind the listener, reciter, or reader of the legal context within which the different kinds of claims are being considered. The different kinds of claims described at A.1., A.2., and B.2. are of interest *insofar as* they are appropriate or inappropriate subjects for the oath of deposit. By rehearsing the dialogue, the Tosephta keeps the proper legal context of the oath of deposit in the forefront of the listener's, reciter's, or reader's mind. The more condensed mishnaic version makes no sense if one does not assume the information supplied in the tosephtan expansion.[30] Whereas the listener, reciter, or reader of the mishnaic version must supply this legal context on his or her own, the tosephtan version asks less of those engaging it.[31] The tosephtan version makes the presentation more vivid

implict four-part structure in MS Vienna and so edited the three clauses down to two, but in the process has lost sight of the basic legal principles expressed by this pericope.

29 See m. Shev. 5:2 where this dialogue appears as part of the basic definition of the oath of deposit. There, the dialogue is presented in response to the question "The oath of deposit. How so?" (שבועת העדות, כיצד?).

30 Though the Mishnah does not state explicitly that this rule concerns the oath of deposit, it establishes this frame of reference in an earlier part of the chapter. See m. Shev. 5:1–2.

31 Foley suggests that audiences in traditional societies are always listening to oral performance against the backdrop of a broader network of associations and motifs. See Foley, *Immanent Art,* 39–60. When considering the traditional contexts in which m.

by taking less for granted and demanding less supplementation on the part of listeners, reciters, and readers.

Comparison of these two sources suggests that continuity between them is achieved by use of a common structural framework, which can be expanded or contracted as needed in different performative settings.[32] Whereas the mishnaic context of performance elicits ornamentation of the debate, the tosephtan context elicits ornamentation in the presentation of the general rule. In his discussion of ornamentation, Lord suggests that several different factors lead the guslari to ornament or refrain from doing so. Time pressures in performance and an audience's impatience can lead a performer to curtail his ornamentation.[33] A performer's fluidity and comfort with the material tend to result in more ornamentation.[34] Finally, Lord notes that intrinsic aspects of the material itself can call forth ornamentation, as with descriptions of the hero that are more heavily ornamented than those of other characters.[35] It is hardly possible to reconstruct the situations in which the mishnaic and tosephtan versions of our source were performed, and therefore, ascribing the ornamention to circumstantial factors or the talents of different performers is beyond the scope of this study.

Shevuot was studied in antiquity, we might think of the broader network of traditional associations as including legal definitions, rules and principles, and contexts.

32 Scholars have often used distinctions like the ones we have noted to ground different theories concerning which source came first. The question of textual priority is important when one is interested in assessing the significance of the differences between the two sources. In other words, do the differences arise because the Mishnah is earlier and the Tosephta comes to comment on and supplement it? Or do the differences arise because the Tosephta represents earlier, less "processed" material, which the Mishnah comes to condense for a more formal and focused presentation? These questions are very important in rabbinic studies and have far-reaching implications. These questions, however, take as their starting point that the significant point of interest in the relationship between the two sources derives from their differences. By way of contrast, this study comes to inquire into the significance of the points of *continuity* between the two sources. What do they tell us about where textual fixity and flexibility were seen to lie?

33 Lord, *The Singer of Tales*, 16–17, 26.

34 Lord, *The Singer of Tales*, 25.

35 Lord, *The Singer of Tales*, 88–89.

It is possible, however, to speculate that the materials preserved in the Mishnah and Tosephta were performed in different contexts with different pedagogical purposes. In so doing, we might account for the different levels and uses of ornamentation by suggesting that more ornamentation may be more well suited to some pedagogical purposes and less well suited to others. One might tentatively suggest that the Mishnah's ornamentation of the debate derives from an interest in fleshing out the ambiguity of the case under consideration, which can plausibly be resolved either according to the sages' or R. Shimon's legal rationales.[36] The more forcefully each side is argued, the less clear-cut becomes the legal resolution. One might likewise speculate that tosephtan expansion of the rule reflects an informal performance setting, in which the student's lack of familiarity with legal issues is accommodated. By way of contrast, the Mishnah's more condensed and cryptic presentation of the rule, bordering on opaque, might indicate an audience more fluent with the legal issues.[37] Drawing on Lord's observation that time constraints in performance lead to less ornamentation, we might speculate that the Mishnah's more condensed presentation of the rule reflects the function of the Mishnah as a crystalized synopsis of legal issues.[38] These remain, however, speculative suggestions that we lack a definite means of confirming or refuting.

[36] See Alexander, "Casuistic Elements," 222–31, which notes that the Mishnah is typically interested in ambiguous cases that can plausibly be resolved according to two or more equally plausible legal rationales.

[37] The idea that the Mishnah would have been used by advanced students goes against the prevailing understanding of the pedagogical purposes of this text. Dominant trends in scholarship understand the Mishnah, instead, as a primer of sorts for novice learners. See, e.g., Gerhardsson, *Memory and Manuscript*, 79–92. Contra this view, see Alexander, "Casuistic Elements," 236–37.

[38] The idea that the Mishnah is a later synopsis of earlier, more expansive tradition formulated for easy retrieval and recall of relevant issues squares well with recent work suggesting the Mishnah's relative lateness with respect to many tosephtan parallels. See Friedman, "The Primacy of Tosefta to Mishna"; Friedman, "An Ancient Tosefta (1)"; Friedman, "An Ancient Tosefta (2)"; Friedman, *Tosefta Atiqta*; and Hauptman, "Mishnah as a Response to 'Tosefta.' "

The important point here is that common to the two sources is a basic structural framework. With greater and lesser degrees of thoroughness, the two sources make the same points, review the same principles, and cover the same ground, all the while treating the issues in the same order. Even as the structure is expanded or condensed to fit the needs of different performative settings, the basic elements of the structural framework constrain the performance. They define an outer limit beyond which the tradition fails to maintain its integrity. Thus, one essential element of the traditions preserved in m. Shevuot as it was conceptualized during the tannaitic period is the **structural frameworks** around which the text is organized. These structures are important because they mark out the fundamental categories of thinking. They establish the "slots" into which the verbatim strings of words (which the two sources do share) can be fitted.[39]

Fixed Phrases in Common: M. Shev. 7:1–7 and T. Shev. 6:1–4

The next set of sources also shares an overarching structural framework, though here it is less pronounced than in the previous set of sources. What I wish to call attention to in this set of parallels is how the use of a **fixed phrase** establishes continuity between the two sources.

[39] The fact that the two sources do have strings of words in common does suggest a certain degree of fixity between performative versions. It is likely that writing did play some role in stabilizing text, even during the tannaitic period. See Jaffee, *Torah in the Mouth,* 100–25. Jaffee, however, makes the important point that the use of writing need not have implied a fixed *conception* of mishnaic textuality. As he writes: "Within such a milieu, written texts enjoyed an essentially oral cultural life, subject to all the vagaries of oral transmission as they were memorized and transmitted in face-to-face performance" (124). Steven Fraade likewise articulates a model of rabbinic textuality wherein the presence of writing need not preclude an understanding of the texts as "orally" fluid: "What emerges, then, is a more 'circulatory' understanding of the interrelation of Rabbinic texts and their oral performative enactments: an orality that is grounded in a textuality that remains orally fluid"; "Literary Composition and Oral Performance," 36.

Even where the overarching structural framework of the two sources is not identical, having certain phrases in common can invoke deeper commonalities than are apparent if we attend only to verbatim reproduction of text. Although the common phrase appears in different "slots" in the overarching framework of each source, the fact that both sources use the phrase to indicate the same legal phenomenon signals continuity between the two sources. The use of a common fixed phrase complements the loose structural commonalities that the two sources share and reinforces the semblance of likeness between them.

The parallel sources begin by reviewing a principle that has functioned in every oath discussed thus far in the tractate. The Mishnah then goes on to elaborate a new principle that pertains to just a few specified cases.

משנה שבועות פרק ז' הלכה א'	תוספתא שבועות פרק ו' הלכה א'
כל הנשבעין שבתורה – נשבעין ולא משלמין.	כל הנשבעין שבתורה – נשבעין ולא משלמין. שנ' ולקח בעליו ולא ישלם כיוון שקיבלו בעלים את השבועה הלז, פטור מלשלם.
ואלו נשבעין ונוטלין: השכיר, והנגזל, והנחבל, ושכנגדו חשוד על השבועה, והחנוני על פנקסו.	

m. Shevuot 7:1	**t. Shevuot 6:1**
All of those that the Torah indicates should take oaths, take an oath in order to be excused from restitution payments.	All of those that the Torah indicates should take oaths, take an oath in order to be excused from restitution payments. As it says, *and the owner shall accept [the oath] and he shall not pay restitution.* Since the owners have accepted this oath, he is exempt from having to pay restitution.

But these take an oath in order to
collect [monies due]: the hired
man, he who has been robbed, he
who has been wounded, he who
[in court] stands opposite one
who is not trustworthy regarding
oaths, and the shopkeeper over
[what is written] in his ledger.

The two sources begin by citing a descriptive principle: All of the oaths prescribed by the Torah are imposed in order to *absolve* the oathtaker of financial responsibility. The Tosephta then offers a brief expansion not present in the Mishnah. It provides a biblical proof text for this principle. The Tosephta's expansion here is similar to those examined in the previous section. It does not add a new element to the conceptual orchestration of legal concepts; it merely supplies information that is presumed or implicit in the more condensed version.[40] The

[40] This is somewhat of a controversial point. Traditionally, expansions of this sort by the Tosephta would be assumed to be a type of "proto-commentary" to the Mishnah. A dominant trend in contemporary scholarship argues that the Mishnah intentionally suppresses references to biblical scripture in order to enhance its own authority as an independent code of law (see, e.g., Halivni, *Midrash, Mishnah and Gemara,* 52–65, and Neusner, *Judaism: Evidence of the Mishnah,* 217–23). When the Tosephta, then, supplies proof texts to the Mishnah's cryptic presentation of the law, this represents a *departure* from the ideological perspective inherent in the mishnaic presentation. By way of contrast, I see no compelling reason to view the Tosephta's presentation as a departure from the mishnaic point of view. As argued by Hannah Harrington, the Mishnah assumes intimate knowledge with biblical scripture and builds its legal edifices upon that knowledge. One should not make too much of the fact that the Mishnah usually presumes, rather than articulates, the nature of those dependencies. See Hannah Harrington, "The Rabbinic Reception of Leviticus," in *The Book of Leviticus: Composition and Reception,* vol. 93, ed. Rolf Rendtorff and Robert A. Kugler, Supplements to Vetus Testamentum (Leiden: Brill, 2003), 383–401. Thus, when the Tosephta supplies the biblical proof text for the mishnaic statement of the principle, I see no reason to think of this as a reactive gesture. I am more inclined to see it on a par with the expansions discussed earlier. As with the other expansions, this one, too, articulates information that is (it can plausibly be argued) assumed in the more condensed version.

Mishnah does, however, add a new structural element. It articulates an additional, secondary principle that complements the first one. The secondary principle states that in certain exceptional instances (to be enumerated), the oathtaker takes an oath in order to *recover* payments due. While the two sources share a common starting point, the Mishnah develops a structural component not found in the Tosephta. The secondary principle that the Mishnah articulates has a certain lexical symmetry with the first principle. Echoing the first principle's prescription to "swear and not pay" (נשבעין ולא משלמין), the second principle instructs that in certain other situations one is to "swear and *collect*" (נשבעין ונוטלין). The Tosephta does not articulate this secondary principle and therefore does not highlight or develop the symmetry latent within the relationship between the first and second principles. It is missing the structural framework of two contrasting principles, which is found in the Mishnah.

The Tosephta does, however, have an alternate method of expressing the same information conveyed by the Mishnah's secondary principle. The phrase that the Mishnah uses to express the secondary principle ("they swear and collect" [נשבעין ונוטלין]) appears intermittently throughout the tosephtan passage, as we shall see. Though none of the usages presents a verbatim reproduction of the mishnaic principle, this fixed phrase alludes to a shared context of legal concepts and vocabulary between the two sources. It invokes a larger context of tradition that the two sources have in common and draw on. While the two sources put the fixed phrase from the common larger tradition to slightly different uses, it nonetheless serves as a link of continuity between them.

Before moving on to discuss the contexts in which the Tosephta uses the phrase "swear and collect" (נשבעין ונוטלין), we must first attend to the final element of the Mishnah's expansion. After articulating the secondary principle that allows certain oathtakers to recover payments due, the Mishnah enumerates the five concrete situations in which this principle operates: when the oathtaker is a hired man (presumably trying to collect his wages), when he is a victim of theft or assault (presumably trying to collect damages), when the other litigant cannot be trusted to swear faithfully, and when he is a shopkeeper testifying with regard to financial records kept in his ledger. In each of these cases, the law presumes in favor of the oathtaker, and if he affirms his claims under oath, the court is authorized to exact payments due. This list suggests a structural framework, which both the Mishnah and the Tosephta adopt. In both sources, each of the five situations is discussed in detail in order to determine the precise conditions under which the plaintiff may take an oath and recover payments due. Both sources treat the situations in the order established by the list, with the single exception that the Tosephta does not include a section on the robbed man (הנגזל). It is in these several paragraphs treating the various situations in which the oath is used to extract payments that the Tosephta uses the phrase "swear and collect" (נשבע ונוטל).[41] Though hardly identical in content, the two sources exhibit strong structural similarities insofar as they discuss the same legal issues in the same order, that is, in the order suggested by the mishnaic list.[42]

The mishnaic version of these paragraphs is a much more tightly controlled composition than its tosephtan counterpart, with each situation being discussed according to more or less the same standardized pattern. Each paragraph begins by identifying the situation to be discussed and asking "How so?" (כיצד). Thus, we read "The hired man, how so?" (m. Shev. 7:1) and again "The man who has been robbed,

41 In the Tosephta, the phrase appears in a singular conjugation ("he swears and collects" [נשבע ונוטל]) as a result of the fact that each case that is discussed is singular in nature. In the Mishnah, the phrase appears in the plural form "they swear and collect" (נשבעין ונוטלין) when the phrase appears as a part of the descriptive principle, which treats several different cases under a single rubric, and in the singular conjugation in each of the descriptive paragraphs.

42 The list may well have existed as an independent source at some point, designed to engender a protracted analysis of the issues surrounding oaths in which the oathtaker "swears and collects." Here, I am imagining a textual source that served to stimulate oral performance as reconstructed by Martin S. Jaffee, *Torah in the Mouth,* 135–40. In this example, the list would have been a tool and resource for performance, and the two different expansions of the list found in M and T would represent two different ways of analyzing the issues at hand.

how so?" (m. Shev. 7:2) and again "The man who has been injured, how so?" (m. Shev. 7:3), and so on. In each case, the introductory question elicits a description of a basic scenario involving litigation between the person in question and another. For example, in response to the first question ("the hired man, how so?"), we find the following scenario: "If [the hired man] said to him: 'Give me my wage, which you still hold in your possession.' And he replies: 'I already gave it [to you]' and he then says, 'I did not collect it' – he swears and collects [his wage](הוא נשבע ונוטל)" (m. Shev. 7:1). The scenario establishes the circumstances under which the person in question (in this case, the hired man) may take an oath in order to collect payment. It clarifies basic legal requirements. Each scenario ends with the declaration "he swears and collects" (נשבע ונוטל), clarifying that contrary to the usual manner in which oaths are imposed, a person in such a situation may take an oath in order to recover funds owed.[43] This pattern is repeated for each of the five situations listed in the second mishnaic principle. Each paragraph also includes some attention to a secondary issue. The Mishnah presents information in a highly regularized manner. The phrase "he swears and collects" (נשבע ונוטל) appears in the same position in each paragraph. In the Mishnah, then, structure and fixed phraseology work hand in hand to express legal concepts and norms.

By way of contrast, the Tosephta's presentation is much less systematic, orderly, and uniform. The fact that the structural framework of the Tosephta is so very inconsistent highlights how the fixed phrase,

[43] Each scenario is followed by a slightly different version of the phrase. After the scenario involving the hired man, we read "**he** swears and collects" (הוא נשבע ונוטל) (m. Shev. 7:1); after the scenarios involving the robbed and wounded men, we read "**behold, this one** swears and collects" (הרי זה נשבע ונוטל) (m. Shev. 7:2–3); after the scenario involving the person who in court stands opposite one who is not trustworthy with respect to oaths, we read "**the one who is opposite him** swears and collects" (שכנגדו נשבע ונוטל) (m. Shev. 7:4); and after the scenario involving the shopkeeper and his record book, we read "**he** swears and collects **and they** swear and collect" (הוא נשבע ונוטל והן נשבעין ונוטלין) (m. Shev. 7:5). These subtle variations suggest that even when a phrase is fixed to represent a particular legal phenomenon, there is flexibility in its deployment.

even by itself, is a powerful mechanism for conveying established legal concepts and norms. Even without the structural framework of the Mishnah, the Tosephta reproduces much of the same tradition found in the mishnaic passage. The haphazard nature of the Tosephta's presentation manifests itself in several ways. In only two of the four cases treated by the Tosephta does the text review the *basic circumstances* in which the oath may be employed to extract payments due. In the other two cases, the text jumps immediately into complicated concerns of a secondary order.[44]

The Tosephta is equally as unsystematic in the language it uses to introduce each paragraph. Whereas the Mishnah consistently begins each paragraph with the question "How so?" (כיצד), the Tosephta

[44] For example, in the first paragraph concerning the hired man, the text assumes fundamental familiarity with the conflict that arises between the hired man and his employer, and so it proceeds directly into a discussion of a secondary issue concerning the timeliness of the claim. Stating "if his time had expired, he may not swear and collect," the text assumes familiarity with the basic scenario that the Mishnah takes the effort to articulate.

Not only does the Tosephta fail to review the basic information that the Mishnah conveys explicitly, but it also treats a different secondary issue than does the Mishnah. By way of contrast to the Tosephta, the Mishnah presents a conflicting opinion about the conditions under which the oath may be administered. The divergent opinion is presented in the name of R. Yehudah, who requires that the employer admit to having withheld at least a portion of the wages. It should be noted that both the mishnaic and tosephtan discussions of the hired man exhibit an internally consistent structural framework. The parallel elements that govern the structure in each case, however, are unique to the source in which they appear. Thus, in the tosephtan source, the second line introducing the concern about timeliness echoes the syntax of the opening line of the paragraph ("The hired man swears and collects; if his time expired, he does not swear and collect" [השכיר נשבע ונוטל; עבר זמנו, אינו נשבע ונוטל] [t. Shev. 6:1]). In the mishnaic source, R.Yehudah's concern that the employer admit to having withheld at least a portion of the wages echoes the concerns of the basic scenario where the employer denies having withheld *any* of the wages. The fact that each source adopts an internally consistent structure not found in the other makes it all the more significant that the phrase "he swears and collects" appears in both. Where no other points of continuity exist, the presence of this common phrase links the two sources.

Likewise, the Tosephta's discussion of the one who stands opposite someone who is not trustworthy with respect to oaths fails to give a basic scenario. It proceeds immediately to consider the secondary issue of what to do when *both* litigants are not trustworthy (t. Shev. 6:3).

alternates between paragraphs beginning with simple declarative statements and those introduced by the question "How so?" (כיצד). Thus, the first paragraph treating the hired man begins, "The hired man swears and collects" (השכיר נשבע ונוטל), but the second paragraph treating the wounded man begins, "The wounded man, how so?" (הנחבל, כיצד). While the third paragraph begins, "the one standing opposite someone who is not trustworthy regarding oaths, how so?" (שכנגדו חשוד על השבועה כיצד?), the fourth paragraph begins "the shopkeeper [may take an oath] regarding records kept in his ledger, but not regarding items sold on terms" (חנוני על פנקסו, ולא במוקף). Even the context in which the repeating phrase ("he swears and collects" [נשבע ונוטל]) appears varies from paragraph to paragraph. As noted, the paragraph treating the hired man begins with the phrase "the hired man swears and collects" (השכיר נשבע ונוטל). By way of contrast, the paragraph treating the wounded man proceeds in exactly the manner as the mishnaic paragraphs, beginning with a question of "How so?" and then continuing with a description of the basic conditions under which the oath can be employed. Finally, it ends with a declaration of "Behold this one swears and collects" (הרי זה נשבע ונוטל).[45] Offering yet more diversity, the paragraph treating the one who stands opposite someone who is not trustworthy with respect to oaths adopts an abbreviated version of the mishnaic pattern. It begins with the question "How so?" but instead of following this question with a scenario outlining the basic conditions under which the oath may be imposed, it goes directly to the final declaration: "The one standing opposite him swears and collects" (שכנגדו נשבע ונוטל). The Tosephta, then, uses a variety of organizational strategies to present information, making it very difficult to identify precise points of continuity with the Mishnah's version of tradition, which is presented in a coherent manner following a single organization format.

I would argue that the common use of the fixed phrase "he swears and collects" (נשבע ונוטל) links the two sources, indicating that they

[45] This represents one of the few verbatim parallels between the two passages.

share a concern for the same legal issues and draw on the same legal definitions and norms. In spite of the varied contexts in which the phrase appears, certain consistencies are maintained. First of all, the phrase is invoked with respect to each of the cases discussed in both the Mishnah and the Tosephta. This creates the general impression that the different items discussed in the different paragraphs are part of a single legal phenomenon. In fact, the Mishnah makes the unity of the phenomenon clear when it states the principle "and these swear and collect" (ואלו נשבעין ונוטלין), to which all of the enumerated cases are subject. But the unity of the phenomenon (and its identity with the mishnaic description) also emerges from the Tosephta's presentation. By employing this key phrase in each paragraph, the Tosephta indicates its own familiarity with and adoption of this principle. Second, regardless of where the phrase is used in the Mishnah or the Tosephta, the verbs appear in third person, participle form. The verbs are conjugated in the plural and singular as appropriate, but the consistent use of the third person, participle form lends the fixed phrase a formulaic quality. Investing the phrase with a formulaic quality enables it to call to mind the same set of legal issues and stipulations irrespective of the context in which it is used.[46] The appearance of the phrase in both the Mishnah and the Tosephta provides an important link of continuity between them. While this set of parallel texts does not have literal or structural convergences as strong as the previous set considered, the presence of the fixed phrase in each attests to a common body of tradition underlying both. It helps us identify the tools and resources available to tannaitic transmitters in preserving and maintaining the integrity of traditions in m. Shevuot. Just as the overarching structural frameworks discussed in the previous section enable transmitters to reproduce a tradition from m. Shevuot with fidelity, so too certain fixed phrases, especially those which express a particular legal concept, help to preserve and maintain tradition in a consistent manner.

[46] Foley explains that formulaic phrases in Homeric, Serbo-Croatian, and Old English epic poetry also invoke certain connotative meanings, irrespective of the context in which they appear. See Foley, *Immanent Art*, 17–33.

In addition to the fixed phrase considered at length here, a number of other fixed phrases are used in a formulaic manner throughout the traditions of m. Shevuot and its parallels.[47] Like the phrase considered here, these other phrases appear in a variety of syntactical contexts and structural frameworks. Their formulaic quality derives from the fact that they (like the phrase discussed at length here) are used in the same grammatical form irrespective of the diverse contexts in which they appear. Also like the phrase considered here, these phrases invoke particular legal concepts and concerns, and thus allude to the broader backdrop of tradition on which the traditions of m. Shevuot and its parallels draw. The ubiquity of fixed phrases among the parallel traditions, especially when they appear in diverse syntactical contexts, suggests that they, like overarching structural frameworks, are a valuable resource for transmitters and formulators of the traditions in m. Shevuot in maintaining continuity in the tradition.

Shared Underlying Conceptual Concerns: M. Shev. 3:4 and T. Shev. 2:1–2

In this final section on tannaitic parallels, I wish to consider an instance in which the points of continuity between parallel traditions

[47] Some of the fixed phrases are more particular to the topic of oaths, and others seem to have broad applicability. Among those particular to the topic of oaths, I would count the following phrases: "from his own mouth" vs. "from the mouth of others" (מפי עצמו ומפי אחרים) (see m. Shev. 3:10–11, 4:1, 5:1; t. Shev. 3:5; Sifra Dibbura d'Hata'ot, Parshata 8:3); "before the court" vs. "not before the court" (בפני בית דין ושלא בפני בית דין) (m. Shev. 3:10, 4:1, 4:3, 5:1–2); "deposit, loan, plunder or loss" (פקדון, תשומת יד, וגל ואבדה) (m. Shev. 4:5, 5:3; Sifra Dibbura d'Hata'ot Pereq 15:2, 16:8–9, 23:3); "wheat, barley and spelt" (חטין שעורין וכסומין) (m. Shev. 3:2, 4:5; Sifra Dibbura d'Hata'ot Pereq 15:3, 16:7, 23:4); "I swear I will not eat" (שבועה שלא אוכל) (m. Shev. 3:1–4, 3:7; t. Shev. 2:1–2; Sifra Per. 15:6–7, 16:2–3). In addition to the formulae specific to the topic of oaths, Neusner also notes patterned elements of mishnaic discourse more generally. He notes certain terms (pure and impure, fit and unfit, liable and not liable) that routinely appear in the apodosis of a mishnaic pericope. These terms might be thought of as formulae that permeate the legal tradition at large, but which also appear in m. Shevuot and its parallels. See discussion of these terms in Neusner, *Oral Tradition in Judaism*, 71–75.

are abstract, rather than concrete. While having overarching structural frameworks and certain fixed phrases in common does not necessarily result in identical versions of a textual tradition, parallels sharing these features do exhibit *concrete* textual manifestations of similitude. By way of contrast, here I wish to concentrate on parallel traditions that allude to or express the same idea in *different* textual terms. In addition to exhibiting concrete textual manifestations of similitude, the set of parallels discussed in this section also displays reliance on a common set of *abstract conceptual concerns.*

In the following example, the two sources do in fact have an underlying structural framework in common, and while they also share some formulaic language, at a key point they employ different language and invoke different legal concepts. These differences – real and extensive though they are – do not prevent the two sources from making the same point. I would argue that the sources succeed in making the same point because the same underlying conceptual concerns propel their composition, even if these concerns get expressed in different textual terms.

Consider the following set of parallel texts.

m. Shev. 3:4

שבועה שלא אוכל, ואכל נבילות וטרפות, שקצים ורמשים – חייב. ר' שמעון פוטר.

(1) [If a person said:] "I swear [lit. "it is an oath"] I will not eat," (2) and then he ate **carrion or torn flesh, forbidden beasts or creeping things** – (3) he is liable. (4) R. Shimon exempts him.

t. Shev. 2:1

שבועה שלא אוכל ואכל אוכלין אסורין, פיגול ונותר וטמא.
שבועה שלא אשתה ושתה משקין אסורין, יין של ערלה ושל כלאי כרם – חייב. ר' שמעון פוטר.

(1) [If a person said]: "I swear that I will not eat," (2) and then he ate **forbidden foods: a sacrificial offering disqualified by improper**

> **intention, sacrificial meat left over beyond the permitted time for its consumption or impure sacrificial meat,** (1^1) [If a person said:] "I swear I will not drink," (2^1) and then he drank forbidden drinks: wine from grapes grown in a vineyard where the laws that prohibit eating fruit produced in the tree's first three years and the laws that prohibit growing more than one species in the vineyard were not observed – (3) he is liable. (4) R. Shimon exempts him.

The issue under consideration in these two sources concerns a type of oath known as the "declarative oath" (שבועת ביטוי). In the event that an individual wishes, he may "declare," or literally "express," his intention under oath to perform or refrain from a certain action. Failure to perform or refrain from the action renders the oathtaker culpable for violating the oath. These sources consider the question of whether the declarative oath "not to eat" (שבועה שלא אוכל) – and in the case of the Tosephta also an oath "not to drink" (שלא אשתה) – is violated when the oathtaker consumes foods (or drinks) prohibited by Jewish law. On the one hand, the language of the oath stipulates that "eating" is prohibited, and since ingesting prohibited foods is a physical act of "eating," one might conclude that the oathtaker should be culpable for violating his oath. On the other hand, since prohibited foods are not generally eaten, one could plausibly argue that the oathtaker would not have had them in mind when formulating the initial prohibition for him/herself.[48] By this way of reasoning, the oathtaker is not culpable for violating the oath. Though s/he violates the oath in a strictly literal sense, the original intent of the oath is upheld. These sources present a classic borderline case, whose interest derives from the fact that it can be resolved according to two equally plausible rationales.[49]

[48] When discussing this case, both gemaras take for granted that the oathtaker *would* have intended his oath to apply only to permitted foods. As a result of this assumption, they struggle to understand why the sages consider the oathtaker liable. See y. Shev. 34b, lines 27–29, and 34c, lines 7–13, and b. Shev. 23b, and also discussion of the amoraic and post-amoraic treatment of this mishnah in Alexander, "Study Practices That Made the Mishnah," 146–72.

[49] See discussion of borderline cases in Alexander, "Casuistic Elements," 222–31.

Whereas the anonymous sages adopt the first rationale, concluding that the oathtaker in such an instance is liable, R. Shimon adopts the second rationale, pronouncing the oathtaker to be free of culpability.

The two sources are strikingly similiar, having both language and structure in common. Both contain a first clause in which the oathtaker establishes the parameters of his oath. He swears not to eat. The second clause of each source introduces a complicating circumstance that opens up the question of the oathtaker's culpability. In each case, he eats a prohibited food. In the third clause, the two sources resolve the question of culpability and pronounce judgment on the oathtaker ("liable"). Finally, in the fourth clause, R. Shimon offers an alternative ruling ("exempt"). The tosephtan version, however, includes an expansion not found in the mishnaic version. Whereas the mishnaic source provides only one example of the scenario in which the oathtaker violates his oath by contravening Jewish law, the tosephtan source includes an illustration of two possible scenarios. In addition to the example cited by the Mishnah (an oath not to eat violated by eating prohibited foods), the Tosephta treats the parallel case of an oath not to drink violated by drinking prohibited drinks (see clauses 1[1] and 2[1]). This expansion by the Tosephta is best considered as ornamentation, rather than adding a new structural element. As with the other examples of ornamentation discussed, it makes the point more vivid by illustrating it a second time, but it does not add information that is not already implicit in the more contracted version.

In addition, the tosephtan source contains a structural element not found in the Mishnah. The Tosephta complements the two cases noted here with the following two converse cases:

t. Shev. 2:2

שבועה שאוכל ואכל אוכלין אסורין, פיגול ונותר וטמא, שבועה שאשתה ושתה משקין אסורין,
יין של ערלה ושל כלאי הכרם – פטור, ור' שמע' מחייב.

> (1) [If a person said:] "I swear I will eat," (2) and then he ate **forbidden foods: a sacrificial offering disqualified by improper intention, sacrificial meat left over beyond the permitted time for its consumption or impure sacrificial meat**, (1^1) [If a person said:] "It is an oath that I will drink," (2^1) and then he drank forbidden drinks: wine from grapes grown in a vineyard where the laws that prohibit eating fruit produced in the tree's first three years and the laws that prohibit growing more than one species in the vineyard were not observed – (3) he is exempt. (4) R. Shimon holds him liable.

This expansion does add a new structural element. It considers a related but slightly different issue. Though both sets of scenarios inquire into the effect of consuming prohibited foods on the status of one's oath, the two sets consider its effect on reverse aspects of the oath. Whereas the first set of scenarios (m. Shev. 3:4 and t. Shev. 2:1) inquires into how the consumption of prohibited foods affects culpability if one *violates* the oath, this set of scenarios (t. Shev. 2:2) considers the issue of whether or not one may *fulfill* an oath by consuming prohibited foods. The Mishnah and the Tosephta, then, draw on the same structural framework but develop it in somewhat different ways.

The two sources also use the same language to articulate the scenario that serves as a context for the tradition. Both sources illustrate the phenomenon of declarative oaths and analyze its complexities with the case of an individual who swears not to eat. Both sources begin with the phrase "I swear I will not eat" (שבועה שלא אוכל). As the Tosephta makes clear and as the Mishnah implies elsewhere,[50] other examples of the declarative oath were available to the composers of this tradition. They might just as well have focused on the oath not to drink, not to give something to someone, not to sleep, or not to throw this stone into the sea. Any one of these other examples of declarative oaths cited elsewhere could have been used in the first clause, where the sources are

[50] See m. Shev. 3:5.

merely concerned to lay out the parameters of an oath. It is noteworthy, however, that a high percentage of mishnayot in m. Shev. Chapter 3 use the oath "not to eat" as the prototypical declarative oath.[51] It would appear that the phrase "I swear I will not eat" (שבועה שלא אוכל) serves in a somewhat formulaic capacity, as a fixed phrase to introduce scenarios that consider various complexities associated with the declarative oath. The language that the two sources have in common, then, can be understood to result from the fact that both sources draw on the same fixed phraseology in their treatment of this issue.

Only in the second clause do the two sources display sharp differences. While both sources suggest that the oathtaker ate forbidden foods, they employ different language and invoke different legal concepts to make the point. Whereas the mishnaic source represents the status of prohibited foods with the biblical categories of prohibited meats ("carrion or torn flesh, forbidden beasts or creeping things" (נבילות וטרפות, שקצים ורמשים), the tosephtan source refers to instances of sacrificial meat that have been disqualified for consumption ("a sacrificial offering disqualified by improper intention, sacrificial meat left over beyond the permitted time for its consumption or impure sacrificial meat" [פיגול ונותר וטמא]). While the two lists both allude to the concept of prohibited foods with illustrative examples, they each draw their terms from different contexts, and the items on each list are disqualified on the basis of different legal concerns.

The items on the mishnaic list have their roots in biblical language from the lists of prohibited meats.[52] The first two items on the mishnaic list ("carrion or torn flesh" [נבילות וטרפות]) appear as a pair already in biblical texts. Lev. 7:24 and 17:15 and Ez. 44:31 include them among the types of meat prohibited to priests and Israelites alike. The prohibition

[51] In fact, this protocol is adopted throughout Chapter 3 of m. Shevuot. See m. Shev. 3:1–4, 3:7, and 3:9.

[52] For an interesting discussion of another instance in which a rabbinic list derives from a biblical context, see Jay Rovner, "Rhetorical Strategy and Dialectical Necessity in the Babylonian Talmud: The Case of Kiddushin 34a–35a," *Hebrew Union College Annual* 65 (1994): 192.

against consuming them is discussed in close conjunction with the prohibition against consuming blood (Lev. 7:26–27, 17:10–14). It is reasonable to assume, then, that the prohibition against eating carrion and torn flesh derives from the fact that the circumstances of the animal's death prevent one from draining the blood properly. The next two items on the mishnaic list ("forbidden beasts and creeping things," שקצים ורמשים) most likely have their origin in Lev. 11, which enumerates a list of impure animals not to be eaten. Lev. 11:41 reads: "All things that swarm (כל-השרץ השרץ) upon the earth are an abomination (שקץ הוא); they shall not be eaten." This verse (along with others in the same chapter)[53] speaks of swarming (or creeping, crawling creatures [*sheratzim*]) and abominations (*shekatzim*), which the rabbis take to be forbidden beasts, in the same breath. For reasons that are not apparent, the sages substituted a different biblical term for the second of these two terms, which also has the meaning of "creeping or crawling creatures": *remasim* (רמשים).[54] The expression "forbidden beasts and creeping

[53] See esp. Lev. 11:10, 20, 23, 41–42.

[54] While the biblical use of the term שקץ (lit. "an abomination") in Lev. 11 explicitly refers to animals that may not be eaten, the biblical use of the term רמש ("creeping or crawling creatures") never appears in a context that implies its status as forbidden food. See, e.g., Gen. 1 in which the term is used descriptively to indicate the creeping creatures that God created to populate the earth. It is tempting to speculate that the pairing of these terms arises in postbiblical literature as the result of rhetorical concerns of diction. While the term רמש (*remes*) is not used in biblical literature to refer to the prohibited status of creeping or crawling animals, the term שרץ (*sheretz*) is. (See Lev. 11 in which a variety of different creeping or crawling creatures are excluded from the category of permitted foods. See also Lev. 5:2, which assumes that certain creeping or crawling creatures are impure.) Pairing the concepts of forbidden beasts (שקצים, *shekatzim*) and creeping or crawling creatures (שרצים, *sheretzim*) may have resulted in a phrase too awkward or infelicitous, and so a different biblical term for creeping and crawling creatures (רמשים, *remesim*) was substituted which avoided the alliteration in the phrase שקצים ושרצים (*sheketzim v'sheretzim*). This suggestion, however, remains pure speculation. It is also interesting to note that these two terms ("forbidden beasts, and creeping creatures," שקצים ורמשים) are paired together in contexts other than as part of this list of four forbidden foods. Equally commonly, the two items appear as part of a different list: "fishes, grasshoppers, forbidden beasts and creeping creatures," דגים חגבים שקצים ורמשים (see, e.g., m. Bekh. 8:1 and m. Ker. 1:5). See also valuable discussion of these formulaic terms and their origins in biblical language in Aharon

creatures" (שקצים ורמשים) would seem to refer to the entire list of prohibited animals in Lev. 11.[55] Thus, the four items appearing on the mishnaic list all employ biblical language and refer to specific biblical injunctions prohibiting certain categories of meat.

The items appearing on the tosephtan list also draw on biblical language but allude to a different set of laws. The laws that form the basis for the tosephtan list appear in Lev. 7:16–21, which discuss several different means by which sacrificial meat becomes disqualified and prohibited for consumption. Although the biblical passage itself only discusses two means by which sacrificial meat becomes disqualified for consumption (if it is left over too long after the sacrifice and if it becomes impure), the rabbis interpret a seemingly redundant term in the passage (*pigul*, lit. "offensive thing") as an allusion to a third category of disqualification. The first term on the tosephtan list, *pigul* (פיגול), is rabbinically understood to indicate sacrificial meat that has been disqualified because of the inappropriate intentions of the officiating priest. As explained in m. Zev. 2:2–3, if at the moment of slaughtering a sacrificial animal or handling its blood (collecting it, walking it to the altar, or sprinkling it on the altar), the priest has the intention to consume the sacrificial meat after the permitted two days, then the sacrifice becomes disqualified because such meat is *pigul*, "an offensive thing." While the language of *pigul* is biblical (appearing in Lev. 7:18), the notion that the priest's *intention* at the moment of sacrifice affects the status of the meat represents a rabbinic extension of the meaning of biblical language.[56] The second term, *notar* (נותר), derives

Shemesh, "Punishments and Sins," in *Punishments and Sins: From the Bible to Rabbinic Literature* (Hebrew) (Jerusalem: Magnes Press, 2003), 190–92.

[55] Shemesh draws the same conclusion in "Punishments and Sins," 191. He concludes that in their stereotyped formulaic usage, the first pair of terms ("carrion and torn flesh") came to refer to all *large* animals that were prohibited for consumption, and the second pair of terms ("forbidden beasts and creeping things") came to indicate *small* forbidden animals.

[56] Neusner discusses the importance of human intention in determining the legal status of objects for the Mishnah. As he understands the matter, the Mishnah's emphasis on human intention is a specifically rabbinic innovation. Neusner, *Judaism:Evidence of the*

from the same biblical passage. Lev. 7:16–18 explains that all sacrificial meat must be eaten within the first two days of sacrificing it. Anything that is left over (*ha-notar* [הנותר]) on the third day must be burned. Eating such leftover meat is explicitly forbidden. Finally, the third term in the list, "impure sacrificial meat" (טמא), is mentioned at the end of the passage in Lev. 7:19–20. There, the text states that any sacrificial meat that has become impure cannot be eaten. The tosephtan list, then, derives from a unified biblical context and reflects a mnemonic synopsis of some of the means by which sacrificial meats become unfit for consumption.[57]

Insofar as each of these lists appears in numerous other contexts in tannaitic literature,[58] they are both formulaic means of expressing the abstract idea of "prohibited foods." The Tosephta even adds an element of ornamentation when it states that these items are "forbidden foods" (אוכלין אסורין). Like the other examples of ornamentation discussed earlier, the addition of this phrase does not add new information but merely makes more explicit and vivid a set of underlying assumptions. The use of the phrase simply clarifies that the items on the list are cited in order to illustrate the phenomenon of prohibited foods.[59] An

Mishnah, 271–81. The rabbinic interest and concern with the role of human intention is, however, by no means limited to the Mishnah. See, e.g., discussion of intention by Urbach, in which he argues that the rabbinic concern with intent permeates post-mishnaic legal materials. Ephraim E. Urbach, *The Halakhah: Its Sources and Development,* trans. Raphael Posner (Tel Aviv: Modan Publishing House, 1996), 191–205.

57 Jay Rovner discusses the phenomenon wherein rabbinic tradents create lists as a mnemonic aid. He discusses the fact that the rabbinic tradents often pattern their thoughts after the structure of bibilical texts. These two lists would seem to offer examples of the phenomenon he identifies. See Rovner, "Rhetorical Strategy," 192–93.

58 The phrase used in the mishnaic passage appears in m. San. 8:2, m. Mak. 3:2, t. Hor. 1:5, Sif. Num. Piska 153, and Midrash Tannaim to Deut. 21:20. The phrase used in the tosephtan passage appears a total of 62 times in tannaitic literature (Bar Ilan Responsa Project, text search). In all cases, the items are listed in the same order, further reinforcing the notion that these phrases are fixed and formulaic in character.

59 This fits into a pattern identified earlier, wherein one source, often the Tosephta, is more expansive or more explicit than the other. For those concerned with issues

important point of continuity between the two sources in the second clause, then, is their shared *conceptual interest* in how ingestion of prohibited foods impacts culpability for an oath not to eat. It is noteworthy, however, that the transmitters and formulators of m. Shev. 3:4 and t. Shev. 2:1 appear to have had different options available to them when composing and constructing tradition. Whereas the mishnaic composers drew on one formula, the composers of the tosephtan source drew on another. There was not necessarily a one-to-one correspondence between abstract conceptual concerns and fixed formulae. Apparently, it is possible for more than one fixed phrase to represent the *same* legal concept. In a case such as ours, where different tradents of the same tradition drew on different formulae to express the same conceptual concern, one gets the sense that the specific phrase employed was not what motivated the composition. Rather, one senses that those formulating tradition were compelled by an underlying conceptual concern, which could be accurately represented by *either* formulation. I would argue, then, that **abstract conceptual concerns** were also among the resources that the formulators of m. Shevuot drew upon when they composed and transmitted tradition. Not only were they masters of concrete formulations of traditional ideas in the form of fixed phrases, but they also were fluent in the conceptual concerns to which fixed phrases and overarching structural frameworks give expression.

Conclusion

A survey of these exemplary passages and their parallels suggests that the tannaitic handlers of the traditions of m. Shevuot did not necessarily conceptualize the text as a linear and lengthy sequence of words. The

of priority between the texts, it seems highly probable, following Hauptman and Friedman, that m. Shev. 3:4 represents a condensed presentation of the issues found in t. Shev. 2:1. See Friedman, *Tosefta Atiqta,* and Hauptman, "Mishnah as a Response to 'Tosefta.'"

presence among the parallels of a shared set of overarching structures, fixed phrases, and underlying conceptual concerns suggests that transmitters of tradition had a strategy for reproducing tradition that did not rely exclusively on memorizing and reproducing lengthy sequences of words in a verbatim fashion. I submit that the nonlinear points of continuity identified in this analysis functioned as the compositional building blocks from which traditions could be constructed anew in different performative settings. The variants among the parallel traditions represent the natural variety that arises among different performative renderings of tradition.[60] Those who handled the traditions of m. Shevuot with attention to the compositional building blocks and their role in stabilizing and reproducing the traditions would likely have understood the traditions to be "orally fluid."[61] For them, the tradition would naturally be viewed as multiform, with no singular version authoritative. Whatever stability the traditions did obtain would have been secured by the use of the compositional building blocks.

It is difficult to know with any certainty at what point in the transmissional history of m. Shevuot such a conception would have prevailed. Was it earlier or later in the tannaitic period? The answer to the question of dating hinges on a number of interrelated inquiries that lie outside the scope of the present project. While I cannot resolve the broader questions of how the Mishnah and Tosephta as we know them came to be, it is my hope that by documenting the presence of the compositional building blocks in the parallel traditions, I can highlight the plausibility of an orally fluid conception of the traditions in m. Shevuot during the tannaitic period. At some point in their early transmissional history, these traditions were not imagined as definitive or authoritative, but as equally valid performative versions of a broader legal tradition.

60 See Lord, *The Singer of Tales,* 99–123, and Jaffee, *Torah in the Mouth,* 109–24.

61 As noted in n. 3 of this chapter, this phrase is coined in Fraade, "Literary Composition and Oral Performance," 36. I find this phrase so useful because even while it acknowledges the conception of textuality that emerges in oral performative settings, it allows for the possibility that the traditions were recorded in writing.

The preceding exercise of exposing the plausibility of an orally fluid conception of mishnaic textuality is valuable insofar as it provides a point of reference for evaluating the difference between this and later conceptions of mishnaic textuality. In the next chapter, I will document the emergence of a different notion of mishnaic textuality. From the evidence of the two Talmuds, it appears that later handlers, transmitters, and students of m. Shevuot regarded the text to be a deliberate and intentional composition. Recognizing that conceptions of m. Shevuot were in flux throughout the rabbinic period highlights what is truly new at the end of the period. While the vast majority of scholars have followed in the footsteps of the latest transmitters of the Mishnah, and viewed the text as if it was *always* as fixed, authoritative, and canonical as it was at the end of the rabbinic period, we can recognize that the authoritative status of the Mishnah is *not* an intrinsic feature of its literary form, evident at the very moment of its promulgation.[62] Rather, we can appreciate that it is a status conferred from without, and over a period of some generations. In this way, we stand to gain a more nuanced understanding of the means by which mishnaic materials come to be authoritative. This insight may be valuable for the study of other scriptural traditions as well, where the question of how sacred texts achieve a canonical standing within the community similarly

62 It is commonplace within rabbinic scholarship to view the Mishnah's authoritative status to be a function of its *literary* form. While this association dates back to the work of Sherira Gaon (see discussion in next chapter), the association is most prominently reflected today in the work of David Weiss Halivni. Halivni argues that the apodictic feature of mishnaic form (its tendency to command directly, without a justificatory clause) is a literary source of its authority. See Halivni, *Midrash, Mishnah and Gemara,* 2–4, 7–8. Halivni's disciple, David Kraemer, makes similar assumptions about the way literary forms generate authority. For his discussion of the Mishnah's literary form, see Kraemer, *The Mind of the Talmud,* 11–15. Neusner draws similar conclusions about mishnaic authority deriving from its literary form. For him, the Mishnah's most relevant literary feature in this regard is that it suppresses the biblical origins of its laws, conveying the laws without linking them to their proof texts. See Neusner, *Judaism: Evidence of the Mishnah,* 217–33. See also n. 6 in the next chapter. In contrast to the work of these and other scholars, I am arguing that authority is a function of how the text is used, transmitted, and handled within a community.

arises.[63] From the work of this and the next chapter, it appears that the authoritative status of m. Shevuot, at any rate, arises in the context of transmission. The devoted handlers of this body of traditions returned to it again and again until the vagaries of a single performative version were viewed as the intentional creation of a single author.[64] In order to gain insight into the post-tannaitic transmissional life of m. Shevuot, we must turn to these issues in the next chapter.

63 Studies that treat how other scriptural traditions have achieved canonicity and authoritative standing have been very useful in shaping my own thinking on this topic. Eugene Ulrich and Hindy Najman spend much energy documenting the emerging authority of the biblical text during the Second Temple period. See Eugene Ulrich, *The Dead Sea Scrolls and the Origins of the Bible* (Grand Rapids, MI: Eerdmans, 1999), 3–120; Ulrich, "From Literature to Scripture: Reflections on the Growth of a Text's Authoritativeness," *Dead Sea Discoveries* 10, no. 1 (2003): 3–25, and Hindy Najman, *Seconding Sinai: The Development of Mosaic Discourse in Second Temple Judasim* (Leiden: E. J. Brill, 2002), Chapters 1 and 2. Boaz Huss also makes valuable distinctions among the different manifestations of a text's sacred and authoritative status at different points in its transmission and among different strata of the community. See Boaz Huss, "*Sefer Ha-Zohar* as a Canonical, Sacred and Holy Text: Changing Perspectives of the Book of Splendor Between the Thirteenth and Eighteenth Centuries," *Journal of Jewish Thought and Philosophy* 7 (1998): 257–307. Likewise, Anne Fitzpatrick-McKinley describes shifts in status in the legal portions of the Hebrew Bible that resonate strongly with the shifts in status I found in m. Shevuot. See Anne Fitzpatrick-McKinley, *The Transformation of the Torah from Scribal Advice to Law* (Sheffield, Eng.: Sheffield Academic Press, 1999). See also the classic essay by Jonathan Z. Smith that breaks down the different aspects of canonicity: Jonathan Z. Smith, "Sacred Persistence: Towards a Redescription of Canon," in *Approaches to Ancient Judaism*, ed. William Scott Green (Missoula, MO: Scholars Press, 1978), 19–27.

64 Martin Jaffee insightfully explains how, why, and under what kinds of conditions free-text transmissional styles alternate with and give way to fixed-text transmissional styles. See Jaffee, "Oral Tradition." He notes that of all the rabbinic compilations, the Mishnah was unique insofar as it did eventually become subject to the rote memorization characteristic of fixed and stable texts (24). Nonetheless, he suggests that the compilation before us most likely began its transmissional life as a "free-text," "viewed by it literary handlers as elements in a larger kaleidoscope of tradition," rather than as a definite statement and "finished product" (23). Only after a certain period did the perceptions of its transmitters and users change such that the document was viewed as an official representation of tradition, rather than as a single refraction of it. His analysis suggests that continued use and reference to adhoc compilations eventually make them into an official measure of tradition.

2

The Scripturalization of Mishnah

A reader of m. Shevuot who encounters the text today takes for granted that this set of traditions is authoritative by virtue of its inclusion within the Mishnah. It is a generally accepted truth that the Mishnah occupies a privileged position as the first installment in the rabbinic canon.[1] Historically, however, these traditions and formulations were not always uniquely privileged within the rabbinic corpus. As discussed in the last chapter, in the earliest phases of composition and transmission, notions of textual continuity existed that did not depend on fixed, linear sequences of words. In such circumstances, it is difficulty to imagine that any single formulation or arrangement of tradition stood out definitively among the others as original, authentic, or privileged. Traditions were performed, read, and studied in a variety of different versions and textual arrangements. By the end of the rabbinic period, however, the situation had changed. Though the verbal content of m.

[1] The idea that the Mishnah achieved an authoritative status upon its promulgation by Rabbi Judah the Patriach is reflected in a number of works. See, e.g., Halivni, "Rabbi Judah's Mishnah," 204–6; Elon, *Jewish Law*, 1061–70, esp. 1069–70; Lieberman, *HJP*, 88–89. See also Joel H. Zaiman, "The Traditional Study of the Mishnah," in *The Modern Study of the Mishnah*, ed. Jacob Neusner (Leiden: E. J. Brill, 1973), 3, who writes that "in terms of tradition the Mishnah was, by definition, authoritative and binding from the day it was published."

Shevuot was not safe from the vicissitudes of minor losses and corruptions in the course of transmission, its structure and content had largely been stabilized. Even more important, the received version of m. Shevuot came to be invested with authority.[2] The emerging authority of the received text was reflected in the reading practices to which the text was now subjected. Many of the hermeneutical assumptions that rabbinic exegetes made about biblical scripture were now made with respect to the mishnaic materials. Likewise, many of the exegetical strategies that the rabbis employed in the study of biblical scripture were now used in the study of mishnaic texts.[3] Albeit in an indirect fashion, the rabbis who read, studied, and interpreted m. Shevuot came to affirm its authority and privileged status by treating it just like scripture. An important question for researchers, then, involves understanding how fluid and informally formulated traditions came to be viewed as deliberately formulated and authoritative scripture.

Traditional accounts of the genesis of the Mishnah tell their own story about how the Mishnah came to be an authoritative document. R. Sherira Gaon (d. 1006), the earliest known chronicler of rabbinic tradition, suggests that the Mishnah's authority derives from the moment of its inception. Sherira explains that the editor, R. Judah the Patriarch (or just plain "Rabbi" as he is known), styled a smooth and harmonious

[2] Goldberg discusses a similar transformation in the authority of mishnaic materials, but he believes that the transformation had happened already by the amoraic period. See Goldberg, "The Mishnah," 243–44. Neusner alludes to the gradual character of this process, which culminated long after the time during which the Mishnah was first composed. He writes: "Why should the Mishnah have been received, as much later on it certainly was received, as half of the "whole Torah of Moses at Sinai"? Jacob Neusner, *The Mishnah: An Introduction* (Northvale, NJ: Jason Aronson, 1989), 37.

[3] This phenomenon has already been noted by a number of scholars. See Moshe Silberg, *Talmudic Law and the Modern State*, trans. Ben Zion Bokser (New York: Burning Bush Press, 1973), 16–17; Hyman Klein, "Some Methods of Sebara," *Jewish Quarterly Review* 50 (1959): 125, n. 4; Abraham Goldberg, "The Babylonian Talmud," in *The Literature of the Sages: First Part: Oral Torah, Halakha, Mishna, Tosefta, Talmud, External Tractates*, ed. Shmuel Safrai (Philadelphia: Fortress Press, 1987), 331; Elon, *Jewish Law*, 400–401, 407–9; Christine Hayes, *Between the Babylonian and Palestinian Talmuds: Accounting for Halakhic Differences in Selected Sugyot from Tractate Avodah Zarah* (New York: Oxford University Press, 1997), 93–94.

text that won followers on the basis of its felicitous expression. Consider the following account:

> In his collection of laws [*halakhot*], Rabbi followed in the manner of R. Meir, which was in the manner of R. Akiva, because Rabbi saw that R. Meir's way was *succinct and easy to teach*. . . . His teachings were *more exact* than any of the other tannaim, *without superfluous language. Each and every word made a vital point* without unnecessary exaggeration. *Nothing was missing or extra*, except in a few instances. *The manner was precise. Great and wonderous things were included in every single word*. . . . When everyone saw *the clarity of the structure*[4] *of the Mishnah*, the truth of its expressions and the *exactness of its words*, they abandoned other tannaitic formulations. . . . The people of Israel relied only on this collection of laws [*halakhot*]. [They] accepted it [the Mishnah] when they saw it, with faith. There is no person who disagrees with them. [Emphasis added.][5]

Sherira's description suggests that the Mishnah's authority is a direct correlative of its literary form. Insofar as Rabbi followed the example of R. Meir and used a precise and exacting literary form, he achieved a following for his Mishnah.[6] Sherira sees in the Mishnah's language a

4 Literally, the "formliness of the structure" (צורתא דתצרתא). Translation is based on idiomatic rendering of one of the meanings provided by Jastrow: "word for word as it is formed." See Marcus Jastrow, *A Dictionary of the Targumim, the Talmud Babli, and Yerushalmi, and the Midrashaic Literature* (New York: Judaica Press, 1989), 1217.

5 Lewin, *IRSG*, 28–30. French recension is provided, following evaluation and preference for it. See Robert Brody, *The Geonim of Babylonia and the Shaping of Medieval Jewish Culture* (New Haven, CT: Yale University Press, 1998), 21–22. Translation draws on Halivni, "Rabbi Judah's Mishnah," 205, and Rabbi Nosson Dovid Rabinowich, trans. and annotation, *The Iggeres of Rav Sherira Gaon* (Jerusalem: Rabbi Jacob Joseph School Press – Ahavath Torah Institute, 1988), 26–28.

6 A number of modern scholars have made an analogous argument that likewise roots the authority of the Mishnah in its literary form. These scholars claim that the Mishnah's authority derives from its commanding style, which forthrightly makes demands of its readers without couching its expectations in the apologetics of scriptural proof texts or explanatory clauses. See, e.g., Jacob Neusner, *Judaism: Evidence of the Mishnah*, 217–22, and Halivni, *Midrash, Mishnah and Gemara*, 40, 54, in conjunction with Halivni, "Rabbi Judah's Mishnah," 204–6. See also Kraemer's discussion of the significance of

simple elegance, which consists of extremely concise expression. Every word expresses exactly what it needs to convey, no more, no less.[7] The Mishnah's literary form, then, stands as an enduring testament by which each generation may reaffirm the authority of this central and important text.

By virtue of having been written hundreds of years after the events that the account purports to describe, Sherira's claims concerning Rabbi's editorial work cannot be taken as historically true in any simple sense.[8] The work of the previous chapter on the shifting verbal content and fluid conception of the traditions of m. Shevuot during the earliest phase of their transmission calls into question Sherira's claim that a process involving deliberate and exacting literary choices produced the text. The account is, however, a useful indicator of where the Mishnah's authority was seen to lie in *Sherira's* day. Apparently, *irrespective* of the historical origins of the mishnaic text, the people who read and valued it as a privileged text *understood* its authority in part to be a function of the precision of its literary form. Accordingly, this chapter traces the genesis and follows the evolution of the *idea* that mishnaic language in tractate Shevuot has a unique precision and expressive power. Although this ideological view of mishnaic language is articulated explicitly only in the post-talmudic writings of Sherira, it impacted how the rabbis read and interpreted m. Shevuot throughout the latter half of the talmudic period.

The emerging ideology about the nature of the mishnaic text manifested itself in two specific ways. First, interpreters increasingly

the choices involved in the construction of mishnaic literary form in *The Mind of the Talmud,* 10–15. See discussion in n. 62 of the previous chapter.

[7] Hayes describes this as a principle of "verbal economy." "It is . . . fair to say that the amoraim increasingly presuppose that the *medium* of the Mishnah was an important part of its message – that syntax, grammar, arrangement of clauses, choice of words, terminology are not accidental but are consciously chosen to convey a particular point." Hayes, *Between the Babylonian and Palestinian Talmuds,* 93.

[8] See Neusner's critique of the dominance of Sherira's account in setting the agenda for contemporary historians of the Mishnah in *The Modern Study of the Mishnah,* introduction. See also the critique in Halivni, "Rabbi Judah's Mishnah," 205 ff.

understood the text before them to be the product of a *deliberate and intentional* compositional process. Those who read and analyzed m. Shevuot compared the received version of the text with alternative formulations that might have been used, and they assumed that the received version had been chosen for a specific reason. In so doing, they attributed intentionality to the compositional process. Second, interpreters assumed that mishnaic language was freighted with significance. They focused their inquiries on increasingly smaller units of text and read phrases and even words as complete semantic units. Atomizing words and phrases and reading them against the grain of their local context was an important means of affirming the intense communicative power of mishnaic language. In these and other ways, the idea that mishnaic language has a unique precision and expressive power increasingly manifested itself in the talmudic interpretations of m. Shevuot.

Using the Talmudic Commentaries

A close examination of the talmudic commentaries to m. Shevuot offers much insight into the question of how the text was studied, understood, and conceptualized during the years following its redaction. Organized around the skeletal structure of m. Shevuot, the two talmudic commentaries provide a partial and heavily edited record of the questions and inquiries that were put to the text. In the asking and answering of these questions, talmudic interpreters reveal fundamental assumptions that they make about mishnaic language in m. Shevuot.

A considerable time lag separates the redaction of the two Talmuds. Scholarly consensus concerning the redaction of the earlier Palestinian Talmud, or Yerushalmi, ranges from the late fourth to the early fifth centuries (370–429 C.E.).[9] Irrespective of whether one follows the

[9] On the early end of the spectrum is Yaakov Sussmann, followed by Christine Hayes, concluding that the Yerushalmi was redacted shortly after R. Jose b. Bun made his contributions, or approximately 360–370 C.E. See Sussmann, "Once More on y. Nezikin"

earlier or the later dating, this event precedes the redaction of the Babylonian Talmud, or Bavli, by at least two hundred years, which current estimates place in the late sixth or early seventh centuries.[10] Several scholars note that this considerable time lag results in the two Talmuds exhibiting very different degrees of literary development and argumentational complexity.[11] In this chapter, I wish to explore an

(Hebrew), in *Mehqerei Talmud (Talmudic Studies)*, ed. Yaakov Sussmann and David Rosenthal (Jerusalem: Magnes Press, 1990), 101, 132, n. 187, and Hayes, *Between the Babylonian and Palestinian Talmuds*, 20. On the later end of the spectrum, pushing the date into the early fifth century are J. N. Epstein, *Introduction to Amoraitic Literature: Babylonian Talmud and Yerushalmi* (Hebrew), ed. E. Z. Melamed (Jerusalem: Magnes Press, 1962), 274, and Alyssa Gray, "A Talmud in Exile: The Influence of PT Avodah Zarah on the Formation of BT Avodah Zarah" (Jewish Theological Seminary, Ph.D. diss., 2001), 304–8. Catherine Heszer leaves the question open, expressing support for either late fourth or early fifth century. See Heszer, "The Codification of Legal Knowledge in Late Antiquity: The Talmud Yerushalmi and Roman Law Codes," in *The Talmud Yerushalmi in Graeco-Roman Culture*, ed. Peter Schafer (Tubingen: J. C. B. Mohr (Paul Siebeck), 1998), 583, 609, 635.

10 See Yaakov Sussmann, *Talmud Yerushalmi According to Ms. Or 4720 (Scal.3) of the Leiden University Library with Restorations and Corrections* (Jerusalem: The Academy of Hebrew Language, 2001), 103–5; Kalmin, *Redaction of the Babylonian Talmud*; Hayes, *Between the Babylonian and Palestinian Talmuds*, 20; Rubenstein, *Talmudic Stories*, 270–72; Heszer, "Codification of Legal Knowledge," 635; and Kaplan, *Babylonian Talmud.*

11 See Sussmann, "Once More on y. Nezikin" (Hebrew), 101–5; Hayes, *Between the Babylonian and Palestinian Talmuds*, 20–23 and 198–99, nn. 43 and 44; Rubenstein, *Talmudic Stories*, 255–60; and Halivni, *Midrash, Mishnah and Gemara*, 82. Integrally related to the issue of the Bavli's later redactional date and its additional literary and argumentational development is the discernment of two redactional layers within the Bavli. Whereas the earlier redactional layer has been characterized by the use of Hebrew, is generally attributed to amoraic sages, and formally has many similarities with amoraic material from the Yerushalmi (characterized by straightforward prescriptive statements), the later redactional layer is characterized by the use of Aramaic, anonymity, and a more discursive, argumentational style. The later redactional layer with all of its attendant argumentational and rhetorical complexity and polish is unique to the Bavli. Important work distinguishing the strata of the Bavli has been done by Klein, Halivni, and Friedman. See Klein, "Gemara and Sebara"; Klein, "Gemara Quotations in Sebara," *Jewish Quarterly Review* 43 (1953): 341–63; Klein, "Some Methods of Sebara"; Halivni, *Seder Moed*; Halivni, *Sources and Traditions*; and Friedman, "A Critical Study of Yevamot X." As a study that stresses the chronological developments between the close of the Yerushalmi and that of the Bavli, this chapter focuses its analysis on the later redactional layer in the Bavli.

additional consequence of this time lag. By virtue of their having been redacted at different points in the reception history of the Mishnah, we would also expect the two Talmuds to reflect differing degrees of maturation in the ideology concerning the precision and intentionality of mishnaic language.[12] Whereas we would expect to see the ideology reflected in a more nascent form in the earlier Yerushalmi, we would expect to find a more fully developed version in the latest redactional layers of the Bavli.[13] Any process as subtle and gradual as the process by which mishnaic language in m. Shevuot came to be viewed as authoritative and scriptural in character eludes precise chronological reconstruction. While we cannot establish the exact point at which certain shifts in the perception of mishnaic language occurred, we can note the presence of trends.

The fact that the Talmuds contain the collected sayings of sages accreted over many generations, along with an editorial hand (or set of hands) weaving the different sources into a whole, makes it difficult to know the date of any particular interpretation with certitude. Nonetheless, the differences in mishnaic interpretation offered in the two Talmuds provide a rough schematic overview of a process that we will probably never be able to reconstruct fully.

[12] Goldberg, "Babylonian Talmud," 331, suggests that the ideology appears fully developed in the Bavli without precedent in the Yerushalmi. One goal of this chapter is to refute the idea that there is no precedent in the Yerushalmi. Hayes notes that the ideology does appear in the Yerushalmi to a lesser degree, but confines her discussion to the footnotes. See Hayes, *Between the Babylonian and Palestinian Talmuds,* 224–25, esp. n. 5, but also nn. 2 and 6. I hope that this chapter supplements her claim with a more forceful presentation of evidence and by exploring the nuances of development in the ideology as reflected in the Yerushalmi and Bavli.

[13] As discussed in n. 11, in order to monitor development over time, this chapter focuses its discussion on the latest redactional layers of the Bavli. Scholars have developed linguistic and conceptual criteria for distinguishing these strata. See n. 11 for key scholars and their work in this area. A particularly important model for the comparison of Yerushalmi materials and Bavli materials as part of a chronological development, with the Bavli's latest redactional layer representing a cultural form that is significantly different from that represented in the Yerushalmi, is found in Rubenstein, *Talmudic Stories,* and Rubenstein, *Culture.*

Omnisignificance, Atomization, and a Narrow Exegetical Focus

The writings of James Kugel document the assumptions that the rabbis make about the biblical text and the reading strategies they develop that reflect their deeply held beliefs about the text.[14] Kugel's observations about rabbinic interpretation of biblical scripture provide a valuable model for thinking about the assumptions that inform talmudic interpretation of m. Shevuot.

Among the strategies identified by Kugel is the rabbinic tendency to focus interpretation on discrete verses, irrespective of their place in a larger narrative. He writes that "the basic unit of the Bible, for the midrashicist, is the verse . . . and it might be said that there simply is no boundary encountered beyond that of the verse until one comes to the borders of the canon itself."[15] The episodic nature of midrash, offering contained answers to discrete questions, results in a focused, rather than wide-ranging, style of commentary: "Our midrashic compilations are in this sense potentially deceiving, since they seem to treat the whole text bit by bit; but . . . these 'bits' are rather atomistic, and, as any student of rabbinic literature knows, interchangeable, modifiable, combinable, – in short, not part of an overall exegesis at all."[16] In other words, the larger patterns of the narrative are lost as the exegete narrows

[14] See James L. Kugel, *The Idea of Biblical Poetry: Parallelism and Its History* (New Haven, CT: Yale University Press, 1981), 96–132, esp. 103–5; Kugel, "Two Introductions to Midrash," in *Midrash and Literature*, ed. Geoffrey H. Hartman and Sandford Budick (New Haven, CT: Yale University Press, 1986), 77–103; Kugel, *In Potiphar's House: The Interpretive Life of Biblical Texts* (Cambridge, MA: Harvard University Press, 1990), and Kugel, *The Bible as It Was* (Cambridge, MA: Belknap Press of Harvard University Press, 1997). For a valuable discussion of midrashic assumptions about the biblical text, see also Jay M. Harris, *How Do We Know This?: Midrash and the Fragmentation of Modern Judaism* (Albany: State University of New York Press, 1986), 7–23; and Yaakov Elman, "It Is No Empty Thing: Nahmanides and the Search for Omnisignificance," *Torah U-Madda Journal* 4 (1993): 1–14.

[15] Kugel, "Two Introductions to Midrash," 93.

[16] Kugel, "Two Introductions to Midrash," 95.

his focus to individual verses and parts thereof. For the midrashicist, the proverbial "tree" is of more interest than the "forest."

The narrow focus of the midrashicist is reflected in the tendency to identify significance in every detail of scripture. In this way of reading, "nothing in Scripture is said in vain or for rhetorical flourish: every detail is important, everything is intended to impart some teaching."[17] The assumption that every detail of scripture is meaningful leads the exegete to focus on all sorts of seemingly pedestrian features in order to extract their significance. The belief that the text is packed full of meaning is closely related to the reading strategy of atomization. Rabbinic exegetes focus their attentions on very small sections of text – a phrase, a word, or even a letter – *because* they believe that these atomized bits of text are "chock-full" of meaning. Unlike other texts, which depend on the surroundings of local context to supply meaning, words and phrases in the biblical text are understood to convey meaning independent of the larger contexts in which they are found. One common technique for affirming the so-called omnisignificance[18] of the biblical text involves identifying and explaining the significance of any *apparent* superfluity in the biblical text.[19] Repetitions, extra words, and extra letters are all probed for some subtle hint of their intended meaning. When interpreted in this manner, the biblical text is shown to be significant as a divine communication and not just as a vehicle for relating information.

As a number of scholars have already noted, the talmudic exegetes of the Mishnah employ many of the same reading strategies in their treatment of Mishnah that the midrashicists use in their explication of biblical scripture.[20] In the talmudic interpretations of m. Shevuot,

[17] Kugel, *The Bible as It Was*, 21.

[18] On the use of this term as a way of describing a rabbinic assumption about the biblical text, see Kugel, *Idea of Biblical Poetry*, 103–5; Kugel, *Bible as It Was*, 21–23; and Elman, "No Empty Thing," 1–14.

[19] See discussion on superfluity in Harris, *How Do We Know This?*, 11.

[20] See sources cited in n. 3 of this chapter.

rabbinic exegetes atomize the mishnaic text (although not to the same degree as biblical exegetes) and focus on these atomized "bits" as semantically loaded.[21] As in midrash, the focus on small sections of text is accompanied by a tendency to read the "bits" as richer in meaning than a plain sense reading of the local context might suggest. Here, too, the assumption of the text's omnisignificance and the strategy of atomization work hand in hand.

As we turn to specific texts that illustrate this phenomenon, it is particularly interesting to reflect how the assumption of omnisignificance is present and the strategy of atomization is deployed with increased intensity as we move from the earlier Yerushalmi to the later Bavli.

The Yerushalmi on M. Shev. 3:1

The following mishnah contains two cases that are meant to be read as a single unit, for together they convey a single principle. Nonetheless, the Yerushalmi reads the two cases as two distinct units, with each case conveying a distinct legal principle. That is, the Yerushalmi atomizes the two cases and reads each one as richer in meaning than a simple reading of the mishnah warrants. The mishnah reads as follows:

m. Shev. 3:1[22]

שבועה שלא אוכל ואכל ושתה – אינו חייב אלא אחת.
שבועה שלא אוכל ושלא אשתה ואכל ושתה – חייב שתים.

a. [If a person said:] I swear[23] that I will not eat, and [then] he ate and drank – he is only liable on one count.
b. [If a person said:] I swear that I will not eat and I will not drink, and [then] he ate and drank – he is liable on two counts.

[21] Klein makes a similar observation in "Some Methods of Sebara," 126.
[22] M. Shev. 3:2 according to numbering system in Palestinian MSS tradition.
[23] Literally, "It is an oath that I will not eat."

This mishnah illustrates the principle that how one formulates an oath influences whether subsequent actions are understood to violate the oath. Whereas in the first case (a) the oathtaker prohibits only eating, in the second case (b) he prohibits both eating and drinking. Since the oathtaker proceeds with the same two actions in both cases (he eats and drinks), the different levels of culpability between the two cases (one vs. two counts) appear to result from the different ways he has formulated his oath. Only when the oathtaker explicitly prohibits *both* eating and drinking do both actions constitute independent violations of his oath. In this way of reading, the first case serves as a foil for the second case, highlighting why in the second instance two counts of culpability follow: because the oath was articulated in a more extensive manner. For the interpreter who is concerned that the mishnaic text exhibit no superfluity, however, the fact that the first case "merely" serves as a foil for the second case raises immediate red flags. Nonetheless, a straightforward reading of the mishnah suggests that the two cases are to be read as part of a single unit, communicating together the following legal principle: Enumerating individual prohibitions in an oath makes the oathtaker susceptible to more counts of culpability if he violates the conditions of the oath.

The next two mishnayot make much the same point in much the same manner. Like m. Shev. 3:1, they contain two complementary cases, in which the first case narrates a more generally stated prohibition and the second case a more explicitly enumerated set of prohibitions.

m. Shev. 3:2–3:3

שבועה שלא אוכל ואכל פת חטים ופת שערין ופת כסמין – אינו חייב אלא אחת.
שבועה שלא אוכל פת חטים ופת שעורין ופת כסמין ואכל – חייב על כל אחת ואחת.
שבועה שלא אשתה ושתה משקין הרבה – אינו חייב אלא אחת.
שבועה שלא אשתה יין ושמן ודבש ושתה – חייב על כל אחת ואחת.

3:2.a. [If a person said:] I swear that I will not eat, and [then] he ate wheat bread and barley bread and spelt bread – he is only liable on one count.

3:2.b. [If a person said:] I swear that I will not eat wheat bread and barley bread and spelt bread and [then] he ate [them] – he is liable on each and every count.

3:3.a. [If a person said:] I will not drink, and [then] he drank many [kinds of] potables – he is only liable on one count.

3:3.b. [If a person said:] I will not drink wine and oil and honey, and [then] he drank [them] – he is liable on each and every count.

In the first case of each of these two mishnayot (a), the oathtaker makes a single general prohibition, and though he follows with several violating actions, he is penalized only one count of culpability. In the second case in each of these mishnayot (b), the oathtaker makes multiple prohibitions, which result in multiple prohibitions. As in m. Shev. 3:1, in each of these mishnayot the two cases jointly convey the principle that a more explicit oath results in more counts of culpability. Whereas a generally stated oath incurs only one count of culpability (a), an oath in which specific foods or potables are enumerated incurs multiple counts of culpability (b), *even though* the oathtaker performs the *same* actions subsequent to his oath. Here again, an interpreter who believes that the mishnaic text should exhibit no superfluity will have difficulty with the fact that m. Shev. 3:1, 3:2, and 3:3 make the same point. Surely three mishnayot were not needed when one would have sufficed.[24]

The Yerushalmi's interpretation of m. Shev. 3:1 wrestles with both of the apparent superfluities that have been noted. First, it infuses each of the two cases in 3:1 with a distinct significance so that neither serves as a mere foil for the other. Second, it differentiates 3:1 from 3:2 and 3:3 so that all three do not rehearse the same point.

[24] It is important to point out that this is not an intrinsic difficulty with the text but only a difficulty if one assumes the principle of no superfluity (what Hayes calls the principle of "verbal economy"). Like the Mishnah, the parallels in the Sifra (HaHova, Perek 15 and 16) bring several different instantiations of this principle.

The Yerushalmi begins its discussion of m. Shev. 3:1 by treating the first case independently of the second case. When divorced from its complementary case, the first case takes on a new significance. As will be recalled, the first case alone reads as follows:

m. Shev. 3:1[25]

שבועה שלא אוכל ואכל ושתה – אינו חייב אלא אחת.

a. [If a person said:] I swear[26] that I will not eat, and [then] he ate and drank – he is only liable on one count.

Without the second case as a point of contrast, it appears that the two actions, eating and drinking, *both* violate the terms of the single oath not to eat. It simply makes no sense to mention both eating and drinking as subsequent actions, unless both violate the terms of the oath. Consequently, the Yerushalmi reasons that though the oath was formulated to prohibit *only eating*, the term "eating" alludes to the act of drinking, as well as eating.[27] Though the oathtaker explictly prohibits only eating, he apparently means to prohibit drinking as well, thereby explaining why the subsequent action of drinking is relevant. From this line of thinking, the following principle emerges:

y. Shev. 34b, line 49

שתייה בכלל אכילה.
ולא אכילה בכלל שתייה.

Drinking is implied by the term eating, but eating is not implied by the term drinking.

[25] M. Shev. 3:2 according to numbering system in Palestinian MSS tradition.
[26] Literally, "It is an oath that I will not eat."
[27] As the Bavli notes, common usage confirms this sense of the relationship between eating and drinking: "A man will often say to his companions: 'Let's go grab a bite,' and then they go and eat and drink" (b. Shev. 22b).

The Yerushalmi opens its discussion of m. Shev. 3:1 by citing this principle. When read as a stand-alone case, the first case of m. Shev. 3:1 conveys information that is replicated neither in the second case nor in the following two mishnayot. This first case is now understood to convey information about the semantic relationship between eating and drinking. It no longer serves as a foil for the second case.

While the Yerushalmi's interpretation of the first case is both reasonable and defensible, it is important to expose the extent to which alternative interpretations – rooted in different hermeneutical assumptions and practices – exist. One might just as easily argue that drinking is mentioned in the first case only in order *to anticipate its relevance for the second case*. In this way of reading, the fact that the oathtaker drinks after his oath not to eat has no real legal significance. It is mentioned only to highlight the comparability of the first case to the second. In the second case, of course, the oathtaker's act of drinking is entirely relevant, since his oath prohibits both eating and drinking. This reading of the mishnah focuses on the two cases as a single unit. I would argue that the Yerushalmi rejects this understanding of m. Shev. 3:1 because it implies that inclusion of the term drinking in the first case is merely incidental. The Yerushalmi's reading attests to an emerging sense that the Mishnah was composed in a deliberate intentional manner. From its perspective, every word has a legal significance. The term "drinking" is included in the first case not as mere rhetorical flourish, but in order to teach the principle that drinking is implied by the term "eating."

After citing this principle, the Yerushalmi presents a number of different sources for the principle. According to R. Yose, however, all the other cases can be learned from our mishnah.

y. Shev. 34b, lines 60–61

ר' יוסי שמע כולהון מיכא:

שבועה שלא אוכל, [ואכל] ושתה – אין חייב אלא אחת.

> R. Yose learned all of them [i.e., all of the instantiations of the principle that "drinking" is implied by the term "eating"] from here: **[If a person said:] I swear I will not eat, and then he [ate and]**[28] **drank – he is liable on only one count.** [= m. Shev. 3:1.a]

R. Yose cites our mishnah – notably only the first case – as the source for the principle. The text indicates that he learned, or deduced, the principle from the case. The significance of the case, then, is that it is a source for this legal principle.

Assuming that references to eating imply drinking also, however, raises a difficulty with the *second* case in m. Shev. 3:1.[29] R. Yose's colleagues put the following question to him:

y. Shev. 34b, lines 61–63

אמר חברייא קומי ר' יוסי:
ומר דבתרה?
שבועה שלא אוכל ושלא אשתה ואכל ושתה – אין חייב אלא אחת?!

> His colleagues said before R. Yose:
> And what do you say about that which comes after:
> **[If a person said:] I swear I will not eat and I will not drink and [then] he ate and drank** [= m. Shev. 3:1.b] – is he liable on only one count?! [No. Such a one is liable on two counts. Therefore the principle that the term "eating" implies drink also must not be at work in this mishnah.]

To R. Yose's colleagues, certain features of the second case lead them to wonder if the principle that eating implies drinking really is assumed in this mishnah. In the second case, the oathtaker promises not to

28 The text in brackets is attested in MS Leiden, but not in the printed edition.

29 The fact that the principle is not obviously compatible with *both* cases serves as further support for the fact that an atomized reading of the mishnah generates this interpretation.

eat or drink. If the term "eating" implies drinking, then the twofold statement "I swear I will not eat and I will not drink" should be understood as a single oath. In this way of thinking, when the oathtaker adds the stipulation that he will not drink, he has added nothing new of substance. R. Yose's colleagues, however, point out the weakness in this interpretation. Were this interpretation to be legitimate, one would expect the two subsequent actions of eating and drinking to yield only one count of culpability, as they do in the first case. The fact that the mishnah holds the oathtaker liable on *two* counts in the second case indicates to R. Yose's colleagues that the principle that drinking is implied by the term eating is not operating in this mishnah and that R. Yose's interpretation of the first case is untenable. Their challenge is a good one.

R. Yose answers his colleagues by showing that the second case teaches a different principle than the first case does, which explains why the oathtaker is there liable on two counts.

y. Shev. 34b, lines 63–65

אמר לון ר' יוסי:
אילו מי שאמר
שבועה שלא אוכל כיכר זו שבועה שלא אוכל כיכר זו, ואכל – חייב שתים!
שמא אינו חייב שתים?!

> R. Yose said to them:
> It is like the case of one who said
> I swear I will not eat this loaf, I swear I will not eat this loaf, and he ate [them] – he is liable on two counts.
> Would you not say such a one is liable on two counts?!

R. Yose explains that having stated explicitly his intention not to eat and drink, the oathtaker indicates that he considers each articulation to be a distinct and separate oath. He likens the second case to an instance in which the oathtaker speaks the same words twice, but with different referents. So, too, even though the oathtaker who says he will neither eat nor drink has twice stated the same intent, each pronouncent has a different referent. Therefore, it is accounted to him as if he made two separate oaths and so he is liable on two counts. As R. Yose understands it, an altogether different principle is communicated by the second case. Though the principle that drinking is implied by eating is assumed here, the real point of the case is to teach the principle that each re-pronouncement is considered as a separate oath. In this interpretation, the second case is distinguished not only from the first case but also from the two mishnayot that follow.[30]

As the interpretation now stands, neither scenario in m. Shev. 3:1 serves as a mere foil for the other. Each imparts a distinct legal principle. The first case teaches that drinking is implied by eating, and the second case teaches that saying the same thing twice with different referents is like making two separate oaths. By identifying these two distinct principles, the Yerushalmi succeeds in distinguishing the two cases from each other and from the mishnayot that follow. Mishnaic language is shown to be significant by virtue of conveying information in a very efficient and elegant manner. Each case is saturated with meaning.

The Bavli on M. Shev. 3:1

The Bavli's interpretation of this mishnah builds on the Yerushalmi's, but it also adds a number of new elements. Where the Bavli replicates moves made by the Yerushalmi, it expresses its assumptions about mishnaic language more directly than the Yerushalmi does. The full extent of the Bavli's commitment to these assumptions, however, can best be seen in the new moves. In the new material, the sheer volume

[30] The two following mishnayot (3:2–3) are not about re-pronouncement but about higher degrees of articulation. The more one articulates with specificity what one intends to prohibit, the more one is potentially liable if one violates the terms of the oath.

of interpretations based on these assumptions indicates how much they are taken for granted and how routine they have become in the intellectual climate.

Like the Yerushalmi, the Bavli begins its interpretation by rooting the principle that the term "eating" implies drinking in the first case of m. Shev. 3:1. In the Bavli, this argument is attributed to Rava. After several attempts are made to find a biblical proof text for the principle that drinking is implied by the term eating, Rava shows that the principle can also be learned from m. Shev 3:1.

b. Shev. 23a

אמר רבא: אף אנן נמי תנינא:
שבועה שלא אוכל אכל ושתה – אינו חייב אלא אחת.
אי אמרת בשלמא שתייה בכלל אכילה, איצטריך ליה לתנא לאשמועינן דאינו חייב אלא אחת,
אלא אי אמרת שתייה לאו בכלל אכילה, שבועה שלא אוכל ואכל ועשה מלאכה, מי איצטריך
ליה לתנא לאשמועינן דאינו חייב אלא אחת?!

> Rava said: We have also learnt it [i.e., the principle that drinking is implied by eating] from a tannaitic tradition, [which states]:
> **[If a person said:] I swear I will not eat and [then] he ate and drank – he is only liable on one count.** [= m. Shev. 3:1.a]
> If one holds the principle that drinking is implied by eating, then the tanna needed to include this passage in the mishnah in order to clarify that the oathtaker is liable on only one count.
> However, if one does not hold the principle that drinking is implied by eating, then did the tanna really need to include this passage in the mishnah [which effectively addresses the case of] a person who said I will not eat and then he ate and did work [i.e., did something else] merely in order to clarify that such a one is liable on only one count?! [Certainly not.]

Rava's argument is rooted in the observation that if you assume the principle, then the first case in m. Shev. 3:1 teaches something that is not at all self-evident. Rava understands the import as follows: Even though logic dictates that he who eats and drinks after taking an oath not to eat should be liable on two counts (because he twice violated the oath), in fact he is liable on only one count. Since this conclusion cannot be deduced by logic alone, the mishnaic text is needed to teach it. On the other hand, if you do not take the principle for granted, then the first case appears to be superfluous by teaching something that is altogether self-evident. Logic alone dictates that he who eats and drinks after an oath not to eat is only liable on one count. Since this conclusion can be deduced by logic alone, the mishnah becomes superfluous. Like R. Yose in the Yerushalmi, Rava is not content to consider the subsequent action of drinking in the first case mere rhetorical flourish. From his point of view, if the subsequent action of drinking has no legal consequence, then it is not worth including in the mishnah. As noted in the discussion of the Yerushalmi, it is entirely reasonable to argue that the term "drinking" is included in anticipation of its relevance for the second case. While such a usage has rhetorical utility, it has no legal significance. For the talmudic exegetes, however, a term without legal significance is a flagrant violation of the assumption that mishnaic language does not waste words. Since only the first interpretation shows the mishnah to be "needed," Rava concludes that the principle is in fact assumed.

Clearly, Rava's argument builds on R. Yose's in the Yerushalmi.[31] Unlike R. Yose, however, Rava uses an expression that conveys his commitment to the idea that every word in the mishnaic text is significant. Nowhere does he state this assumption directly, but he does use language that has elsewhere been linked with this point of view. According

[31] For more on how the Bavli often uses elements present in the Yerushalmi's sugya as a starting point, see Gray, "A Talmud in Exile." See also Shamma Friedman, "Historical Aggadah in the Babylonian Talmud" (Hebrew), in *Memorial Volume for R. Saul Lieberman,* ed. Shamma Friedman (New York and Jerusalem: Jewish Theological Seminary, 1993), 119–64. See also Rubenstein, *Talmudic Stories,* whose work examines the Babylonian extensions of Palestinian sugyot, and Elizabeth Shanks Alexander, "Art, Argument and Ambiguity in the Talmud: Conflicting Representations of the Evil Impulse," *Hebrew Union College Annual* 73 (2002): 97–132.

to Christine Hayes, the sages whose interpretations are recorded in the Bavli "rarely concede that one phrase of the Mishnah is a gloss or reformulation of another, but insist that each phrase is *necessary* (צריכא) in its own right." Likewise, "if a teaching appears self-evident, the amoraim will show that it is not self-evident, that on the contrary, it is *necessary* (צריכא) in order to preclude some plausible, but erroneous alternative" (emphasis added).[32] The talmudic concern that the Mishnah be neither self-evident nor redundant flows from the belief that the mishnaic text exhibits what Hayes calls "verbal economy." In other words, the talmudic interpretation of the Mishnah assumes that it expresses its ideas using the fewest words possible. While Rava does not use the phrase "it is necessary" (צריכא), which is the direct subject of Hayes's discussion, he does use a cognate form of the same root when he points out that the mishnah either is or is not "needed to teach" (איצטריך לאשמועינן) something we would not otherwise know. Thus, Rava not only repeats the argument of R. Yose that rests on the assumption that the Mishnah does not waste words but also uses language that reflects a self-conscious awareness of this assumption.

Like R. Yose's interlocutors, Rava's traditional interlocutor Abaye refutes the claim that the principle is assumed in m. Shev. 3:1. As in the Yerushalmi, the refutation focuses on the difficulties the principle poses for a proper understanding of the *second* case in m. Shev. 3:1.

b. Shev. 23a

אמר ליה אביי:
אלא מאי שתייה בכלל אכילה?
אימא סיפא: שבועה שלא אוכל ושלא אשתה ואכל ושתה – חייב שתים.
כיוון דאמר שלא אוכל איתסר ליה בשתייה,
כי אמר שלא אשתה, אמאי חייב?
אילו אמר שלא אשתה תרי זימני, מי מיחייב תרי?!

32 Hayes, *Between the Babylonian and Palestinian Talmuds*, 93–94.

Abaye answered him:
But is drinking really implied by the term eating?
Recite the second half of the mishnah, [which disproves this assertion]:
[If a person said:] I swear I will not eat and I will not drink and [then] he ate and drank – he is liable on two counts. [= m. Shev. 3:1.b]
Now, when he says "I swear I will not eat" he already prohibits drinking.
Why then does he become liable on an additional count when he adds the words "I swear I will not drink"?
If he had said "I swear I will not drink" twice, would he be liable on two counts?! [Surely not!]

Like R. Yose's colleagues before him, Abaye notes an inconsistency in the second case of m. Shev. 3:1 that arises if one assumes that the term "eating" implies drinking also. The reader will recall that the second case discusses the person who swears not to eat and drink and then goes ahead and does both. Like R. Yose's colleagues, Abaye argues that such a person should be liable on only *one* count if the principle is operative. He reasons as follows: The oathtaker who swears not to eat implicitly prohibits drinking also. When he goes on to state the prohibition against drinking *explicitly*, nothing changes. According to Abaye then, he should be liable on only a *single* count when he subsequently violates the terms of the oath. The mishnah, however, holds the oathtaker liable on two counts. On the basis of the inconsistency that arises from assuming the principle, Abaye concludes that the principle is not assumed by this mishnah.[33]

[33] It will be recalled that R. Yose responded to this challenge by pointing out that each new articulation of the prohibition is like a new oath. See previous discussion. It is noteworthy that the Bavli formulates Abaye's initial challenge to Rava in a manner that both anticipates and addresses R. Yose's rejoinder. By likening the oath not to eat and drink to a twice-repeated oath not to drink, the Bavli undermines R. Yose's rejoinder. It will be recalled that R. Yose buttresses his interpretation of the second case by likening it to a twice-stated oath not to eat a particular loaf of bread. R. Yose assumes that

Up to this point in the argument, the Bavli essentially re-presents elements of the debate already attested in the Yerushalmi. From this point forward, however, the Bavli introduces analysis without a parallel in the Yerushalmi. It is noteworthy that the new materials rely heavily on the assumption that mishnaic language conveys meaning in a powerful and efficient manner. Every move from this point forward takes for granted the belief that the Mishnah communicates in the most efficient manner possible. Since the talmudic material is lengthy and complicated, I will cite text only selectively and paraphrase the basic moves of the argument.

Two new assumptions inform the next part of the argument. The first assumption is that it makes a difference whether the oathtaker says "I swear I will not *eat*" or "I swear I will not *drink*" first. If, on the one hand, the oathtaker says "I swear I will not *drink*" first, then the second statement is *not* understood to overlap with the first. Having explicitly prohibited drinking as a discrete act, the oathtaker makes clear that the subsequent mention of eating refers to eating alone and not to both eating and drinking. The two-part statement is understood to be a two-part oath, for which the oathtaker who violates it is liable on two counts. If, on the other hand, the oathtaker says "I swear I will not *eat*" first, then the second statement is considered redundant. Having stated his intention not to eat first, the oathtaker prohibits *both* eating and drinking, and so any additional prohibition of drinking has no additional legal consequences. Under these circumstances, even though

such a pronouncement renders the oathtaker liable on two counts. Abaye's challenge dismisses the viability of such a retort at the outset when he simply assumes that a twice-repeated oath yields only a single count of culpability. One wonders here how familiar the Bavli is with the Yerushalmi and if it has been formulated in such a manner as to anticipate any perceived weaknesses in the Yerushalmi's argument. Alyssa Gray notes that the Bavli often addresses questions left unresolved by the Yerushalmi as part of a larger argument on the Bavli's familiarity with our version of Yerushalmi. See Gray, "A Talmud in Exile," 61–62, 84–85, 254–68, where she discusses the Bavli picking up questions left unresolved by the Yerushalmi. See also Alexander, "Art, Argument and Ambiguity," for another example of how the Bavli works with questions elicited by the Yerushalmi's argumentation.

the oathtaker may eat *and* drink, he is only liable on one count, since he is subject to only a single generalized oath. This assumption attributes great significance to word order, indicating how the Bavli is narrowing its focus to the finer details of the text.

The second assumption at work in the next section of the Bavli's argumentation is that the narration of the mishnaic case does not necessarily represent an actual chronology of events, but only a schematic enumeration of the events that happened.[34] Where the second case of the mishnah states that the oathtaker says "I swear I will not eat and drink," with the narration mentioning eating before drinking, the Bavli assumes in point of fact that the two prohibited acts, eating and drinking, could have been mentioned in either of two possible orders. It is equally likely that the oathtaker said "I swear I will not *drink* and eat" (drinking first) as that he said "I swear I will not *eat* and drink" (eating first). This second assumption is somewhat counterintuitive. At first glance, it appears to contradict the text, which clearly mentions eating first. I would argue, however, that this assumption sees the text in which the oathtaker says "I swear I will not eat or drink" as *so freighted with meaning* that it can bear *manifold* meanings. It suggests that the text is not transparent or readily decipherable in any straightforward sense, and so is deserving of intense scrutiny. The idea that this text might refer *both* to an oath in which the prohibition against drinking precedes the prohibition against eating *and* vice versa is in fact quite attentive to the details of the text. It attends to the fact that the oath in the text is two-part, and it is attentive to the significance of word order; it simply does not slavishly assume that the stated order is the only possible way to arrange events.[35] From a legal perspective,

[34] A similar assumption is at work in b. Shev. 27b; see the discussion in Alexander, "Study Practices That Made the Mishnah," 57–59.

[35] It is also possible to argue that in attributing to the mishnaic text two equally plausible interpretations, one of which appears to contradict the plain-sense meaning directly, the Bavli is coming close to seeing the mishnaic text as omnisignificant. When it bears multiple interpretations that are mutually exclusive, the mishnaic text is shown to be neither self-evident nor transparent. Its meaning is not readily apparent. Rather, the

this is in fact a legitimate assumption. Legal texts usually offer an idealized and schematic representation of events. There will always be some difference between how the text describes circumstances and the actual events with which a judge is faced. By considering both possibilities ("drinking" stated first and "eating" stated first), the Bavli acknowledges this disparity and tries to account for the full diversity that actual events may bring.[36]

Rava's reply to Abaye's challenge takes for granted these two assumptions. It will be recalled that Abaye questions the existence of the principle that the term "eating" implies drinking because holding it leads to the conclusion that the oathtaker in the second case is liable on only one count. Since the mishnah states that he is liable on two counts, Abaye concludes that the principle is not assumed in m. Shev. 3:1. In order to refute Abaye, Rava must come up with a plausible explanation for why the oathtaker in the second case is in fact liable on two counts.

b. Shev. 23a

אמר ליה:
התם, דאמר שלא אשתה והדר אמר שלא אוכל . . .
אבל אמר שבועה שלא אוכל ושלא אשתה ואכל ושתה, מאי? אינו חייב אלא אחת!

text must be scrutinized intensively and mined for meaning. In this description of the Bavli's interpretation, I am reminded of Kugel's description of midrash as "holy *recherche*." He suggests that the midrashic stance toward the biblical text implies that it is worthy and deserving of extensive investigation. See Kugel, "Two Introductions to Midrash," 91–92.

36 It might be argued that here we see firm evidence of the Bavli treating the Mishnah like a legal code. This move is also part of the shifting perception of mishnaic materials, even though it is not the chief focus of this chapter. For an analysis that focuses more directly on the gradual amalgamation of the viewpoint that the Mishnah is a law code, see the analysis by Dov Zlotnick in which he argues on behalf of the gradual adoptation of this viewpoint by the amoraim. See Dov Zlotnick, *The Iron Pillar: Mishnah,* 194–217. See also Halivni's discussion of the amoraic reception of and use of the Mishnah as a law code in "Rabbi Judah's Mishnah," 208–9.

He [Rava] replied:
There [= the case which you note carries two counts of culpability], the reference is to a person who said [first] "I swear I will not drink," and then went back and said, "I will not eat" . . .
But if he said "I swear I will not eat and I will not drink," and [then] ate and drank, what is the ruling? He is only liable on one count [as you suggest]!

Rava explains that the oathtaker is liable in Abaye's hypothetical case on two counts because he stated his intent not to drink *before* stating the intent not to eat. Having mentioned drinking as a discrete action first, the subsequent mention of "eating" refers to eating alone and includes no implicit reference to drinking. Two counts of culpability follow because two discrete actions (drinking and eating) have been prohibited. Rava points out that the consequences that Abaye describes, in which only *one* count of culpability follows, result when *the word "eating" is stated before the word "drinking."* As discussed earlier, Rava makes the highly unusual move of assuming that the order of events narrated in the mishnah is not in any way determinative. For Rava, the language of the mishnah sets out certain parameters, and within those he freely explores the interpretive possibilities.

Abaye dismisses Rava's interpretation of the second case by showing it to be redundant with the first case. Here again, the assumption that mishnaic language does not waste words informs the analysis.

b. Shev. 23a

אי הכי, אדתני רישא שבועה שלא אוכל ואכל ושתה,
ליתני שבועה שלא אוכל ושלא אשתה ואכל ושתה – אינו חייב אלא אחת,
וכל שכן שלא אוכל ליחודיה.

> [Abaye answered]:
> If what you say is correct, then in the first case where the mishnah actually states "If a person took an oath, saying 'I swear I will not eat' and then he ate and drank,"
> It should instead state, "If a person took an oath saying 'I swear I will not eat and I swear I will not drink,' and then he ate and drank – he is liable on one count."
> [If such is the ruling when the oathtaker states both "eating and drinking" in the oath,] then certainly it is the ruling when he states only "eating" in the oath.

Abaye argues that the mishnah certainly cannot be commited to the position that a person who says "I swear I will not eat and drink," and then subsequently eats and drinks, is only liable on one count. Abaye astutely points out that when one is commited to that position, the first case in the mishnah becomes superfluous, as it can be learned from inference and need not be stated explicitly. The force of Abaye's argument comes from the fact that he assumes that the Mishnah will not waste words. Rava must concede the point, since he, too, shares the assumption. Fundamental to the interpretive sparring between Rava and Abaye is the underlying assumption that mishnaic language is efficient.

With one final interpretive insight, Rava puts to rest all of Abaye's challenges to his position. In the end, he demonstrates the viability of the principle that the term "eating" implies drinking too by successfully showing how it operates in the second case of m. Shev. 3:1.

b. Shev. 23a

כיון דאמר שלא אוכל והדר ואמר שלא אשתה,
גלי אדעתיה דהך אכילה דאמר אכילה גרידתא היא.

> [Rava replied:]
> Having stated "I will not eat" and then gone back and stated "I will not drink,"

> [the oathtaker] clarified that his intent when he initially spoke the word "eating" was to indicate eating alone [and not drinking also].

Rava explains that when the oathtaker follows the prohibition against eating with a prohibition against drinking, he makes clear that his initial use of the term "eating" was limited in scope. Even though the oathtaker states his intent not to eat before he states his intent not to drink, the statement is countenanced as a double oath, for which he is doubly liable. Thus, under *all* circumstances (irrespective of word order), the oath not to eat and drink results in two counts of culpability. Having definitely demonstrated that the second case yields two counts of culpability, the rest of the argument falls into place. The first case is no longer considered superfluous.

It is interesting to note that Rava ends up where common sense alone could have taken us. Often, when we say "eating," as in "Let's go grab a bite to eat," we mean both eating and drinking. Sometimes, however, the term "eating" is used in a more restrictive sense to mean eating alone. An explicit mention of "drinking" alongside the term "eating" is a pretty good indicator that the reference to "eating" is a reference to eating alone. The difference between this argument from common sense and Rava's final argument, however, is the way that Rava draws his evidence from mishnaic language. He is attentive to the fact that eating is mentioned before drinking in the mishnaic formulation and is at pains to account for that particular arrangement of the words. For Rava, the fact that drinking is mentioned after eating creates an impetus for overriding the regnant assumption about drinking and eating. The subsequent mention of drinking reveals important information about the meaning of the initial usage of the term "eating," namely, that it indicates eating alone. Rava's final interpretation of the second case is noteworthy because of the extent to which it focuses on the fine details of the mishnaic formulation.

Although this argument is lengthy and complicated, it is worth making the effort to understand its subtleties because of the manifold ways in which assumptions about mishnaic language impact the interpretive process. Though the interlocutors disagree about the significance of particular words and phrases, they share a fundamental commitment to the idea that mishnaic language communicates in a powerful and effective manner. Both agree that an interpretation that implies that the mishnaic text is redundant or self-evident is unacceptable. While the Bavli's interpretation of m. Shev. 3:1 builds on the atomized reading of the mishnah recorded in the Yerushalmi, the Bavli takes the impulse to focus narrowly one step further when it distills the significance of the word order in the second case. What for the Yerushalmi is a nascent interpretive posture becomes for the Bavli a fully developed and mature ideology about the mishnaic text. I would further speculate that interpretations like this one shape Sherira's understanding of the text. Whereas the Bavli's interpretation simply takes for granted that mishnaic language has an efficient elegance and expressive power, Sherira states these ideas outright. The very descriptions he offers of mishnaic language – "exact," "without superfluous language," "with nothing missing or extra," and "with great wonders contained in every word" – are presumed by the talmudic exegetes at every turn. Talmudic exegesis like that explicated here, then, plays an important role in fixing these associations in the communal consciousness.

Ascribing Increasingly Intense Degrees of Authorial Intention

Alongside the assumption that mishnaic language conveys meaning in a powerful and efficient manner, another assumption about the *intentionality of mishnaic composition* was concurrently emerging. Interpreters assumed that the text of m. Shevuot was a carefully considered and precisely crafted composition. As part of the project of clarifying textual significance, they reconstructed the deliberative process from which the received text emerged. Though interpreters today often despair of knowing what a given author had in mind at the time of composition,[37] ancient rabbinic interpreters were more sanguine about the prospects of reconstructing the composer's initial intent. Talmudic interpreters juxtaposed the received text with other *possible and plausible* formulations that they assumed were rejected for good reasons. They assumed that the mishnah could have been formulated in any number of possible ways. Instead of the received text X, the composer might have taught Y or Z. "Let the mishnah teach it" this way (ניתני in the Yerushalmi or ליתני in the Bavli) or "he could have stated it" this way (הוה ליה למימר), the interpreters propose. But each alternative formulation is shown to be inappropriate to the current context. By indicating the imprecise locutions that the composer rejects, the interpreter succeeds in isolating the significance of the text at hand, but he also reveals an underlying assumption that the composer works with a high degree of intentionality and deliberateness. The more alternative formulations the composer of a tradition rejects, the more insight we are held to gain into the compositional process and the intention behind the choices made. This interpretive strategy seeks to rehabilitate and reconstruct the paths not taken in order for us to understand better the signifcance of the path that was taken.

As we turn to specific textual illustrations of this principle, it is again important to note how the Bavli adopts this interpretive strategy that is attested in the Yerushalmi, but deploys it with an additional degree of intensity.

[37] Some of the more extreme positions in literary criticism deny any relevance of the author and his/her intentions in the interpretation of the text s/he has produced. See, for example: "Still newer critics . . . construe the text as isolated from every context other than a purely textual one and consider the term 'author' and the history of cultural usages to be impediments to the workings of the textual environment" from Donald E. Pease, "Author," in *Critical Terms for Literary Study*, ed. Frank Lentricchia and Thomas McLaughlin (Chicago: University of Chicago Press, 1990), 112. Even the so-called "new historicists," who are committed to the idea that historical context is relevant to the interpretation of texts, can often and easily be stymied in their attempts to discern matters of intent.

The Yerushalmi on M. Shev. 3:8

The following mishnah is subject to an interpretation that compares the received text to other plausible formulations.

m. Shev. 3:8

איזו היא שבועת שוא?... נשבע על דבר שאי אפשר:
ואם לא ראיתי גמל שפורח באוויר, ואם לא ראיתי נחש כקורת בית הבד.

> What is a vain oath? . . . When one swears concerning a matter which is impossible:
> [For example, if one says, I swear] if I didn't see a camel flying through the air, or if I didn't see a snake like the beam of an olive press.

This mishnah seeks to define the vain oath. A general definition explains that a vain oath occurs when one affirms under oath something that is patently impossible. The general definition is then followed by several illustrative examples. He who swears that he saw a camel flying through the air or that he saw a snake as wide as the beam of an olive press makes exaggerated and impossible claims. The rhetoric of the mishnah makes clear that it takes these eventualities to be impossible.[38] The person who swears that such things really did happen is held liable.

The Yerushalmi begins its interpretation by questioning the fundamental assumption in m. Shev. 3:8 that these eventualities are impossible.

[38] This same assumption is reflected in m. Ned. 3:2. There, the phrase "if I didn't see a snake like the beam of an olive press" (אם לא ראיתי נחש כקורת בית הבד) appears as an illustrative example of an exaggerated vow (נדרי הבאי). In this mishnah, the rhetoric reflects the tacit assumption that such a claim is impossible. In the case of exaggerated vows, however, the votive is not held responsible for his exaggerated statement. By way of contrast, the oathtaker who makes the exact same claim under oath is held liable.

y. Shev. 34d (= y. Ned. 37d)

והא חויוא דשפור מלכא בלע גמלין בלע קר־נין? . . .
במרובע.

> What about the snake of the king Shapur, who swallowed camels and swallowed carriages [whole]? . . .
> As a square, then.

The Yerushalmi challenges the mishnah's assumption that it is impossible to find a "snake like the beam of an olive press." The Yerushalmi testifies that the Persian king Shapur had a snake so large that it swallowed camels and carriages whole. Though unusual, there are snakes as large as the beam of an olive press. The conclusion follows that the impossibility of the comparison of snake to beam is *not a function of size but of shape.* If it is highly unlikely but possible to find a snake as *big* as the beam of an olive press, it is certainly impossible to find a snake with squared-off corners, that is, *shaped* like the beam of an olive press. As in the examples discussed previously, here too there is a narrowing of exegetical focus. The interpreter attends to the minute details of the text, irrespective of its importance for the text's overall message. The mishnah is not itself overly concerned with whether or not snakes as large as the size of an olive press exist. The overall import of the mishnah depends more on the *rhetorical* function of the comparison (we *assume* it is impossible) than on its actual impossibility. The Yerushalmi, however, is not content to accept the mishnah's assumptions that this claim is impossible without thorough investigation and verification. The interpretive inquiry that follows does not really affect the legal significance of the mishnah, but it does confirm the conclusions: talmudic interpretation is highly attentive to subtle textual details.

Once the interpretative possibility focused on size is eliminated, the question arises as to why the mishnah was not formulated so as to avoid confusion.

y. Shev. 34d (=y. Ned. 37d)

ואם במרובע, ניתני אפילו קטן?
אמר ר' יודן אבוי דר' מתנייה:
כיני. אלא דלית אורחא דתנייא מיתפוס אלא מילה רובא,
דתנינן "גמל פורח באוויר," ניתני עכבר פורח באוויר.

> If [the intent is to compare the beam to the snake with regard to its] square [shape], then let the mishnah be phrased [so as to include the possibility of a] small [snake]?
> R. Yehudah, father of R. Matniah said:
> It is in fact so. But it is the style of the mishnah to refer to large things [rather than small things].
> [For example,] where the mishnah states, "**a camel flying through the air**" (= m. Shev. 3:8), let it state: "a mouse flying through the air." [Why doesn't it? Obviously because of the mishnah's stylistic preference for large things].

The Yerushalmi wonders why the composer misleads the reader to think that size is significant when it is not. Certainly the mishnah could have invoked a simile that is applicable to *small as well as large* snakes. This move is important for our discussion. The interpreter makes clear that he believes that the mishnaic composer had other options available to him. He *might* have compared the snake to a small squared-shaped object. The technical term "let it teach" or state (ניתני) introduces the alternative formulation: "Let the mishnah state a small thing."

R. Yehudah explains that the received text, which compares snakes with beams, can in fact be used to describe small snakes. He argues that the mishnaic composer simply has a stylistic preference for drawing on large things as examples. To illustrate his point, R. Yehudah points to the first part of our mishnah, which speaks about a flying *camel.* Here again, the received text is compared to an alternative formulation in order for us to better understand the choices made by the composer.

The Yerushalmi again introduces the alternative formulation with the technical term "let it teach" or state (ניתני): "Let the mishnah state a *mouse* flying through the air." Though the mishnah could plausibly have spoken of a flying mouse and made the same point, it did not because of the composer's stylistic preferences. Apparently, the composer uniformily chooses to invoke large, rather than small, things, which accounts for his choice of language.[39] Both "the beam of an olive press" and a "camel" are large things.

Central to the interpretive strategy employed here is the idea that the composer had a range of options before him as he set about his task. At two critical junctures where the composer could have spoken of small things, he chose instead to speak of large things. In documenting the available alternatives, the Yerushalmi makes clears that mishnaic composition required the making of informed choices. Though we can imagine that in other cases the choices might hinge on more substantive issues, here stylistic preference accounts for the choices. In any event, mishnaic composition is assumed to be a deliberate and intentional process.

The Bavli on M. Shev. 3:2–3

As in the Yerushalmi, so too in the late, editorial stratum of the Bavli, talmudic exegetes discern the composer's intent by comparing the received text to alternative formulations that the composer presumably rejected. Interpretations employing this strategy attest to the Bavli's commitment to the idea that the mishnaic composer made conscious

[39] This is a somewhat problematic claim, since one can certainly think of mishnayot that speak of small things (e.g., m. Shev. 5:3, which describes a scenario involving a single grain of wheat, barley, and spelt, respectively). This discomfort may account for the fact that the Bavli reproduces the first part of the Yerushalmi's argument but not the second part, which rests on the assertion that the author of the mishnah has a stylistic preference for large things. See b. Shev. 29b. Gray notes that the Bavli often restructures material from the Yerushalmi so as to resolve the questions left hanging there. See Gray, "A Talmud in Exile," 61–62, 84–85, 254–68.

and deliberate choices when composing his text. The following mishnah is the subject of one such interpretive exercise.

m. Shev. 3:2

שבועה שלא אוכל ואכל פת חטין ופת שעורין ופת כסמין – אינו חייב אלא אחת.
שבועה שלא אוכל פת חטין ופת שעורין ופת כסמין ואכל – חייב על כל אחת ואחת.

> [If a person took] an oath, [saying "I swear] I will not eat," and he ate wheat bread, barley bread and spelt bread – he is only liable on one count.
> [If a person took] an oath, [saying "I swear] I will not eat wheat bread, barley bread and spelt bread," and he ate [them] – he is liable on each and every count.

This mishnah juxtaposes two cases that are similar, but which have very different legal outcomes. Although in both cases the oathtaker eats three different kinds of bread, only in the second instance when he prohibits them explicitly is the oathtaker held liable for each and every act of eating. At first glance, the reasoning behind this ruling appears quite straightforward. The oathtaker in the second case carries a higher degree of culpability because he outlined the nature of his prohibition more extensively. Were this interpretation correct, however, the legal import of this mishnah would be redundant, as m. Shev. 3:1 and 3:3 discussed in the previous section make much the same point.[40] We have already come to anticipate that the Bavli does not rest content accepting an interpretation of the mishnah that renders it redundant. In this view, there must be another reason that the oathtaker is held

[40] As noted several times already, this interpretation *will not* pose a problem for the interpreter for whom redundancy is *not* a difficulty. I see no reason to discount this interpretation a priori. It strikes me as quite plausible that m. Shev. 3:1–3 make much the same point. In this way of thinking, each is a different performative version of the same tradition along the same lines that parallel traditions represent different performative renditions of the same tradition, as discussed in Chapter 1.

liable to a greater degree in the second case. Though the reason is not immediately apparent, it does emerge after intensive and extensive examination of the language used in this mishnah in comparison with other available options.

The Bavli's interpretation focuses on the key point of difference between the two cases in the mishnah. Whereas in the first case the oathtaker prohibits eating only in the most general sense, in the second case he prohibits eating specifially three kinds of bread. What is it about the more specific articulation that renders him culpable to a higher degree?

b. Shev. 23a–b

ודלמא למיפטר נפשיה מאחרנייתא קאתי
הוה ליה למימר: חטין ושעורין וכוסמין
ודלמא לכוס

דהוה ליה למימר: פת חטין ושעורין וכוסמין
ודלמא פת חטין לאכול, שעורין וכוסמין לכוס

דהוה ליה למימר: פת חטין ושל שעורין ושל כוסמין
ודלמא ע"י תערובת

אימא וכן של שעורין וכן של כוסמין

<u>פת</u>, <u>פת</u> למה לי?
שמע מינה לחלק.

1.a. Maybe [the higher degree of specification in the second case is intended not to differentiate three different oaths, but] to permit other kinds [of grain breads].

1.b. [If the intent of the oath was to permit other kinds of bread,] it could have said: [I swear not to eat] wheat, barley and spelt.

1.c. [That cannot be. If the text were as you suggest, then the intent would have been to prohibit] chewing individual grains.

2.a. [If the intent of the oath was to permit other kinds of bread,] it could have said: [I swear I will not eat] bread of wheat, barley and spelt.

2.b. [That cannot be. If the text were as you suggest, then the intent would have been to prohibit] wheat bread for eating as a whole loaf, but barley and spelt for chewing as individual grains.

3.a. [If the intent of the oath was to permit other kinds of bread,] it could have said: [I swear I will not eat] bread of wheat, and of barley and of spelt.

3.b. [That cannot be. If the text were as you suggest, then the intent would have been to prohibit] multigrain bread [i.e., a single loaf made of wheat, barley and spelt].

4. [If the intent of the oath was to permit other kinds of bread] it could have said: [I swear I will not eat] wheat bread, and that of barley and that of spelt.

5. So, why does the text include [the superfluous words] "bread" "bread"? Learn from this [that it was the oathtaker's intent] to distinguish [between three separate oaths].

The structure of this interpretive exercise is complicated and worth fleshing out in some detail. The argumentation begins by responding to an unstated position that the specificity of the oath ("I swear I will not eat *wheat bread, barley bread,* and *spelt bread*) functions to impose multiple oaths. An anonymous interloculor attempts to refute this unstated position by claiming that the specificity functions not to *include* stated items in separately delineated oaths but to *exclude* unstated items from a single generalized oath.[41] In other words, the oathtaker did not mean with his words to impose three separate oaths (one for each type of bread, respectively). Instead, he meant to ensure

[41] According to his logic, the oathtaker in the second case should not be liable on each and every count (as the mishnah rules), but only on a single count. For this understanding, see Rashi ad loc ד''ה ודלמא למיפטר נפשיה מאחרנייתא קאמר.

that he *would be able to eat* the unstated kinds of bread (e.g., oat or rye bread). The argument opens with the claim that the specificity is intended *to permit* the unnamed kinds of bread.

In order to refute this claim, the Bavli must show that another formulation can better, that is more economically, express this intent. The exercise introduces one formulation after another in the hopes of finding one that can express this intent. The formulations, however, are one by one shown to be insufficient to the task. Each conveys its own distinctive meaning, and cannot at the same time express the oathtaker's interest in permitting the unnamed breads. The search is rewarded in the end. The Bavli does finally succeed in identifying an alternative formulation that expresses the oathtaker's interest in permitting the unnamed breads. If the oathtaker wished to permit unnamed breads, he might have said: "I swear I will not eat bread of wheat, and that of barley and that of spelt." The key difference between this formulation and the mishnaic one is the fact that the word "bread" is repeated two additional times in the mishnaic formulation ("I swear I will not eat wheat bread, barley *bread,* and spelt *bread*"). In accordance with the Bavli's belief that the mishnah should exhibit no superfluity, the presence of the repeated term "bread" must be explained. The argument concludes by suggesting that the "bread" is repeated in order to indicate the oathtaker's intent to impose multiple oaths. Apparently, the multiple counts of culpability result not from the higher degree of specificity in the second case but from the repetition of the word bread.

Several features of this interpretive exercise are noteworthy. First, as we have remarked throughout this chapter, the analysis is narrowly focused. The exegete observes the presence of the repeated word "bread" and attempts to discern its significance. Many a reader might gloss over such a repetition, but not the exegetes of the latest editorial stratum of the Bavli. For them, every detail has important consequences for meaning. Second, reconstructing the alternative formulations available to, but rejected by, the mishnaic composer helps clarify the significance of the received text. The mishnah's meaning emerges most clearly when it is juxtaposed with a different but plausible formulation. In this case, the exegete tries to identify an alternate formulation that conveys a specific meaning (that unnamed breads are excluded from the oath, i.e., permitted). It can then be shown that the mishnaic composer rejected this alternate formulation because he wished to make a *different* point. In the course of trying to locate the formulation that can be said to have been rejected, the talmudic exegete considers a variety of formulations. According to the logic and structure of the argument, these formulations were never considered by the mishnaic composer and therefore were never formally rejected by him. The rhetoric of the talmudic argument suggests that only the last of the proposed formulations (the one that permits unnamed foods) was formally rejected by the mishnaic composer. Only this formulation is directly juxtaposed to the mishnaic formulation in an effort to discern the distinction of the mishnaic formulation. In spite of this fact, this exercise does reconstruct a plethora of different formulations that are similar to the mishnaic formulation. The similarities notwithstanding, each formulation is shown to convey its own distinctive meaning. Their collective presence has an impact beyond their function within the argument.[42] Together they indicate the full range of options theoretically available to the mishnaic composer.

In the eyes of the Bavli's exegetes, mishnaic composition is an exacting science. Each expression conveys a distinctive nuance of meaning, and within the range of possibilities, the mishnaic composer chose his words very carefully. While the Yerushalmi speculates that each

[42] Aryeh Cohen talks about reading the sugya against the grain. He suggests that the linear flow of the sugya is only one way to read the sugya. Important perspectives emerge when one attends to repeated motifs and other literary features. In this case, the repeated motif is the invocation of alternate textual versions. See Cohen, *Rereading Talmud*, 131–51, esp. 141. David Kraemer's work is also attentive to the rhetorical impact of the flow of claims in an argument over and against the explicit legal claims of the sugya. See Kraemer, *Reading the Rabbis: The Talmud as Literature* (New York and Oxford: Oxford University Press, 1996). See also Louis Jacobs, *The Talmudic Argument: A Study in Talmudic Reasoning and Methodology* (Cambridge: Cambridge University Press, 1984), who offers valuable insight on literary readings of legal sugyot in his conclusion.

element in the received text has a single alternative formulation, the Bavli reconstructs the numerous options that were available to the composer. The more options he might have had, the more his choices can be shown to be deliberate and intentional.

Conclusion

By the end of the talmudic period, the textual traditions of m. Shevuot were well on their way to being viewed as authoritative and privileged traditions. Their language was assumed to be charged with meaning, and they were assumed to have been composed with a high degree of intentionality. No explicit claims were made concerning their divine origins, but exegetes did routinely submit them to interpretive strategies that took their scriptural character for granted.[43] In time, a fully developed theory of Mishnah as divinely inspired Oral Torah would emerge and reinforce the suggestion in our sources that mishnaic language is special.[44] The sources of talmudic interpretation are interesting precisely because they give us insight into a process in formation. Whereas the Yerushalmi uses strategies that assume the power of mishnaic language in restrained and limited ways, the Bavli exploits the full potential of these strategies and so the assumptions on which

[43] Kugel makes an interesting suggestion in his discussion of the assumptions governing ancient Jewish biblical exegesis. He notes that three of the formative assumptions (of scripture's cryptic character, its relevance, and its perfection) are attested in early exegesis, whereas the fourth assumption (of scripture's divine character) is attested much less and only in the later materials. He makes the suggestion that the three assumptions of cryptic character, relevance, and perfection do not *follow* from the idea that scripture is divine, but rather *precede* it. As I understand Kugel, what he seems to be saying is that the habits of reading scripture according to the first three assumptions ultimately *lead to* the belief that scripture was divine. I would suggest we might speculate that a similar sequence of events occurred in the domain of conceptions of mishnaic textuality. The strategies discussed here, which embody certain assumptions, would have ultimately *preceded* the idea (and maybe even led to the idea) that mishnaic materials are divinely inspired. See Kugel, *Bible as It Was*, 22–23.

[44] Jaffee discusses the gradual process by which halakhic materials came to be seen as Oral Torah in *Torah in the Mouth*, 84–99.

they are based echo through it more strongly. By the time we get to Sherira's writings, the assumptions about the special character of mishnaic language are articulated explicitly. For Sherira, the authority of Mishnah follows from the beauty, subtlety, and power of its literary form.[45] Mishnaic form, however, is not intrinsically authoritative. Only in the hands of a devoted community of learners, a community attuned to extracting every morsel of significance sequestered within the folds of its language, do the literary features of m. Shevuot take on a meaning beyond that of their message.

I would argue that the devoted community of learners had the power to change the way the materials were understood, grasped, and conceived over time by the sheer power of the way in which they handled them themselves. The transmission of m. Shevuot did not happen in a sterile environment. Rather, mishnaic traditions were transmitted and received in a specific cultural environment with specific cultural understandings.[46] Those who passed on materials transmitted not only verbal content but also their conceptions of the materials as expressed in their interpretive framings of the materials. Sherira represents the culmination of this process – when the sensibilities nurtured by generations of intensive study finally became explicit. In the next chapter we will begin to explore the habits of study engendered by study of m. Shevuot and discuss how they accompanied the text in the course of the text's transmission.

45 The extent to which the Mishnah's authority becomes rooted in the elegance of its literary form offers an interesting parallel to the way in which Muslims conceptualize the Quran. I have often heard it said that the beauty of the Quran's language is testament to its divine origins. The language of the Quran is so closely associated with divine revelation that all translations are considered to fail to convey the original elegance and so are labeled "interpretations" rather than true "translations."

46 On the importance of the sage's transmissional act in the conveyance of rabbinic tradition, see Martin S. Jaffee, "A Rabbinic Ontology of the Written and Spoken Word: On Discipleship, Transformative Knowledge and the Living Texts of Oral Torah," *Journal of the American Academy of Religion* 65, no. 3 (Fall 1997): 27–61.

3

Modes of Legal Analysis in the Mishnah

The previous chapter explores ways in which post-tannaitic handlers of m. Shevuot fashioned a communal conception of it as scriptural. Rather than being passive agents for the mere conveyance of sources, transmitters of m. Shevuot played an active role in shaping how the materials were conceived and conceptualized. In this chapter, I wish to examine further how ways of thinking about m. Shevuot were crafted in the course of transmission.

Typically, scholars who discuss oral transmission of mishnaic materials focus on that aspect of transmission which involves the conveyance of verbal content. They suggest that mishnaic formulations distilled the key points of complex analytic discussions in summary form suitable for rote memorization. David Weiss Halivni succinctly summarizes this point of view:

> The Mishnah and Braitha (Tannaitic material not included in the Mishnah) consist almost entirely of fixed law; they contain very little discursive material. This is so despite the almost certain fact that the authors of the Mishnah and Braitha too discussed and argued (sometimes fiercely) before they arrived at conclusions. It can be assumed a priori that conclusions are always preceded by discussions and arguments. In addition,

> occasionally one encounters enough arguments in the Mishnah and Braitha to indicate that there were initially many more that were not subsequently preserved. Apparently, to the authors of the Mishnah and Braitha, law was to be officially transmitted only in the apodictic form. Arguments and discussions were necessary – indeed, indispensible – but only as a means of arriving at decisions, not as ends in themselves. Once the end was achieved, the means was left to wither away, to be forgotten.[1]

In other words, the discursive and analytic component of the learning process was excluded from the formal transmission process. Since it would have been too difficult to preserve complex analysis in any reliable form, transmitters preserved only the legal conclusions that were reached; they focused their attention on the legal "upshot," which, in their estimation, *could* be reliably preserved. Implicit in this reconstruction is a perceived mutual exclusivity between the rote memorization associated with mishnaic transmission and the vigorous analytic activities that preceded the formulation of the mishnaic shorthand.[2] From the standpoint of traditional scholarship, the repetition of mishnaic materials once they had been formulated simply did not engage its practitioners in any deep level of analysis.[3] By way of contrast,

1 Halivni, *Midrash, Mishnah and Gemara,* 2–3. For a similar understanding of the way in which mishnaic formulations encapsulate and summarize complex discussions and arguments, see Gerhardsson, *Memory and Manuscript,* 136–48. Kaplan and Klein assume that a similar process operated in the amoraic period, when complex analytic discussions were reduced to short, pithy amoraic statements suitable for memorization. See Kaplan, *Babylonian Talmud,* 196–97, 220, 234, and Klein, "Gemara and Sebara," 69, esp. n. 7, and 90.

2 Scholars have used the same dichotomy between rote memorization and discursive analysis to understand the transmissional life of halakhah and aggadah. According to typical scholarly understandings, halakhah is formulated in a precise manner, so as to facilitate accurate verbatim transmission. By way of contrast, in this view, aggadah is by nature discursive and so not capable of being transmitted with as much precision. See Gerhardsson, *Memory and Manuscript,* 96, 146–47. See also Faur, *Golden Doves,* 87, and Lauterbach, "Midrash and Mishnah," 182 ff.

3 If anything, the opposite would be assumed: Oral performance of Mishnah was intended for the simpleminded and the young and inexperienced. See Lieberman, *HJP,*

I wish to consider the possibility that transmission of m. Shevuot did engage practitioners in analytic thinking, *even while* it conveyed textual materials. I argue that when one reconstructs ancient mishnaic transmissional practices, conveyance of verbal content and cultivation of analytic skills need not be thought of as mutually exclusive activities.[4]

The conventional wisdom that analytic activity does not occur when mishnaic materials are transmitted is rooted in the classic understanding of mishnaic transmission as unreflective regurgitation of fixed verbal content. The work of the previous two chapters, however, calls into question the appropriateness of assuming that in the earliest stages of transmission, m. Shevuot was textually fixed in a way such that it could have been reproduced mechanically. The orally informed view

88: "Those *Tannaim* were pupils chosen for their extraordinary memory, though they were not always endowed with due intelligence. The Rabbis characterized these reciters as follows: 'The magian mumbles and understands not what he says. [Similarly] the *Tanna* recites and understands not what he says.' Indeed the stupider the *Tanna,* the more reliable his text; he was not suspected of doctoring it." On the relative youth and academic inexperience of those studying Mishnah, see Gerhardsson, *Memory and Manuscript,* 126–27.

4 The work of Mary Carruthers has been particularly valuable in helping me imagine the way in which analytic activity is integral to the reproducing of text in rhetorical settings. She writes in *Craft of Thought,* 8–9: "The orator's 'art of memory' was not in practice designed to let him reiterate exactly in detail a composition he had previously fabricated. For one thing, to sound as though he were reciting from memory like a parrot was one of the worst faults a Roman orator could commit. . . . The goal of Roman oratory was to speak eloquently *ex tempore*. . . . Thus the orator's 'art of memory' was not an art of recitation and reiteration but an art of invention, an art that made it possible for a person to act competently within the 'arena' of debate, . . . to respond to interruptions and questions, or to dilate upon the ideas that momentarily occurred to him. . . . All scholars who study the subject of rhetorical memory remain much indebted to Frances Yates. But for all her pioneering strengths, her work unfortunately does reinforce some common misconceptions about the possible cognitive uses of the 'art of memory.' . . . Yates herself believed that the goal of the art of memory was solely to repeat previously stored materials: she characterized the medieval versions of the ancient art as 'static,' without movement, imprisoning thought. She could not have been more wrong." In an earlier work, Carruthers likens the ancient and medieval image of memory to a storehouse in which bits of data are stored and inventoried. In the context of oral performance, the bits of information get manipulated into meaningful relationships; raw data becomes usable and useful knowledge. See Carruthers, *Book of Memory,* 16–45.

of rabbinic textuality presented in this book offers another way to view the textual artifacts preserved from antiquity. Martin Jaffee suggests that rabbinic texts and compilations as they have come down to us today be thought of as "a kind of freeze frame of... [orally fluid] tradition, temporarily stilled by the compilational activity itself. But such activity was not conceived as the product of a finished 'work.' It was, at best, a 'work in progress,' finished only at the point that the perception of its transmitters and users began to define the compilation as a text representing 'tradition' itself."[5] In the last chapter, we demonstrated how the perception of m. Shevuot's transmitters and users eventually did define the materials therein as an official and authoritative version of tradition. Before that point, however, Jaffee's image of the rabbinic texts as a "work in progress" is more fitting.

Such a view leaves open the possibility that the texts before us today functioned in antiquity within a complex cycle that led from the fluidity of oral performance to the fixity of written transcription and *then back again* to the fluidity of oral performance.[6] In this way of thinking, written transcriptions are not seen as fixed and finalized versions of text, *notwithstanding* the fixity that comes in the wake of writing. Instead, it is granted that written texts can be manipulated with

[5] Jaffee, "Oral Tradition," 23. See also Peter Schäfer, "Research into Rabbinic Literature: An Attempt to Define the Status Quaestionis," *Journal of Jewish Studies*, 37, no. 2 (1986): 139–52.

[6] The following statement by Jaffee is quite suggestive: "The resulting [mishnaic] tractates are thematically guided anthologies that function both as mnemonic aids in the preservation of the material and as springboards for restoring textually fixed traditions to the aural/oral world of analysis and debate generated by the curriculum"; "Oral Tradition," 25. The piece from which this citation is drawn has been enormously powerful in shaping my thinking. See also Jaffee, *Torah in the Mouth*, 100–125. Similarly powerful has been Fraade, "Literary Composition and Oral Performance," and his book *From Tradition to Commentary*. The work of Ruth Finnegan has also proved very influential to me for thinking through the complex nonlinear interactions between oral performance and literary forms of textual preservation. See especially her discussion of the interaction between the oral and the literary in the transmission of the broadside ballads, in *Oral Poetry*, 160–68.

the same fluidity that is generally associated with oral performance.[7] Steven Fraade talks about the textual artifacts before us today as "the literary face of an otherwise circulatory system of study and teaching."[8] What Fraade's image of a circulatory system makes clear is that rabbinic texts have an oral life that both precedes *and* follows them. In this understanding, the textual artifacts before us today are seen both as the summary of oral exercises already performed *and* a script that teaches or guides disciples in future such performances. Here, the text is not a final product but a jumping-off point for future improvisations. In Chapter 1, I tried to imagine something of the oral life of m. Shevuot *before* it reached its current form. I reconstructed the oral compositional building blocks that plausibly could have been used in the formulation of individual traditions in m. Shevuot. In this chapter, I wish to try to understand something of the oral life of m. Shevuot *after* it reached its current form. That is, I wish to gain insight into the nature of the performanace for which m. Shevuot serves as script.

Adopting Fraade's point of view that rabbinic texts are part of a complex cycling between literary consolidation and oral improvisation suggests that m. Shevuot serves not only as a summary of oral exercises already performed but also as an invitation to reenact similiar such exercises in the future.[9] Insofar as performing textual materials

[7] On this perspective, see also Finnegan, *Oral Poetry*, 52–87, and Calinescu, "Orality in Literacy."

[8] Fraade, *From Tradition to Commentary*, 19. Fraade further develops his thoughts on the metaphor of the oral circulatory system in "Literary Composition and Oral Performance," 35–36, 46.

[9] Neusner expresses a similar idea when he writes, "The Mishnah calls one to participate in the process of discovering principles and uncovering patterns of meaning." See Jacob Neusner, trans., *The Mishnah: A New Translation*, with an introduction by Jacob Neusner (New Haven, CT: Yale University Press, 1988), xxvii. As he describes it, reading Mishnah is an active process that involves recreating the logic that underlies its compositions. Susan Handelman also discusses the idea that engaged reading of a text can serve pedagogical purposes, teaching the readership how to reproduce the thought patterns and methods of the text being read. In her critique of Paul deMan, she suggests that rhetoric, language, and texts be thought of "as an *action* or effect on a public audience . . . and by extension as *teaching*." In the same context, she writes

requires "thinking the thoughts" that produced the formulations in the first place, the practitioner is initiated into particular habits of thought. If we can reconstruct something of the analytic activites required for the construction of the legal scenarios of m. Shevuot, we will also gain insight into the analytic activities that were *generated through* or *engendered by* performance of these materials. Identifying the habits of thought that were transmitted in conjunction with the verbal content of m. Shevuot is valuable because it provides us with a clearer perception of the intellectual environs within which the materials were subsequently received.[10]

My discussion of mishnaic texts begins with the simple observation that the casuistic form dominates tractate Shevuot.[11] In its most basic form, the casuistic form presents short legal prescriptions using an "if... then..." formulation: "If X set of circumstances occurs, then legal resolution Y should be employed." It is easy to see how one might not recognize that this form provides access to the analytic activity that would have been central to the construction of such a formulation. When viewed as a fixed text, the casuistic form appears to do no more than convey a legal norm. As Halivni writes, "Logically, an 'if' clause possesses the same relationship... that a non-'if' clause possesses, except that the former's assertion is hypothetical. However, when that assertion actually does occur – and the law is designed for precisely that eventuality – the difference between it and the non-'if' clause disappears."[12] In Halivni's view, the use of the "if... then..."

that "the literary form of midrash teaches us how it must be taught." See Susan Handelman, "The 'Torah' of Criticism and the Criticism of Torah: Recuperating the Pedagological Moment," in *Interpreting Judaism in a Postmodern Age,* ed. Steven Kepnes (New York: New York University Press, 1996), 236. I would likewise argue that m. Shevuot teaches its students how to think about the legal cases it records.

10 The next chapter more fully develops the idea that oral performance of m. Shevuot cultivates a way of thinking that impacts how the text of m. Shevuot is subsequently studied and interpreted.

11 Jacob Neusner has already called attention to the fact that the Mishnah's use of the casuistic form played an important role in its construction as oral tradition. See Neusner, *Oral Tradition in Judaism,* 61–100.

12 Halivni, *Midrash, Mishnah and Gemara,* 7.

formula, which distinguishes the casuistic form, is merely a rhetorical convention. The use of the conditional is significant only insofar as it anticipates those eventualities that will come before the law. Seeing the significance of mishnaic formulation as the conveyances of legal norms, a good many scholars have argued that the primary purpose of the Mishnah was to serve as a law code.[13] When we abandon the literary lens that conceptualizes texts as fixed, however, the legal verdict of mishnaic cases no longer appears to be as central. What we notice instead is the diverse ways in which the casuistic form is employed. Recognizing the subtle differences in how casuistic formulations are presented suggests that more was at stake in formulating them than just recording legal verdicts.

The Casuistic Form in Biblical and Ancient Near Eastern Codes

Scholars of the Bible and ancient Near East have expended considerable energy analyzing the casuistic form in biblical and cuneiform codes. Although their interest in the casuistic form is motivated by an entirely different set of concerns,[14] their work proves useful to the

[13] A long-standing debate in mishnaic studies concerns whether or not the Mishnah was intended to function as a law code or pedagogical handbook. See n. 1 in the Introduction.

[14] Much of the interest in these fields has been shaped in response to the work of Albrecht Alt, who advanced a very provocative theory in the 1930s about the distinctiveness of Israelite law. He distinguished between casuistic law, which was widespread in the ancient Near East, and apodictic law, which formulates legal norms as direct commands and which he claimed was unique to the Israelite legal system. On the basis of this distinction in legal forms, Alt argued that Israelite law was unique in the ancient Near East in the fact that it was grounded in the morality of a divine lawgiver on whose authority the apodictic commands rested. See Albrecht Alt, "The Origins of Israelite Law," in *Essays on Old Testament History and Religion* (Garden City, NY: Anchor, 1966), 103–71. These very bold claims provoked considerable interest in comparative legal studies focusing on the Bible and the ancient Near East. Reuven Yaron offered an important moderation of Alt's theories by showing that the apodictic form can be found in ancient Near Eastern legal codes. See Reuven Yaron, "Forms in

current study because it attends to subtle differences in how the casuistic form is presented. Insofar as this body of work observes noteworthy features of the form above and beyond the fact that it records legal norms, it can sensitize us to the other kinds of work the casuistic form performs.

The defining feature of casuistic legal materials is, of course, the presence of what is usually translated as the "if... then... " formula.[15] The first clause, the "if... " clause or protasis, states the facts or circumstances of a particular case. The second clause, the "then... " clause or apodosis, provides a legal resolution. Scholars of the biblical and ancient Near Eastern materials have argued that the casuistic formulation was the closest correlate the ancients had to generalized speech.[16] Scholars have speculated that in at least some instances, the cases they record once came before the court.[17] In their current formulation, however, they function as aids for future decisions and so contain no details other than those considered relevant to future rulings. All references to specific individuals and specific events have been suppressed in order to highlight that which is most broadly applicable about the case. Taking

the Laws of Eshnuna," *Revue internationale des droits de l'antiquité, 3e Série* 9 (1962): 137–53, and Reuven Yaron, *Laws of Eshnuna* (Jerusalem: Magnes Press, 1969).

15 See R.A.F. MacKenzie, S. J., "The Formal Aspect of Ancient Near Eastern Law," in *The Seed of Wisdom: Essays in Honor of T. J. Meek,* ed. W. S. McCullough (Toronto: University of Toronto Press, 1964), 33–35, for a discussion of the use of the English idiom of "if... then... " to convey the conditional meaning of the original. As MacKenzie notes, the conditional meaning is communicated in the original Semitic languages by the use of "two grammatically coordinate statements, two successive affirmations, one states *what is,* the other what *shall be*" (33).

16 See Jean Bottéro, *Mesopotamia: Writing, Reasoning and the Gods* (Chicago: University of Chicago Press, 1992), 170–72. Raymond Westbrook reflects a similar view of the function of the first clause of the casuisitic formulation when he writes that it was the means "whereby raw data could be cast into generalized, objective form, stripped of any connections with circumstances irrelevant to their universal application." See Raymond Westbrook, "What is the Covenant Code?" in *Theory and Method in Biblical and Cuneiform Law: Revision, Interpolation and Development,* ed. Bernard Levinson, JSOT Supplement Series 181 (Sheffield, Eng.: Sheffield Academic Press, 1994), 30.

17 Bottéro, *Mesopotamia,* 170–72, and Raymond Westbrook, "Biblical and Cuneiform Law Codes," *Revue Biblique* 92, no. 2 (April 1985): 252–54.

our own interest in the analytic processes central to the composition of the casuistic form into account, we may conjecture that someone who constructed such a case had to abstract from the particular to the general. He had to consider which of the myriad circumstantial details in the complex "real-life" scenario accounted for the ruling.

Beyond observing the presence of the basic casuistic form, scholars of the biblical and ancient Near Eastern law codes have also noted the tendency for cases to appear as parts of a series. In a typical series, the first case serves as a prototype,[18] and each successive case introduces a hypothetical variable into the prototype. Representing cases in all their possible permutations continues the work of generalizing begun by casting particular circumstances into casuistic form. According to Raymond Westbrook, introducing the variables makes the already generalized case even more "universally applicable (by exhausting all the possible alternatives)."[19] J. J. Finkelstein stresses the academic nature of the exercise of generating the cases by suggesting that the related cases were merely hypothetical.[20] In imagining the hypothetical variants of the prototype, those formulating the law anticipated an even greater number of circumstances that the law could cover.

Jean Bottéro suggests that the series as a whole (in conjunction with other similar series) functioned like a multiplication table. The reader or student of the different series instinctively made associative links between repeated elements within the protasis and repeated elements in the apodosis. From the repeating patterns, the reader could intuit the

[18] For the language of prototype, see J. J. Finkelstein, *The Ox That Gored* (Philadelphia: The American Philosophical Society, 1981), 18–21.

[19] Westbrook, "Biblical and Cuneiform Law Codes," 259. He suggests that this method of generalizing can be contrasted with modern systems "where the process of generalization consists in creating abstract principles of law rather than variants of the precedent." See also Bottéro, *Mesopotamia*, 175: "They also know that scientific knowledge is, in itself, universal and much broader than a single observation or the simple passive contemplation of what goes on before our eyes. That is why a scientific work had to foresee *everything* that related to its subject" [emphasis added]. This accounts for the inclusion of the variant cases.

[20] J. J. Finkelstein, *Ox That Gored*, 21.

overarching principles at work in the system as a whole.[21] For Bottéro, this manner of presenting overarching principles suggests that the casuistic codes served an academic or pedagogical function: "The cuneiform treatises are nothing else but types of paradigms or tables. It was by the repetition and the variation of particular cases . . . that the substance of the discipline in question was assimilated, that the habit of scientific judgment was formed, that the sense of correct reasoning was acquired."[22] Bottéro's observations are very suggestive for our forthcoming discussion of the analytic activities engendered by oral performance of the casuistic form. He highlights how both the construction and repetition of the tables of related cases engaged the practitioner in exercises of compare and contrast, leading to a more refined understanding of the system's legal principles.

Scholars of the Bible and ancient Near East have also noted that casuistic materials exhibit a particular interest in the *highly improbable* case. Finkelstein notes that some of the cases "chosen for illustrative purposes are the most unusual, sometimes even bizarre kinds of occurrences."[23] In such cases, it seems unlikely that the case was recorded to serve as a normative guide should the precise circumstances related therein occur. The improbable case is improbable precisely because it posits a variety of circumstances (each one uncommon in and of itself) occurring simultaneously. As I will argue more extensively later in the chapter, the disparate circumstances of the case are chosen because each one invokes or alludes to a different legal principle. The improbable case, then, seems designed to allow students of the law to consider how diverse and competing legal concerns from different domains of law interact with one another. Here again, we can anticipate how the construction of this type of casuistic formulation engaged the performer in a particular type of analytic activity.

21 Bottéro, *Mesopotamia*, 178–79.

22 Bottéro, *Mesopotamia*, 178.

23 J. J. Finkelstein, *Ox That Gored*, 19. Bottéro makes a similar observation about both medical treatises and the Code of Hammurabi. See Bottéro, *Mesopotamia*, 175–76.

Finally, scholars of biblical and Near Eastern law have also noted that the casuistic codes display a preference for borderline, as opposed to straightforward, cases. Borderline cases are those that can plausibly be interpreted according to two different principles. Consideration of borderline cases trains the reader to negotiate competing but mutually plausible considerations. It attunes and sensitizes the reader to ambiguities in the legal system. An additional feature of the borderline case, which apparently explains its ubiquitous presence, is the economical conveyance of general principles that it affords.[24] Not only does the borderline case suggest a basis for resolving the ambiguous case, but it also provides clarity as to the legal principle informing the straightforward or basic case. As Westbrook explains, if the borderline case of the seduction of a betrothed virgin requires the execution of the two offending parties, then certainly the straightforward case of the married woman should be resolved in like manner.[25] Presentation of borderline cases, then, is an economical way to express the legal principles that undergird the system as a whole.

In sum, while it is certainly true that the casuistic form communicates a set of legal norms, it is equally true that the form does much more than that. It engages both those who construct or compose it and those who review it in certain kinds of analytic activities. One is led to 1) abstract general principles from particular cases, 2) compare similiar cases in a series, 3) consider how diverse legal principles interact in the improbable case, and 4) evaluate the concerns of competing legal considerations in the borderline case.

What I wish to do now is show how the legal cases of m. Shevuot present the casuistic form in a similarly diverse set of manifestions. Recognizing the subtle differences among different ways of presenting the casuistic form helps us appreciate that the form does more than merely present legal norms. The observations that have been made

[24] See Raymond Westbrook, *Studies in Biblical and Cuneiform Law* (Paris: J. Gabalda et Cie., Editeurs, 1988), 4.

[25] Westbrook, *Biblical and Cuneiform Law*, 4.

with respect to the casuistic form in biblical and ancient Near Eastern materials will help us identify the analytic activities embodied by the construction of and perpetuated by the performance of m. Shevuot.

Basic Casuistic Form: Using Particular Cases to Illustrate General Rules

First, it must be observed that a large proportion of mishnaic pericopes employ an "if . . . then . . . " structure, in which the first clause describes a set of circumstances and the second clause provides a legal resolution. As in the biblical and ancient Near Eastern examples, the conditional meaning is conveyed through the use of two successive clauses, one stating what is the case, and the other what shall be. In a total of 50 mishnayot in m. Shevuot 3–8, the casuistic form (protasis + apodosis) appears 93 times. In a number of mishnayot, there are two, four, or even six casuistic formulations.[26] Only 9 mishnayot out of the 50 contain no casuistic formulations at all.[27] While the casuistic form is not the only literary convention employed in the tractate, it certainly is a dominant form.[28]

Just as scholars observed with respect to the ancient Near Eastern and biblical materials, the casuistic form in m. Shevuot provides a language of generalization. The casuistic formulations express norms that can be broadly applied. This is particularly evident in the following mishnah.

[26] For four casuistic formulations in a single mishnah, see m. Shev. 4:3, 4:4, 4:5, 6:1, 6:7, 7:6, and 8:6. For five casuistic formulations in a single mishnah, see m. Shev. 8:3. For six casuistic formulations in a single mishnah, see m. Shev. 5:3, 5:5, and 6:3.

[27] See m. Shev. 3:5, 3:8, 3:10–11, 4:2, 6:4–6, and 8:1.

[28] Jacob Neusner calls attention to the prominence of this formal trait of mishnaic discourse when he uses the terms protasis and apodosis in his analysis of the smallest units of mishnaic discourse. See Neusner, *Oral Tradition in Judaism,* 61–98. It must be noted, however, that when Neusner uses the language of protasis and apodosis, his intent is purely descriptive and he appears to be making little of the parallels with casuistic formulations elsewhere.

m. Shev. 4:3

1. שבועת העדות כיצד?
2. אמר לעדים:[29] בואו והעידוני
3. שבועה שאין אנו יודעין לך עדות,
4. או שאמרו לו: אין אנו יודעין לך עדות,
5. משביע אני עליכם, ואמרו אמן
6. – הרי אלו חייבין.

1. A testimonial oath. How so?
2. If he said to [potential] witnesses, [whom he believes know evidence which supports his claim:] Come and testify on my behalf,
3. [And they said to him:] We swear we know of no testimony on your behalf,
4. Or, if they said to him: We know of no testimony on your behalf, [and he said to them:] I adjure you, and they said, Amen [indicating they accepted the conditions of the oath],
5. [If they swore falsely]
6. – Behold, they are liable.

Lines 2–5 narrate a situation in which a testimonial oath is administered. A litigant who believes recaltritrant witnesses know evidence in support of his case may submit them to a testimonial oath, in which they swear that they in fact do not have knowledge of information relevant to his case. By this means, the litigant is able to reassure himself that no pertinent evidence is being withheld from the court. The narrated scenario includes just the appropriate number of details to convey how a testimonial oath is to be administered. Two possible procedures for administering the oath are indicated (lines 3 and 4). In one procedure the witnesses adjure themselves, and in the other the force of the oath is initiated by the litigant, and they indicate their

[29] MS Kaufman and MS Cambridge have לעידים, and MS Parma has לעדים. Printed edition has לשנים.

acceptance of the terms of the oath by saying "Amen." What about line 1? What is the purpose of the introductory clause "a testimonial oath, how so?" (שבועת העדות כיצד)? This introductory clause makes clear that the particular case is intended to serve as a general paradigm.[30] The Mishnah thus makes explicit that the function of this particular case is to illustrate a generally applicable rule. Not only does the Mishnah use the basic casuistic formulation to convey a general rule, but it also understands that it is doing so.

Interestingly enough, this illustrative case appears *after* several rules have already been stated with respect to the testimonial oath. M. Shev. 4:1 deals with the question of who may be submitted to the testimonial oath, and m. Shev. 4:2 outlines the consequences for swearing falsely when subject to the testimonial oath. (Neither m. Shev. 4:1 nor 4:2 uses a casuistic formulation.) Each of the preceding mishnayot presumes a basic understanding of what is meant by the term, "testimonial oath." The fact that the casuistic formulation appears only after rules concerning the testimonial oath have been stated suggests that the casuistic form is not being used to give expression to, that is, "call into existence," a legal principle. Rather, the casuistic formulation appears to provide a clarifying illustration of what is already assumed and known about the phenomenon of the testimonial

[30] J. N. Epstein discusses the fact that the term כיצד is among those formulaic terms that were used quite fluidly. While many MSS may attest a certain instance, others are just as likely not to. See Epstein, *ITM*, 1032–39. In a private communication, Judith Hauptman indicated that she had found many instances in which the term כיצד appears in the Mishnah, but not in the tosephtan parallel. She surmises that the term כיצד was in many instances added by the redactor or editor of the Mishnah to smooth over awkward segues. Conversely, there are also numerous instances in which the Tosephta responds to an opaque mishnah by supplementing with the term כיצד ("how so?") and offering illustrative examples, as in the relationship between m. Kid. 1:1 and its tosephtan parallel. While the current example conforms to none of these patterns (i.e., it has no tosephtan parallel and it is attested in all the MSS), the work of Epstein and Hauptman has more general implications about the formulaic character of the term. Their work suggests that it was a standard term whose purpose and function extended beyond any specific usage. It was among the arsenal of tools available to formulators and transmitters of text. It played a conceptual role in terms of framing how material was understood.

oath.[31] In other words, the Mishnah is *illustrating* an already implicit rule, rather than expressing a rule de novo.[32] If this is so, then the Mishnah uses its awareness of how particular cases illustrate general rules in a particularly versatile manner. In addition to using the casuistic form to express general rules, the Mishnah demonstrates here that it can also start with a known legal category and translate it into casuistic form to help make it more concrete. For the Mishnah, the concrete details of particular cases are intimately connected with the broader legal principles they come to illustrate and express, irrespective of whether the starting point is the particular or the general.[33] Constructing this mishnah, then, engaged the performer in a dialectical negotiation between the general and the particular. If such activity was required for the initial composition of such a form, we must imagine that the performance of it engaged the practitioner in the same analytic activities.

The Mishnah demonstrates a fluidity in moving back and forth between the particular details of specific cases and broadly conceived

[31] For this insight I am indebted to Christine Hayes, who offered a formal response to an earlier version of this chapter at the Annual Conference for the Association of Jewish Studies in Washington, DC, in 2001. In his commentary, HaMeiri suggests that the purpose of this mishnah is to "detail the qualities of how the testimonial oath proceeds" (היא לפרט בתכונת שבועת העדות היאך).

[32] By way of contrast, in the ancient Near Eastern and biblical examples, the casuistic formulation is necessary to *express* the legal principles. For this astute insight I am again indebted to Christine Hayes.

[33] In a formal response paper, Hayes suggests that the principle illustrated here was "probably extracted from the very casuistic formulation that now serves to illustrate rather than express it." In this particular case, it is not possible to isolate with certainty the casuitic formulation from which the general principle would have been deduced. The mishnayot immediately preceding m. Shev. 4:3, which assume the general principle that m. Shev. 4:3 comes to illustrate, do not employ the casuistic formulation. They themselves are formulated as general rules. A more likely scenario is that a borderline case (e.g., the second half of m. Shev. 4:3) that takes the basic case for granted was considered too cryptic, and so the basic case (that is, the first half of m. Shev. 4:3) had to be articulated explicitly. I suspect that the Mishnah's use of borderline cases derives more from their theoretical interest as ambiguous cases, and less because they are an economical way to present information. Thus, as we find in this case, the Mishnah does not always resist stating the basic case explicitly. See discussion of borderline cases later in the chapter.

rules in other ways, as well. On two occasions in m. Shevuot, a series of casuistic cases is followed by a summary statement: "This is the general rule" (זה הכלל).[34] In such cases, the text signals explicitly that a summary principle can account for the diverse rulings in the preceding cases. These examples additionally illustrate the Mishnah's comfort with moving from the specific to the general, as in the following instance.

m. Shev. 8:6

1. אמר לנושא שכר והשוכר: היכן שורי?
אמר לו: מת, והוא שנשבר או נשבה
נשבר, והוא שמת או נשבה[35]
נשבה, והוא שמת או נשבר;
נגנב, והוא שאבד
אבד, והוא שנגנב;
משביעך אני, ואמר: אמן – פטור.
2. מת או נשבר או נשבה, והוא שנגנב או אבד
משביעך אני, ואמר אמן – חיב.
3. אבד או נגנב, והוא שמת או נשבר או נשבה
משביעך אני, ואמר אמן – פטור.
4. זה הכלל:[36] כל הנשבע להקל על עצמו – חיב.
להחמיר על עצמו – פטור.

[34] In addition to m. Shev. 8:6, discussed at length in this chapter, see also m. Shev. 5:5. Birger Gerhardssohn offers an interesting discussion of the mishnaic use of the technical term זה הכלל. See Gerhardsson, *Memory and Manuscript,* 138–39, 141. See also Epstein *ITM,* 1039–43, where he lists the many instances in which the formula appears.

[35] MS Parma reverses the order of this line and the next.

[36] The printed edition inserts an additional general rule before the one given here: "This is the general rule: Anyone who [by their false oath] changes [the outcome] from 'liable' to 'liable,' from 'exempt' to 'exempt,' and from 'exempt to 'liable' – is exempt; [anyone who changes the outcome] from 'liable' to 'exempt' – is liable." Epstein suggests (and I concur) that the version in the printed edition represents an amalgamation of the general rule found in the Tosephta and the general rule found in the earliest MSS of the Mishnah. The printed version, with its two

1. [If the owner] said to a paid guardian or to one who has hired [his ox]: Where is my ox?
   And he said: "It died," but really it was lamed or carried off;[37]
   "It was lamed," but really it died or was carried off;
   "It was carried off," but really it died or was lamed;
   "It was stolen," but really it was lost;[38]
   "It was lost," but really it was stolen;
   [If the owner] submitted him to an oath, and the [guardian or hirer] said "Amen," [indicating he accepted the terms of the oath] – he is exempt [from liability regarding the false oath].
2. [If he said:] "It died" or "it was lamed" or "it was carried off," but really it was stolen or lost;[39]
   [If the owner] submitted him to an oath, and the [guardian or hirer] said "Amen," [indicating he accepted the terms of the oath] – he is liable [for swearing falsely].

statements of general rule, presents a particularly interesting illustration of the Mishnah's movement from the specific to the general. After the specific cases comes a general rule that is expressed in language drawn from the specific cases. This rule is then followed by a second statement of the rule that draws on more abstract conceptual language.

37 If an animal in the care of the paid guardian or the hirer dies, becomes lame, or is carried off, the paid guardian or the hirer is not liable for compensating the owner, since these are considered to be beyond his reasonable control. See m. Shev. 8:1 (= m. BM 7:8) based on Ex. 22:6–14. The case treated here is of interest to the Mishnah because though the bailee does not accurately report what has happened to the owner's ox, the misrepresentation does not change his degree of culpability. He is equally liable for the death, laming, and carrying off of the ox.

38 The point here is similiar. If the ox is stolen or lost while in the care of the paid guardian or the hirer, they are required to compensate the owner, since the paid guardian and the hirer are expected to accept a certain level of responsibility for the goods in their care. The important point for this mishnah is that theft and loss obligate the bailee at the same level. So though the bailee who states "it was stolen," when really it was lost, is not representing the situation accurately, his deception does not have legal consequences. He will not be any less or any more liable for having misrepresented the situation.

39 Here the bailee's falsehood does seem designed to avoid culpability. Here he claims that something for which he would not have to pay compensation happened, when in fact something for which he *would* have to pay compensation happened.

3. [If he said:] "It was lost" or "it was stolen," but really it died, was lamed or was carried off
   [If the owner] submitted him to an oath, and the [guardian or hirer] said "Amen," [indicating he accepted the terms of the oath] – he is exempt [from liability regarding the false oath].
4. This is the general rule: Anyone who swears [falsely] in order to lighten his liabilities [i.e., to avoid compensatory payment] – is liable [for his false oath].
   Anyone who swears [falsely] with the effect of increasing his liabilities – is exempt [for his false oath].

M. Shev. 8:6 offers a concluding statement to a chapter that is devoted more or less[40] to illustrating the general principle stated in line 4. In order to understand how the cases narrated here illustrate the general principle stated in line 4, we must first fill in some of the information assumed by this mishnah.

M. Shev. 8:1 outlines the basic legal framework within which the cases narrated in Chapter 8 must be understood. Building on biblical precedents,[41] m. Shev. 8:1 explains that individuals may keep the property of others in their custody according to four different types of financial arrangement, and in each case with differing levels of responsibility if the property becomes damaged or lost. The four different types of financial arrangement mark out the categories of what the Mishnah terms four different types of guardians or bailees (ארבעה שומרים). One who watches over someone else's property as a favor is known as the unpaid guardian (שומר חינם), and he has no liability in the event of loss or damage because he offers his services without compensation. A guardian who is paid (נושא שכר) has a higher degree of liability, but not complete financial responsibility, since some circumstances are considered beyond his control. One who has the property in his custody because he has hired it out for his own benefit or use is called the hirer

[40] Only the cases narrated in the second half of m. Shev. 8:3 and 8:4 are not illuminated by the general rule offered at the end of the chapter.

[41] See Ex. 22:6–14.

(שוכר), and like the paid guardian has a higher degree of liability than the unpaid guardian, but not complete financial responsibility. Finally, the borrower has the highest degree of culpability because the property is within his custody solely on the basis of the goodwill of the owner. By outlining the differing levels of financial responsibility carried by each of the four bailees at the very beginning of the chapter, m. Shev. 8:1 provides fundamental information necessary for understanding the rationale for the rulings in the cases that follow.

The degree of the bailees' financial responsibility is drawn from Exodus 22:6–14, which outlines five different situations in which property in the custody of another might come to harm. Assuming that it is an animal in the custody of another, the Mishnah anticipates the following eventualities: The animal might die, become lamed, be abducted, get lost, or be stolen.[42] The borrower, with the highest degree of financial liability, is responsible for compensating the owner for the loss of the animal under all of these circumstances, whereas the paid guardian and hirer, who have some, but not complete, financial responsibility, are responsible for compensating the owner in cases of theft and loss, which they can be reasonably expected to guard against, but not in the cases of death, laming, or abduction, which are considered to be circumstances beyond their control.

The tractate on oaths includes a discussion of the four bailees because it is expected that the bailees will confirm the circumstances under which the animal disappeared by means of an oath. Chapter 8 (including m. Shev. 8:6 cited here) narrates a number of cases in which the bailee misrepresents the circumstances by which the animal disappeared. For example (from m. Shev. 8:6, scenario 1), "He

[42] At first glance, instances of abduction and theft of the animal might appear to be similar, making it unclear why two separate categories are needed to describe the relatively similar sets of circumstances. In fact, the categories of theft and abduction are marked by important differences. The rabbis distinguish between theft by stealth, which happens in the dead of night when one is not present, which a reasonable person should be able to guard against by properly securing the property, and abduction under threat of violence, which even a responsible person cannot prevent or guard against.

said, 'It died,' but really it was lamed or carried off." In the course of the chapter, every single combination of circumstances is considered. The bailee might be either a paid or unpaid guardian, a hirer, or a borrower.[43] Likewise, he might misrepresent the truth in any number of possible ways, as can be seen from m. Shev. 8:6:

1. . . . And he said: "It died," but really it was lamed or carried off
   "It was lamed," but really it died or was carried off
   "It was carried off," but really it died or was lamed,
   "It was stolen," but really it was lost
   "It was lost," but really it was stolen . . .
2. [If he said:] "It died" or "it was lamed" or "it was carried off," but really it was stolen or lost . . .
3. [If he said:] "It was lost" or "it was stolen," but really it died, was lamed or was carried off . . .

At least ten different combinations of circumstances are considered with respect to each of the four bailees, and in each case the Mishnah offers a ruling as to whether or not the bailee who misrepresents the truth under those circumstances is liable for his false oath.[44] In a surprisingly high number of cases, the lying bailee is actually *not* liable for his false oath.

The general rule at the end of the chapter explains the basis for the ruling in each of the individual cases narrated in the course of

[43] M. Shev. 8:2–3 deal with the unpaid guardian, 8:5–6 with the borrower, and 8:6 with the paid guardian and the hirer.

[44] This mishnah (and the chapter in which it appears) is constructed by introducing a number of variables into a basic prototype case. As such, it could be profitably analyzed under the rubric of a series of related cases (see next section). The variables all come from the biblical context from which this oath is exegetically derived (Ex. 22:6–14). The biblical passage suggests four different finanical arrangements by which the property of one party is in the domain of another party and five different circumstances under which the property becomes lost to its owner. These nine factors function as variables, which the Mishnah combines according to standard patterns to form the cases.

the chapter.[45] Apparently, the lying bailee is culpable for his false oath only when his misrepresentation of the situation works to his financial benefit. An example from m. Shev. 8:6 will again help illustrate the point. As will be recalled, the paid guardian is liable for compensatory payments only under circumstances he can reasonably be expected to prevent, that is, in cases of theft by stealth and by loss. He is not, however, liable for unforeseeable circumstances that he is helpless to prevent, like death, laming, and abduction. Therefore, though the paid guardian might misrepresent the situation in any number of ways, he is only culpable for swearing falsely when his lie helps him avoid compensatory payment. Thus, we read in scenario 2:

> [If he said:] "It died" or "it was lamed" or "it was carried off" [circumstances that do *not* require compensating the owner], but really it was stolen or lost [circumstances that *do* require compensating the owner,]
> [If the owner] submitted him to an oath, and the [guardian or hirer] said "Amen," [indicating he accepted the terms of the oath] – he is liable [for swearing falsely].

Since this false oath seems designed to circumvent compensatory payments, the bailee is held culpable for the false oath. However, in cases where the false oath does not affect the level of compensation due to the owner, the bailee is not culpable for the false oath, *even though* he has misrepresented the truth.[46] In m. Shev. 8:6, scenarios 1 and 3

[45] As noted before, only the second half of m. Shev. 8:3 and 8:4 cannot be explained by the general rule at the end of the chapter.

[46] Rambam and HaMeiri explain that the bailee is not culpable for the false oath that does not affect compensatory payments because this oath is an example of an "oath of deposit." (For a basic definition of the oath of deposit, see m. Shev. 5:3.) Under certain circumstances, when one person believes his property is in the custody of another, he may submit him to an oath to confirm that the property is rightly his. This procedure is known as the oath of deposit. The contested property may be either a disputed sum of money or a concrete object. One special stipulation of the oath of deposit is that one is only culpable for swearing falsely if there does indeed exist disputed property between the two parties. (See m. Shev. 5:4–5 for specific rules about features of the disputed property that might exclude it from being subject to the oath of depos-

provide examples of situations in which the misrepresenation of the truth does not affect the compensation due the owner.

The general rule that accounts for all of the particular cases narrated in the course of the chapter reads as follows:

> This is the general rule: Anyone who swears [falsely] in order to lighten his liabilities [i.e., to avoid compensatory payment] – is liable [for his false oath].
> Anyone who swears [falsely] with the effect of increasing his liabilities – is exempt [for his false oath].

As should be evident from the lengthy explanation with specific illustrations necessary to make this general rule comprehensible, the rule is not a freestanding statement, but rather a synthesis of patterns evident in the many particular cases narrated throughout the chapter.[47] Though the Mishnah employs generalized language, it is not so general, broadly stated, or abstract as to be able to stand independent of the cases it comes to illustrate.[48] The chapter narrates more than 30 different cases, each resulting from a slightly different configuration of the variables (which bailee, what he said, and what really happened). If the cases were merely illustrative of the principle stated at the end of the chapter, one might reasonably ask if all *30* configurations were

it.) Thus, even though an oath may misrepresent the truth, when it does not create a property dispute between the two parties, the oath is not countenanced as an oath of deposit and so the bailee is not culpable for swearing falsely. Rambam, however, expresses discomfort with the Mishnah's ruling in this matter and suggests that even though the lying bailee is not culpable for the oath of deposit, he *is* culpable for the declaratory oath (שבועת ביטוי), that is, for having made a false declaration under oath. See Rambam in *Mishnah im Perush Rabbenu Moshe ben Maimon,* trans. Joseph Kapah, vols. 3–4, Jerusalem: Mossad HaRav Kook, 1976, רע''ט (269), siman 7, and HaMeiri in *Perushei ha-Mishnah le-ha-Meiri, Vol. 5, Seder Nezikin,* ed. Menachem Mendel Meshi Zahar, Jerusalem: Dvar, 1974, ק''לה (135), intro. to chap. 8.

47 Gerhardsson makes a similar point about the extent to which mishnaic rules (*kelalot*) are not freestanding statements of rule, but rather concise summaries of principles undergirding disparate cases. See Gerhardsson, *Memory and Manuscript,* 138–39.

48 An early Palestinian amora, R. Yohanan, reflects a similar sensibility about the insufficiencies of general rules, even when they have been stated: "One may not learn from general rules, even where exceptions are stated" (b. Kid. 34a, b. Eruv. 27a).

really necessary.[49] The fact that the Mishnah runs through all of the possible combinations before turning to the general rule suggests that what we have before us is a spelled-out version of a thinking process, rather than an effort at succinct expression of the law.[50] In presenting the individual cases in toto, the Mishnah invites its students, readers, or audience to do the analytic work of inferring the general principle. In this particular mishnah (m. Shev. 8:6), we see the stages of the thinking process delineated: first the cases, then inference of the general rule.[51] It is noteworthy that the formula "This is the general rule: . . . " (זה הכלל)[52] and the accompanying statement of principle appear *after* the specific cases that illustrate it.[53] I would speculate that the general rule follows

[49] Neusner remarks upon the Mishnah's tendency to illustrate general rules with numerous exemplary illustrations: "The Mishnah is scarcely satisfied to give a single instance of a rule from which we may generalize. It strongly prefers to give us three or six or nine instances, on the basis of which we may conclude that there is, indeed, an underlying rule"; *Oral Tradition in Judaism,* 120. For Neusner, the value in having several cases is that such a textual format engenders a thinking process. It leads to a process of abstraction. I find this interpretation of the data compelling.

[50] This is a somewhat controversial claim, since it is often assumed that the Mishnah expresses itself in a most succinct manner. See, e.g., Halivni, *Midrash, Mishnah and Gemara,* 52; Elon, *Jewish Law,* 1078. Examples like the present one, however, hardly display economy of expression. As a result, the commonplace assumption that the Mishnah always uses the most economical, succinct, and direct method of expression needs to be rethought.

[51] The printed edition contains two versions of the general rule, one stated in more general language than the other. From a text-critical perspective, it is clear that the second version of the general rule (which was actually inserted before the general rule we cited) was amalgamated from a parallel text in the Tosephta. See the discussion in Epstein, *ITM,* 1043. Nonetheless, it is interesting to speculate that the printed version (with two successive statements of the general rule, the latter more generally stated than the former) represents an even more drawn-out version of the thinking process: first, specific cases; then, general rule stated in language that reflects the specificity of the cases; finally, a general rule stated in more abstract language.

[52] For a bibliographic survey of scholarship on the formula "this is the rule" (זה הכלל), see Leib Moscovitz, *Talmudic Reasoning: From Casuistics to Conceptualization* (Tübingen: Mohr Siebeck, 2002), 51.

[53] This order of affairs (first particular cases, then general rule) is not unique to the current example. See also, e.g., m. Shevu. 5:5, m. Peah 1:4, m. Shevi. 7:1–2, m. Maas. 1:1, m. Shab. 7:1. See also Moscovitz, *Talmudic Reasoning,* 53, who notes that this phrase and others like it generally *follow* the specific cases.

the specific cases because it is seen as being derivative from them. The general rule is a product or result of the thinking process engendered by the many specific cases.[54]

Summing up, then, we find that m. Shevuot has a strong preference for the casuistic form and that it does recognize that particular cases come to express or illustrate general rules.[55] For the Mishnah, as for the biblical and ancient Near Eastern materials alluded to earlier, the casuistic form provides a means of expressing general principles with broad applications. The Mishnah's occasional tendency to articulate a general principle explictly suggests that even in the many casuistic formulations where no general principle is stated, one is implied. Insofar as the Mishnah generally employs the casuistic form without an explicit statement of general principle, it leaves that work of inference to its students, audience, or readers.[56] Reading the casuistic form in m.

54 The Mishnah also has other means of indicating it recognizes that the particular cases come to express general principles. On a number of occasions, after the legal resolution in the apodosis, the mishnah includes a short explanatory clause. The explanatory clause may be introduced by a variety of different terms (עד ש..., מה הטעם?, מפני ...ש), but in each case the clause explains the basis for the ruling in more general terms. Here I distinguish myself from David Weiss Halivni, who writes that the use of motive clauses is anomolous in the Mishnah. In Halivni's view, only belatedly does the mishnaic form include reference to logical or scriptural motives for the cases. In his understanding, motive clauses represent a deviation from what he sees as the Mishnah's main purpose: presentation of rabbinic law in condensed form suited for memorization and transmission. See Halivni, *Midrash, Mishnah and Gemara,* 57. By way of contrast, I do not believe that one needs to see the explanatory clauses as a departure from the essence of the mishnaic task. In my view, the articulation of explanatory clauses is a natural extension of the Mishnah's conscious understanding that particular cases function to express generally applicable rules.

55 Lieberman, *HJP,* 95, suggests that the movement from specific cases to general rules played a role in the formation of mishnaic discourse even at the time of R. Akiva.

56 Neusner uses slightly different language to stress the importance of general rules behind the specific cases. He speaks in terms of deep-seated underlying logic that gets expressed in the nitty-gritty details of ordinary life. My sense is that his "underlying logic" is more universal than the general rules to which I have tried to point. He understands the deep-seated logic to be reflective of patterns that underlie *all* phenomena. For him, the underlying logic of reality is the intellectual domain of philosophers, and he characterizes the authors of the Mishnah as philosophers. See Neusner, *Oral Tradition in Judaism,* 105–6. While I agree with Neusner that one important consequence

Shevuot as a so-called work in progress allows us to see that readers, listeners, and students are not merely presented with a set of legal norms. Equally as important, they are invited to participate in the work of moving from the particular to the general and back again.

The Series of Related Cases: An Exercise in Compare and Contrast

In addition to employing the basic casuistic formulation to represent general rules, the Mishnah also generates a series of related cases by introducing variables into a prototype case. The following example offers a slightly abbreviated series of only two cases. The variable elements are highlighted in bold.[57]

m. Shev. 6:1

שבועת הדינין – הטענה שתי כסף, והודאה בשוה פרוטה;
ואם אין ההודאה ממין הטענה, פטור.
כיצד?
שתי כסף לי בידך
אין לך בידי[58] – פטור.
שתי כסף **ופרוטה** לי בידך
אין לך בידי **אלא פרוטה** – חיב.

of the Mishnah's literary form is that it engenders and facilitates an abstract mode of thought, I do not associate that activity with philosophers. E. P. Sanders suggests that the abstract thinking which can be found in the Mishnah is that which is typical of legal and semilegal writing. It need not be associated with philosophers. See Sanders, "Jacob Neusner and the Philosophy of the Mishnah," in *Jewish Law from Jesus to the Mishnah: Five Studies* (Philadephia: Trinity Press International, 1990), 313–15.

57 The version cited here is according to MS Parma. The different MSS attest great variability in this mishnah. Though each is structured according to the format of two contrasting cases, the two cases that are contrasted with each other are different in each attestation.

58 The printed edition adds the bold-faced text: אין לך בידי **אלא פרוטה**.

> The judges' oath is imposed [to clear the defendant of responsibility] when the claim is [at least] two silver pieces, and [when the defendant] admits to [a minimum] of one *perutah* [a penny's worth].
> And if the admission is not of like kind with the claim, [then the defendant] is exempt from any liability [concerning the judges' oath].
> How so?
>
> 1. [If the claimant said:] You have two silver pieces of mine in your possession. [And the defendant replied:] I have nought of yours in my possession – this one is **exempt** [from the judges' oath].
> 2. [If the claimant said]: You have two silver pieces **and one *perutah*** of mine in your possession. [And the defendant replied:] I have nought of yours in my possession save **a single *perutah* – this one is liable** [to take the judges' oath, and so may be cleared of financial responsibility to the claimant].

As we found in the examples discussed in the preceding section, this mishnah combines explicit articulation of general principles with illustrative examples narrated casuistically. The mishnah begins by stating a general rule that the judges of the court may submit a defendant to an oath to clear him of financial obligation under certain circumstances. The circumstances stipulated here require that the claim be at least two silver pieces, and that the defendant partially admit to the claim, at least a *perutah's* worth. As in the cases treated previously, the casuistic formulation makes the general rule concrete by narrating a particular case. Unlike the previous cases, however, this example uses *two* contrasting cases to make the generally applicable rule vivid and concrete. Whereas the first case narrates a set of circumstances that falls *outside* of the domain of the general rule, the second case narrates an example that *conforms* to the standards stipulated by the general rule. Taken together, they illustrate what is meant by saying that "the claim must be a minimum of two silver pieces and the admission a minimum of one *perutah*."

The two cases abound with structural and linguistic parallels. Both cases begin with a statement by the claimant: "You have two silver pieces of mine in your posession" (שתי כסף לי בידך). Likewise, both cases convey the reply of the defendant in the same manner: "I have nought of yours in my posession" (אין לך בידי). In addition to the parallel elements, however, the two cases also contain significant variants. The second case adds an additional phrase to the words of both the claimant and the defendant. In the second case, the complete words of the claimant read: "You have two silver pieces **and one *perutah*** of mine in your possession." Likewise, the complete words of the defendant read: "I have have nought of yours in my possession **save a single *perutah*.**" The highlighted points of difference between the two otherwise parallel cases are precisely the features of the cases that account for the divergent rulings between the two. One might reasonably ask, however, why these subtle alterations to the scenario lead to the fact that the defendant must submit to a judge's oath. It is fairly self-evident why adding the phrase "save a single *perutah*" to the words of the defendant impacts the ruling. Without that phrase, he does not meet the basic condition of the rule (that "the defendant must admit"); otherwise, his denial of debt is outright and complete. When the phrase is included, he does meet the basic condition of the rule – he admits to some debt, even if it is not the complete amount the claimant is claiming.

The significance of the second point of difference between the two cases is less self-evident. Why should having the claimant claim "two silver pieces **and one *perutah***" impact the ruling? Apparently, this addition is needed to clarify the other condition of the rule, namely, that "the claim must be a minimum of two silver pieces." The language of the general rule is somewhat ambiguous. The term "claim" might refer *either* to the total amount claimed by the claimant *or* to the *differential* between what the claimant is claiming and what the defendant is admitting. Given the fact that the defendant admits to owing one perutah, the fact that the claimant admits to "two silver pieces *and* one *perutah*" suggests that the Mishnah assumes the second definition. Apparently, the differential between what the claimant is claiming and what the defendant is admitting must be at least two silver pieces. Otherwise, this special kind of oath, known as a "judge's oath," cannot be administered. Although the two cases have very strong linguistic and structural parallels, the sharply divergent rulings suggest that the minor variations between the two cases are highly significant. In this case, the difference between the two cases suggests what is meant by a minimum claim of two silver pieces. For this mishnah, the term "claim" is understood to be the *disputed* amount between the two parties, that is, the difference between what the claimant is claiming and what the defendant is acknowledging.

The form of two contrasting cases is a standard formulaic mechanism in mishnaic discourse for highlighting the difference between *inclusion* versus *exclusion* in a general rule.[59] Whereas the first case falls outside the general rule, the second case falls inside the general rule. The formulaic format, with strong structural and linguistic parallels, highlights patterns from which the reader can infer the broader principles and rules that account for the divergent rulings. While the current example articulates the legal reasoning assumed by the two cases in an explicit manner, it is just as often the case that the general principle must be inferred on the basis of subtle differences between the two cases alone. Thus, just as was suggested with respect to the series of

[59] The form of two contrasting cases accounts for a high percentage of the casuistic formulations in m. Shevuot, 74 out of a total of 93 cases. For instances where the contrast in the two apodoses is between "liable on one count" vs. "liable on each and every count," see m. Shev. 3:1, 3:2, 3:3, 4:5, 5:3. For a contrast in the two apodoses between "exempt" and "liable," see m. Shev. 4:6–7, 5:5, 6:1, 6:2, 6:3, 6:6, 6:7. In rare cases, the contrast in the apodosis will be conveyed by other terms. See, e.g., m. Shev. 7:7. In other tractates, contrast in the apodoses of two adjacent cases can be conveyed by a variety of other terms, among them "fit" vs. "unfit" and "pure" vs. "impure." Jacob Neusner, *Oral Tradition in Judaism,* 69 also notes the importance of the opposing rulings in structuring mishnaic discourse.

related cases in the biblical and ancient Near Eastern materials, the juxtaposition of related cases with subtle but significant variables between them exposes patterns and alludes to overarching legal principles.

On a number of occasions, including the current example, the form of two contrasting cases repeats several times in a row.[60] The successive pairs of cases often illustrate the same or a related point of law. In these cases, the commonalities with the series as a form in the biblical and ancient Near Eastern materials are even more pronounced. As noted in the section on biblical and ancient Near Eastern materials, treating several related cases gives the impression of dealing with an issue comprehensively and helps reinforce the generalizability of the basic case. The successive pairs of contrasting cases likewise broaden the applicability of the basic case and give it an air of universality. Neusner has remarked on the repeated syntactical patterns in the Mishnah – akin to the successive pairs of contrasting cases discussed here – and noted how they are unified by an underlying logic.[61] He suggests that the repeated syntactical patterns conveying a single underlying logic are intended to serve a philosophical purpose: to give "symbolic expression to the notion that beneath all the accidents of life are a few, comprehensive relationships: unchanging and enduring patterns lie deep in the inner structure of reality."[62] While it may be overstating the case to suggest that the underlying logic behind several adjacent parallel cases expresses a pattern intrinsic to *all* reality, Neusner is correct to note that the specific and particular cases of the Mishnah (especially when they appear as part of a series) do engender a tendency toward more generalized thinking.

The following mishnah consists of four different cases. It offers a slightly different perspective on how the Mishnah adopts the literary format of the series and uses it for its own purposes.

60 See m. Shev. 3:1c–3:3, 4:3, 4:5, 5:2–3, 5:5, 6:1–3, 6:7, 7:6, 8:2–4, and 8:6.
61 Neusner, *Oral Tradition in Judaism*, 66–69, 109.
62 Neusner, *Oral Tradition in Judaism*, 109.

m. Shev. 4:4

כפרו שניהן כאחת – שניהן חיבין.
זה אחר זה – הראשון חיב.
כפר אחד והודה אחד – הכופר חיב.
היו שתי כיתי עדים, כפרה הראשונה ואחר כך כפרה השניה – שתיהן חיבות,
מפני שהעדות יכולה להתקים בשתיהן.

1. If two witnesses deny together [under oath that they know information relevant to a case, and later it turns out that they did] – both are liable.
2. If they denied one after the other [that they know information relevant to the case, and later it turns out that they did] – the first one is liable [and the second one is exempt].[63]
3. If the one denied [that he knows information relevant to the case] and the other admitted [to knowing relevant information] – the one who swore falsely is liable.
4. If there were two pairs of witnesses, and the first pair of witnesses denied [that they know information relevant to the case], and afterward the second pair denied [that they knew testimony, and later it turns out that they all did] – both [pairs of witnesses] are liable,
5. Since the testimony of either pair would stand in court.

Knowing that for the purposes of valid testimony, two witnesses will function as a unit, this mishnah considers the question of whether they also function as a unit when they *deny* knowing any information relevant to the case at hand. The first case is straightforward. When the two witnesses swear falsely at the same time, both are equally liable for disqualifying the potential testimony, and so both are equally culpable for the testimonial oath. Each of the cases that follow (2–4) considers

[63] This last phrase in brackets is added by the printed edition, and we must asssume that it is implicit in the version attested in MSS Kaufman, Parma, and Cambridge.

a hypothetical variable of the basic case. How should culpability be determined when the witnesses deny one after the other, or when one denies and one admits knowing relevant information, or when they are followed by another set of falsely swearing witnesses? As suggested by Westbrook with respect to the biblical and ancient Near Eastern codes, the full complement of the variant cases gives the impression of dealing with an issue comprehensively.

It will be recalled that Bottéro suggests with respect to the biblical and ancient Near Eastern materials that the variant cases highlight the underlying but unarticulated legal principles by allowing the reader to see how circumstances in the protasis are paired with legal resolutions in the apodosis in a variety of different situations. Variant cases in the Mishnah would likewise seem to highlight fundamental legal principles. Here, however, the legal principle does not remain implicit, since the basis for the ruling in all four cases is provided in line 5.[64] Potential witnesses who under oath deny knowing any information relevant to the case at hand are culpable *if and only if* their testimony would have stood in court. By articulating the reasoning behind the rulings explicitly, this mishnah displays the same tendency noted previously of recognizing explicitly the relationship between particular cases and the more broadly formulated rules they embody.

As in the biblical and ancient Near Eastern materials, the Mishnah uses the variant cases to highlight the precise nature of the underlying legal principles. In this particular example, the Mishnah introduces the variants that will be most efficacious in clarifying the legal principles behind the ruling in the generic first case. From the first case alone, one might think that deniers are culpable simply by virtue of having denied knowing relevant information. The second case, however, excludes this broad interpretation of the first case. In the second case, after the first witness has denied knowing any testimony, the testimony of the

[64] See n. 54, which discusses some of the alternative formulas by which the Mishnah makes clear that it is stating the general principle expressed by the particular cases. The formula used in this case is "since . . . "(מפני ש . . .).

witness is of no use to the court. Even if he were to admit that he did know testimony, the testimony of one witness alone is not considered sufficient for the purposes of the court. For this reason, the second denier is not liable for the testimonial oath, even though he swore falsely. The variant case, then, comes to limit the student's or reader's understanding of the first case and to clarify the parameters of the underlying principle. In addition to denying knowing relevant information, the witnesses must offer the court potentially useful testimony in order to be held culpable for their false oath.

The third and fourth cases similarly come to refine the reader's understanding of the principle at hand. The ruling in the second case demonstrates that on certain occasions, even if one swears falsely, one is not held liable for the false oath. The second case appears to present an instance in which the one who swears falsely is not held culpable because his testimony is not offered in concert with the testimony of the other witness. On this basis, one might conclude that the criterion for absolving oneself from the responsibility of one's false oath entails swearing as a discrete individual. The third case comes to exclude this possible interpretation of the second case. The third case considers the situation in which one witness denies knowing relevant information while the other admits. One might think that the fact that he swore falsely as a lone individual relieves him of responsibility for his false oath. The third case, however, makes clear that such reasoning is problematic. The one who swore falsely is culpable for his false oath. Though it remains unstated, we must assume that his culpability derives from the fact that *had* he offered his testimony, it would have stood in court, since the other witness *did* admit to knowing information relevant to the case. The third case, like the second then, comes to introduce a more nuanced understanding of the legal principle undergirding the entire set of four cases.

The fourth case, too, refines the reader's understanding of the legal principle at work throughout the four cases. While the second case clarifies that only the testimony that would be of use to the court is subject to the testimonial oath, one might think that the second witness to deny in a serial manner is exempt from the testimonial oath because he swore *after* the first witness already denied. In other words, the reader might interpret the case to indicate that in the case of serial denials, only the first to deny is held culpable. The fourth case comes to exclude this possible interpretation. It clarifies that the second set of witnesses is equally subject to the testimonial oath as the first set, since their testimony is of *as much use to the court* as the first set's testimony. The fourth case, then, reveals the underlying principle to be an *inclusive*, as well as restrictive, one. Whereas in the second case the fact that the testimony is of use to the court *excludes* the second falsely swearing witness from culpability, in the fourth case the fact that the testimony is of use to the court *includes* the second set of falsely swearing witnesses as culpable individuals. Comparison of variant cases, then, allows the student, audience, or reader of the materials to consider the underlying principle from a variety of perspectives, which, taken together, provide a more subtle understanding of the principle at hand.

The value of the variant cases, then, extends beyond completing a paradigm and so providing a comprehensive treatment of the subject at hand. By treating a subject from a variety of perspectives, the Mishnah exposes its readers, students, and listeners to subtleties of legal reasoning. The reader becomes attuned to the fact that the principle stated at the end of the mishnah functions in both an inclusive and exclusive manner. The generation of variant cases enables the reader to grasp the principles behind the rulings with greater specificity than the prototype case alone would permit. The Mishnah, then, exploits the conventions of casuistic form to refine the understanding of legal principles. Not only does the Mishnah do what the biblical and ancient Near Eastern materials did, which is reveal patterns and suggest overarching principles by introducing standard variables; the Mishnah also exploits the form to introduce a more limited interpretation of the cases at hand. The Mishnah uses the variant cases to plumb the depths of a specific principle. Oral performance of such a mishnah would have engaged the student in a sophisticated analysis of the principle stated at the end.

Improbable Cases: Exploring How Different Legal Principles Interact

Like the casuistic materials in the biblical and ancient Near Eastern codes, the casuistic formulations in the Mishnah demonstrate a disproportionate interest in improbable cases and circumstances. The pigeon found exactly halfway between two domains (m. BB 2:6), the man who tithes doubtfully-tithed-produce (*demai*) while naked (m. Dem. 1:4), the man taking a vow upon seeing a *koy* that it is neither wild animal nor domesticated cattle (m. Bik. 2:11),[65] and the edible sprouts that appear in the dirt scattered about on a boat anchored to the shores of Israel (m. Hal. 2:2) are all of interest to the Mishnah because of the complex legal issues they present when a legal resolution needs to be determined. Though situations that involve such a pigeon, sprouts, koy, or naked tither are unlikely to occur, the Mishnah turns again and again to such improbable cases because of their theoretical interest. As Neusner notes in his discussion of the intellectual agenda of the Mishnah, the Mishnah "consistently ask[s] the same sorts of questions, about gray areas, doubts [and] excluded middles."[66] The Mishnah's interest in situations that fall in between clear-cut legal categories leads it to construct the most bizarre cases, which bring "diverse legal principles into juxtaposition and conflict."[67]

The following mishnayot adopt the format of two contrasting cases discussed in the previous section. They each narrate a scenario that is highly improbable. The scenarios are of interest to the Mishnah because they give expression to a subtle point of law. When persons

[65] This mishnah is treated by Neusner in his discussion of gray areas of the law within the Mishnah. Specifically, he is concerned with instances in which the Mishnah considers cases that might be interpreted according to one of two possible legal principles. As such, they are clearly subsumed by neither legal principle and so fall in between clear-cut legal categories. See Jacob Neusner, *Judaism: Evidence of the Mishnah*, 256–69, esp. 261.

[66] Neusner, *Judaism: Evidence of the Mishnah*, 256.

[67] Neusner, *Judaism: Evidence of the Mishnah*, 257.

swear falsely about not knowing information relevant to a case, they are held liable *if and only if* the testimony they were to have provided would have resolved a *financial* dispute. If the testimony would not have resulted in the *payment of funds* due to the plaintiff, then even if the potential witnesses swear falsely concerning what they know, they are not held liable. In an effort to illustrate this principle, the following two cases are presented.

m. Shev. 4:6–7

משביע אני עליכם אם לא תבואו ותעידוני . . . שהדליק את גדישי ביום הכיפורים – הרי אלו חייבין.
משביע אני עליכם אם לא תבואו ותעידוני . . . שהדליק את גדישי בשבת – הרי אלו פטורין.

1. [If a man submitted two potential witnesses to an oath, saying:] I adjure you to come and testify on my behalf... *that [a certain person] ignited my grain pile* **on Yom Kippur** [and they swore falsely that they knew no information relevant to the case] – behold, they are liable [for their false oath].
2. [If a man submitted two potential witnesses to an oath, saying:] I adjure you to come and testify on my behalf... *that [a certain person] ignited my grain pile* **on the Sabbath** [and they swore falsely that they knew no information relevant to the case] – behold, they are exempt [from liability for the false oath].

As with the example of two contrasting cases considered earlier, these two cases contain strong linguistic and structural parallels. Only a single detail distinguishes them: The relevant act of vandalism might be committed on either Yom Kippur or the Sabbath. In spite of the striking similarities between them, however, the two cases are resolved with different legal rulings. Whereas denial of information concerning a crime committed on the Sabbath yields no liability at all, the exact same behavior concerning a crime committed on Yom Kippur does render the falsely swearing witness liable. The format of two contrasting cases indicates that the single variable of difference between the two cases (that is, whether the vandalism occurred on the Sabbath or Yom Kippur) contains the key to understanding the rationale behind both rulings. Why is testimony concerning crimes committed on the Sabbath *included* within the rule, while testimony concerning crimes committed on Yom Kippur *excluded* from the rule?

Before answering this question, it is important to consider another issue. Why construct this scenario at all? Why is testimony about burnt grain piles on the Sabbath and Yom Kippur of interest to the Mishnah? Was this a regular occurrence in tannaitic times? Did people often find themselves in need of such testimony? I would argue that the Mishnah's interest in this case was most likely not generated by practical concerns, but rather by theoretical concerns.[68] Each detail in these two scenarios (including the single variable of difference between the two cases) results from attention to a distinct theoretical concern. The peculiarity of the resulting cases derives from the Mishnah's interest in treating three different theoretical concerns in a single setting.

First, the cases consider the possibility that comparable acts of destruction might be committed either on Yom Kippur or on the Sabbath. These details are included to call to mind the rule (expressed

[68] In trying to develop a methodology for extracting historically reliable information from the two Talmuds, Christine Hayes argues that it is important to recognize when the Talmuds take a certain position as the result of their dependence on early texts and use of standard reading practices. Not all stated legal positions reflect actual historical practice. She suggests that it is inappropriate to attribute historical significance to legal positions that flow from the exegetical and hermeneutical agenda of the Talmuds. See Hayes, *Between the Babylonian and Palestinian Talmuds*, esp. 8. Extending Hayes's insights to the field of mishnaic studies, I would argue that one should not assume that the Mishnah considers all the legal cases that it does on account of practical judicial concerns. That is, not all cases reflect the historical circumstances in which the "code" of the Mishnah was produced. Just as when reading the Talmuds we must be attentive to the exegetical nature of literature, so too when reading Mishnah we must be attentive to the pedagogical nature of the literature. Some cases are brought forward for consideration simply because of their heuristic value.

in m. Meg. 1:5) that violations of the Sabbath are punishable by court-administered death penalty, whereas violations of Yom Kippur are punishable by *karet*, which the rabbis understand to be death at the hands of heaven.[69] This technical difference between the Sabbath and Yom Kippur violation becomes relevant when attending to a second aspect of the scenarios, namely, that they involve damage to a fellow's property and so require reparation payments. A principle expressed in m. BK 8:5 and 3:10 suggests that in certain situations one is not required to pay damages, even if one truly did damage to another or to his property. Appparently, when a single act violates both civil and criminal norms, the offender is culpable only for the criminal offense; payment for civil damages is waived. This principle protects the offender from a certain kind of double jeopardy. Returning to our case, then, when one vandalizes his fellow's property on the Sabbath, civil damages are waived and the offender need only suffer the death penalty, since he has both violated the Sabbath (a capital crime) and damaged property (a civil crime). If a comparable act is performed on Yom Kippur, however, the damage payment is *not* waived because there is no possibility of double jeopardy for a crime committed on that holy day. Since violations of Yom Kippur are punishable by *karet*, death at the hands of heaven, the human court plays no role in the adjudication of such criminal activity. The third legal concern addressed by these scenarios devolves from the fact that they each involve a testimonial oath, which (it will be recalled) is operative *if and only if* the testimony would have resulted in financial remuneration.

We are now in a position to return to the initial question about the different degrees of liability conferred upon the person who withholds testimony concerning damage committed on the Sabbath and the person who withholds testimony concerning damage committed on Yom Kippur. Since testimony regarding damage committed on the Sabbath would *not* have resulted in financial remuneration (on account

[69] See m. Meg. 1:5.

of the principle of double jeopardy, since the court already administers the death penalty to such an individual), the person who swears falsely about such an occurrence is not held liable. Conversely, since testimony regarding damage inflicted on Yom Kippur *would* have resulted in financial remuneration (since the court does not administer the death penalty to such an individual, the damage payments are not dismissed by virtue of the double jeopardy principle), the person who swears falsely about such an occurrence *is* held liable.

At first glance, it may appear that this mishnah does no more than illustrate the general rule that testimonial oaths may be administered only in cases where the testimony results in financial remuneration. It might seem no different from the example of the two contrasting cases considered in the previous section. This interpretation, however, privileges the legislative function of the Mishnah over and against its pedagogical function. It suggests that the most important function of the Mishnah is to establish legal norms. From a pedagogical perspective, the particular mode of expressing this principle offers the student, audience, or reader more than a simple legal norm. By invoking principles from three altogether different domains of law – 1) Sabbath versus Yom Kippur violations, 2) reparation for acts of vandalism, and 3) testimonial oaths – this mishnah compels the student, audience, or reader to synthesize principles from across the spectrum of the legal system. An important part of the intellectual exercise engendered by this mishnah entails recalling legal principles from diverse arenas of Jewish law and applying them to the situation at hand in relevant ways. Neusner points out that the Mishnah delights in creating scenarios that force laws from different domains to intersect. Indeed, he writes, the Mishnah is at its best "when [it] force[s] into conflict laws which, to begin with, scarcely intersect."[70] Such cases lead the students, audience, or readers of the Mishnah to explore the implications of diverse legal principles from diverse legal spheres in relation to one another.

70 Neusner, *Judaism: Evidence of the Mishnah*, 257.

Borderline Cases and Disputes: Fleshing Out Legal Ambiguities

Just as the biblical and ancient Near Eastern material's casuistic formulations gravitate toward borderline or ambiguous cases, so too in the Mishnah a substantial portion of the casuistic formulations explore scenarios in which there is no single clear-cut resolution.[71] These cases are borderline because they might reasonably be interpreted according to one of two mutually plausible paradigms.

In the following example, the mishnah begins by narrating a case whose resolution *is* clear-cut. The mishnah then proceeds, however, to explore the secondary implications of the basic principle, which are less clear-cut.

m. Shev. 7:4

ושכנגדו חשוד על השבועה כיצד?
אחת שבועת העדות ואחת שבועת הפקדון, ואפילו שבועת שוא.
היה אחד מהם משחק בקביא, ומלוה ברבית, ומפריחי יונים וסוחרי שביעית – שכנגדו נשבע ונוטל.
שניהן חשודין – חזרה השבועה למקומה, דברי רבי יוסי.
רבי מאיר אומר: יחלוקו.

1. "He who [stands in court] opposite one who is not trustworthy regarding oaths," how so?

[71] Hannah Harrington likewise notes the Mishnah's interest in exploring ambiguous cases. In her research, she focuses on the ambiguities within Scripture that capture the Mishnah's interest. An oral presentation of her work at the Annual Conference for the Society of Biblical Literature in November 2001 first alerted me to her interest in these issues. See also Harrington, *The Impurity Systems of Qumran and the Rabbis* (Atlanta: Scholars Press, 1993), 2, 6–8; and Harrington, "The Halakhah and Religion at Qumran," in *Religion in the Dead Sea Scrolls*, ed. John Collins and Robert Kugler (Grand Rapids, MI: Eerdmans, 2000), 75–78.

2. [The rule ilustrated below applies] equally in cases when the testmonial oath is administered as in cases where the oath of deposit is administered, and even in cases where it is a vain oath.
3. If one of them was a dice-player, a usurer, a pigeon flyer, or a trafficker in produce from the seventh year – the one [standing] opposite him in court may take an oath and collect [payments due].
4. If they were both suspect [with regard to oaths] – the oath returns to its proper place, these are the words of R. Yose.
5. R. Meir says: They should divide [the disputed claim between them].

The basic case in this mishnah provides an example of someone who takes an oath in order to recover payments due. This type of use of an oath is exceptional within the tractate.[72] For the most part, taking an oath *absolves* one of the responsiblity to pay. In this case, however, taking the oath *entitles* one to receive payments. This mishnah makes an exception to the general rule that one takes an oath to absolve oneself of payments due because the litigant who is due to take an oath is not considered trustworthy.[73] Though formalistic procedures dictate that in a number of specific situations the defendant can take an oath and absolve himself of payments, the fact that he himself is not trustworthy means that his oath will not be believed, and therefore the mechanism that would normally absolve him of financial responsibility is not operative. Therefore, the defendant remains liable to pay the disputed amount (be it a damage payment, a deposit, or some other type of debt). In such situations, the court submits

[72] Four other cases exist in which someone may take an oath and thereby recover payment due to him: the day laborer, a person who has been robbed or wounded (and is thus due damage payments), and a shopkeeper who has kept records of monies owed in his register. See m. Shev. 7:1–6.

[73] M. San. 3:3 supplies a standard of trustiworthiness for testimony that is adopted here. The following people neither may give testimony in court nor are considered trustworthy when submitted to an oath: dice-players, usurers, dove-flyers, and traffickers in produce of the seventh year.

the plaintiff to an oath (assuming that he is trustworthy) in which he confirms his position that he is owed money. Having administered this oath, the court is reassured that the debt is genuine. The court can then feel confident about forcing the defendant to pay his debt.

What happens, however, if *both* plaintiff *and* defendant are not trustworthy? This question is a natural outgrowth of the basic case, which takes for granted the trustworthiness of the plaintiff. Lines 4 and 5 present this borderline case and explore possible resolutions. As with most borderline cases, at least two possible resolutions present themselves.[74] On the one hand, the dilemma might be resolved in the manner suggested by R. Yose: "the oath returns to its proper place." That is, since the plaintiff is no more trustworthy than the defendant, there is no reason to privilege his oath over that of the defendant. In R. Yose's way of thinking, the fact that both are equally unreliable suggests that the situation should revert back to the status quo and be adjudicated according to the mechanisms used to resolve the typical case where neither litigant is more or less trustworthy than the other. Since the defendant is typically granted the benefit of the doubt, R. Yose believes that the defendant should be given his due and allowed to absolve himself of the debt by taking an oath. According to R. Meir's way of thinking, however, there is no such thing as reverting back to the status quo. The fact that *both* parties are untrustworthy makes this case wholly unlike the typical case. From R. Meir's perspective, the collective untrustworthiness of the two litigants requires a totally different type of resolution to be implemented, one suited to the peculiar features of this case. Since neither litigant can be believed over the other, R. Meir thinks they should essentially "split the difference" and each take financial responsibility for *half* of the disputed sum.[75]

[74] Yet a third resolution is suggested by the tosephtan parallel. T. Shev. 6:3, proposes that no oath be imposed at all.

[75] This dispute represents the divergent opinions of R. Yose and R. Meir. According to Goldberg, the differences between their points of view can be understood in light of

The ambiguity of the second case, the borderline case, is emphasized by the fact that two possible legal resolutions are offered.[76] By concretely stating two or more possible resolutions, the dispute form makes vividly clear that the scenario in question might be plausibly understood according to two different paradigms. It is interesting to consider the possibility that the dispute form is as ubiquitous as it is in the Mishnah because it promotes a nuanced understanding of borderline cases.[77] The presence of the dispute helps students, readers,

their interpretative approaches to the view of R. Akiba: "Thus R. Meir always gives a literal interpretation to what R. Akiba teaches. R. Yehuda, on the other hand, will usually limit R. Akiba's teachings to a specific situation. R. Yose almost invariably takes a middle position between these two." See Goldberg, "The Mishnah," 218. See also Abraham Goldberg, "Everyone According to the System of R. Akiba" (Hebrew), *Tarbiz* 38 (1969): 231–54. As Yaakov Elman notes, however, it is difficult to understand how R. Akiba's disciples would have arrived at such strongly conflicting interpretations of their master's teachings. See Elman, "Order, Sequence and Selection: The Mishnah's Anthological Choices," in *The Anthology in Jewish Literature,* ed. David Stern (New York: Oxford University Press, 2004) 63–65. Furthermore, it is difficult to guage the extent to which the disciples of R. Akiva are interpreting his opinions when Akiva's view on the matter is not cited at all. For this reason, Elman questions whether the Mishnah's editor's intent was in fact to present the teachings of R. Akiva (64–65), and I see the merits of his argument. It seems equally plausible to suggest, as I have, that the divergence of opinions results from diverse principles that can be invoked to resolve the legal conundrum at hand.

76 On the relationship between textual ambiguities and conflicting interpretations, see Aryeh Cohen, who notes that textual ambiguities (which he calls "ungrammaticalities") are often the site of conflicting interpretations, in *Rereading Talmud,* 166. See also Alexander, "Art, Argument and Ambiguity."

77 Abraham Goldberg makes a similar point about the pedagogical value of diverse legal interpretations. He argues that the Mishnah's editor intentionally included a variety of legal interpretations of the views of R. Akiva in order to expose students to a wide range of views. As he writes in "The Mishnah": "The chief aim of the final editor was to present the gamut of possible interpretations.... In particular... the editor is interested in presenting the teachings of R. Akiva as they become reflected in the interpretative teachings of his prime pupils" (214). See also Goldberg, "The Mishnah," 223–24. The view represented here, which sees the value of the dispute form in its pedagogical function, need not be at odds with other theories about the significance of the dispute within rabbinic, but especially mishnaic, literature. Shaye Cohen, for example, suggests that the dispute form was a manifestation of the nascent ideology of pluralism that proliferated after the destruction of the Tem-

or listeners tease out the various resolutions warranted by a particular case. It sensitizes them to the nuance of detail on which the different legal resolutions rest and models a kind of legal analysis they can repeat on their own in other contexts.

As in the biblical and ancient Near Eastern materials, borderline cases help develop skills of legal reasoning. The progression from the basic case to the borderline case proceeds in a logical manner. The basic case is predicated on a basic difference in trustworthiness between the litigants: Whereas the defendant is not trustworthy, the plaintiff *is* trustworthy. Consideration of the basic case naturally leads to the borderline case: If the basic rule is contigent upon the trustworthiness of the plaintiff, one naturally asks the "what if" question. What if the plaintiff *is not* trustworthy? Part of the value of the borderline case consists in attuning students, readers, or listeners to the complicating circumstances that might lurk within the basic case and that make for a less clear-cut legal resolution. Proper application of the law requires being able to distinguish the competing aspects of a case and discern appropriate principles for resolving them.[78] By modeling considered legal reasoning, the Mishnah also teaches its students how to do so.

It is interesting to note that some of the more nuanced and subtle borderline cases not only include a dispute form but also draw out the logic of each side.[79] The following mishnah offers one example.

ple. See Shaye J. D. Cohen, "The Significance of Yavneh: Pharisees, Rabbis and the End of Jewish Sectarianism," *Hebrew Union College Annual* 55 (1984): 47–49. For an elaboration of traditional explanations of disputes within the Mishnah, see Elon, *Jewish Law*, 1070–72.

78 It will be recalled that Westbrook argues that casuistic legal collections were a resource that judges consulted when facing particularly difficult cases. See Westbrook, "Biblical and Cuneiform Law Codes," 254.

79 In addition to the example treated here, see also m. Shev. 3:1 (the debate between the sages and R. Akiba) and m. Shev. 5:4 (the debate between R. Yehudah and the sages) for other instances where the dispute form draws out the logic inherent in each position.

m. Shev. 3:6

נשבע לבטל את המצוה ולא ביטל – פטור.
לקיים את המצוה, ולא קיים – פטור,
שהיה בדין שיהא חייב, כדברי ר' יהודה בן בתירה.
אמר ר' יהודה בן בתירה: ומה אם הרשות, שאינו מושבע עליה מהר סיני, הרי הוא חייב עליה, מצוה, שהוא מושבע עליה מהר סיני, אינו דין שיהא חייב?
אמרו לו: לא. אם אמרת בשבועת הרשות שכן עשה בה לאו כהין, תאמר בשבועת מצוה, שלא עשה בה לאו כהין?

> [If a person] swore to violate a commandment, and he did not violate it – he is exempt [from liability for violating the intent of the oath].
> [If a person] swore to uphold a commandment, and he did not uphold it – he is exempt [from liability for violating the intent of the oath],
> It would have been logical that [in this second case] he would have been liable, as in the opinion of R. Yehudah b. Beterah.
> R. Yehudah b. Beterah said: Just as one is liable [for oaths] with respect to voluntary actions, for which one does *not* become subject by way of [the revelation at] Mt. Sinai, one must certainly be liable [for oaths] with respect to commandments, for which one *does* become subject by way of [the revelation at] Mt. Sinai.
> They said to him: No. [The two are not comparable.] Can you say that oaths concerning voluntary actions, [to which one may just as easily say] "no" as "yes" are like oaths concerning commandments, [to which one may not just as easily say] "no" as "yes"?

This mishnah discusses two cases, with the second provoking a complicated and subtle debate. Even though the first case is presented without an alternative ruling, it (like the second) explores the ambiguous gray areas in between more clearly defined principles.

The first case considers an instance in which someone takes an oath to violate a commandment. The intellectual interest of this case derives from the way it brings two clearly defined principles into conflict.[80] Taking an oath to violate a command essentially subjects the oathtaker to two mutually conflicting authorities. On one hand, the authority of Jewish law in general requires that he uphold the commandment. On the other hand, the authority of the oath requires that he violate the commandment. This mishnah is concerned with the question that naturally arises from such a conflict: To which authority does the oathtaker owe his allegiance? This borderline case provides a forum for considering such conflicts of authority.

The mishnah resolves the question in favor of the authority of Jewish law in general. The mishnah rules that one who does not fulfill his or her oath to violate a commandment is not liable, because such an oath is essentially invalid.[81] The mishnah's ruling makes clear that the norms of Jewish law are eternally binding and so cannot be modified by external means, such as an oath. While the question of which authority should prevail is clear-cut enough so as not to provoke a dispute, the question remains open-ended in a theoretical sense. Even if no sage takes the position that the authority of the oath should prevail over the authority of Jewish law in general, the position remains theoretically plausible. I would argue that even if the plausibility of two mutually conflicting legal resolutions is merely theoretical, the case nonetheless remains intellectually interesting and engaging as a borderline case.

80 As noted with respect to improbable cases, Neusner comments that the Mishnah's intellectual agenda is largely taken up with bringing competing principles into conflict. See Neusner, *Judaism: Evidence of the Mishnah*, 256–61.

81 In their commentaries, Rambam and HaMeiri clarify the ways in which the oathtaker is both liable and not liable for his oath, by distinguishing between two different categories of oaths. On the one hand, the oath has elements of a declarative oath (שבועת ביטוי), in which one declares or expresses via the oath what one will or will not do. On the other hand, the oath has elements of a false oath (שבועת שוא), in which one swears concerning a falsehood. M. Shev. 3:8 stipulates that one type of false oath involves swearing to violate a commandment. Rambam and HaMeiri explain that while swearing to violate a commandment does not incur liability as a declarative oath, the act does incur liability as a false oath. See Rambam, *Mishnah im Perush Rabbenu Moshe ben Maimon*, trans. Joseph Kapah, vols. 3–4, Jerusalem: Mossad HaRav Kook, 1976, רנ"ז, and HaMeiri, *Perushei ha-Mishnah le-ha-Meiri, Vol. 5, Seder Nezikin*, ed. Menachem Mendel Meshi Zahar, Jerusalem: Dvar, 1974, ק"ט.

Indeed, a large percentage of borderline cases do not include a dispute form.[82] In cases where no dispute form is present, the Mishnah offers its students, readers, or listeners an intellectual challenge. They must tease out on their own the two mutually plausible resolutions that might theoretically be invoked to resolve the case. Identifying the ambiguity in the case establishes the import of the resolution to which the Mishnah does in fact commit.[83]

The second case in this mishnah exemplifies more than just theoretical ambiguity. In this case, two disputants independently arrive at different legal resolutions using accepted methods of legal reasoning. The second case considers an instance in which an oathtaker swears

[82] Detailed examination of m. Shev., chaps. 3 and 4, reveals the following statistics: 11 examples of basic borderline cases (m. Shev. 3:4a, 3:4c, 3:6a, 3:7, 3:9, 4:4, 4:8–12) and 4 instances where the ambiguity of the borderline case is highlighted by a dispute (m. Shev. 3:1b, 3:4b, 3:6b, 4:1).

[83] The Bavli's interpretive strategies with regard to the Mishnah attest to the fact that the Mishnah cultivates this reading strategy. As we will have ocassion to discuss more extensively in the next chapter, the Bavli routinely assumes that a given case is included in the Mishnah in order to exclude an alternative, but plausible, ruling not provided by the Mishnah. This reading strategy assumes that the Mishnah expresses itself with extreme verbal economy. Chapter 2 describes the broader context in which the Bavli's tendency to view mishnaic texts as efficient expressions of their message occurs. One way to justify the presence of a given case in the Mishnah is to assume that the case might have been adjudicated according to another equally plausible legal principle (yielding a different legal resolution). By this way of thinking, the Mishnah has "bothered" to include the case in question in order to communicate that the alternative legal principle and the alternative legal resolution are unacceptable. See, e.g., Rava's interpretation of m. Shev. 3:1 on b. Shev. 23a. There, he reads the first case of two contrasting cases as a borderline case. When the Bavli employs this reading strategy by assuming the Mishnah expresses itself with extreme verbal economy, it essentially raises the possibility than any case might be read as a borderline case. For a discussion of the Bavli's assumptions concerning the Mishnah's extremely concise expression, see Hayes, *Between the Babylonian and Palestinian Talmuds*, 92–121, esp. 116–21. By way of contrast to the Bavli's way of reading the Mishnah, I am not arguing that every case in the Mishnah is potentially a borderline case. As I hope to have already demonstrated, the casuistic form has a number of typical manifestations in the Mishnah (explicitly illustrative, as a part of a series, highly improbable cases, and borderline cases). Each manifestation of the casuistic form engenders a different sort of legal analysis, so that no single type of analysis should be applied to every single mishnaic case.

to *uphold* a commandment. On the face of it, this case would seem to be more clear-cut than the previous one. In the first case, the conflict between the authority of Jewish law in general and a particular oath makes for an unclear resolution. As will be recalled, one intuitively wonders which authority will prevail. This second case appears to present no such conflict, since the oath works to *reinforce*, rather than subvert, the authority of Jewish law. Since an oath to uphold a commandment does not conflict with the authority of Jewish law, one might anticipate such an oath will be valid. In that case, however, the Mishnah would have ruled that he who violates such an oath *is* liable. The fact that the Mishnah rules that he who violates an oath to uphold a commandment is *not* liable suggests that the case is more ambiguous than this initial analysis would indicate. Apparently, there are two equally plausible ways to rule in this case, too.

Although the Mishnah rejects the position that an oath to uphold a commandment is a legitimate oath, it recognizes the apparent logic of that position and acknowledges its appeal. After stating its own position that an oath to uphold a command is *not* a valid oath (expressed by the ruling that violating such an oath incurs no penalty), the Mishnah proceeds to flesh out the logic of the alternate view. It states (translating loosely) that a certain kind of logic, as exemplified by the words of R. Yehudah b. Beterah, renders such an oathtaker liable (שהיה בדין שיהא חייב, כדברי ר' יהודה בן בתירה), suggesting that an oath to uphold a commandment is a valid oath. The Mishnah then presents R. Yehudah b. Beterah's reasoning, spelling out how he reaches his conclusions. R. Yehudah b. Beterah argues on the basis of an a fortiori argument. The rabbinic a fortiori argument is a type of analogy that argues by way of inference.[84] It argues that certain factors known to be the case in situation X may also be assumed for situation Y. The analogy gains its legitimacy from the relative "strength" of the two cases: What applies in the less strong case can be inferred to apply in the stronger case, as well.

[84] See Moscovitz, *Talmudic Reasoning*, 240, where he implies that a fortiori inferences constitute a type of legal analogy.

As R. Yehudah b. Beterah sees it, oaths concerning voluntary actions are a less "strong" case, since no authority other than the oath itself compels the action. By way of contrast, he sees the oaths concerning commandments as a "stronger" case, since such oaths are compelled both by force of the oath and by the giving of the law at Mount Sinai. They are, in a sense, "doubly" commanded. Making these assumptions, he reasons that if one is liable for violating an oath concerning a voluntary action (the less strong case), one should certainly be liable for violating an oath concerning a commandment (the stronger case). Stated in a slightly different manner, he argues that if one's own act of adjuration is enough to incur liability for failure to comply, then certainly one should incur liability for an action that is additionally required by Sinaitic revelation. This mishnah, then, not only acknowledges a viewpoint other than the one that it sanctions, but it also spells out the legal reasoning on which the alternative view is based.

After presenting the legal reasoning of R. Yehudah b. Beterah, the mishnah develops the reasoning behind its own sanctioned point of view and indicates the shortcomings of R. Yehudah b. Beterah's view. The sages reject R. Yehudah b. Beterah's a fortiori argument because they see oaths concerning voluntary actions and commandments as fundamentally dissimilar. They argue that voluntary actions are, as their name makes explicit, voluntary. One is free either to do or not do them. By way of contrast, they point out that one may not freely choose to do or not do commandments. One is eternally obligated by the authority of Sinai to do them. As a result of this profound difference between voluntary actions and commandments, the sages argue that oaths concerning the one may not be likened or treated analogously to oaths concerning the other. For this reason, they conclude that one is *not* liable for oaths concerning commandments. While their view stands in sharp contrast with that of R. Yehudah b. Beterah, both views are shown to be based on the accepted methods of legal reasoning.

Borderline cases, then, provide training in fleshing out the ambiguity of legal cases. Sometimes the ambiguity is merely theoretical, as when no dissenting view is provided. When the dispute form is present, however, the Mishnah offers concrete evidence of the ambiguity of the borderline case.[85] Finally, in certain exceptional cases, the Mishnah not

[85] It would be interesting to examine how many borderline cases, for which no dissenting view is expressed in the Mishnah, have dissenting views expressed in the Tosephta or other parallels. Compare, e.g., m. Shev. 3:9 with t. Shev. 2:3–4. The presence of such cases leads one to wonder why the Mishnah would have suppressed the dissenting view, especially if it has an intellectual interest in making explicit the ambiguity of borderline cases, as has been argued in the preceding section.

Traditional theories suggest that the Mishnah's editor(s) excluded from the final document those views which he wished to discount. Inclusion of a particular view, especially in the anonymous voice, has generally been read as a sign of the editor's preference for that position. This interpretation of the Mishnah's suppression of dissenting views expressed in parallels to the Mishnah takes for granted that the Mishnah functioned as an authoritative code of normative law. Inclusion within the Mishnah indicates an authoritative stamp of approval for the included position and disapproval for the excluded position(s). On this point of view, see Elon, *Jewish Law,* 1069–70: Epstein, *ITL,* 213.

The ubiquity of the dispute form, however, poses a challenge to this view. If the Mishnah's intended purpose was to serve as a normative code of law, how are we to explain the many instances in which no single norm is granted presumptive authority? Proponents of the "Mishnah as law code" theory have adopted from the Talmud a complex set of rules, which they ascribe to the editor(s) of the Mishnah. These rules indicate which opinion is authoritative when several opinions are present. See e.g., b. Yeb. 42b: "If a dispute is followed by an anonymous opinion, the law follows the anonymous opinion. If the anonymous opinion follows a dispute, the law does not follow the anonymous opinion." See discussion of the various rules articulated in the two Talmuds in Zlotnick, *The Iron Pillar,* 206–11. See also Frankel, *Methods of the Mishnah* (Hebrew), 224 ff, 284, 287 ff; Epstein, *ITL,* 225–26. As Zlotnick makes clear, the presence of a system of rules formulated by amoraim (chiefly the school of R. Yohanan) tells us more about how the Mishnah *was used by the amoraim* than about the intentions of the editor. See Zlotnick, *The Iron Pillar,* 209.

Just as the ubiquity of the dispute form stands as an unresolved challenge to the view of the Mishnah as law code, the instances where the Mishnah suppresses a dispute that is attested in parallel sources challenge the view that the Mishnah served a solely pedagogical function. If the Mishnah did not take every available opportunity to train its students in negotiating the ambiguity of borderline cases by clarifying the two or more legal resolutions that one might provide to a given case, one can reasonably question the pedagogical purpose that I have been arguing underlies the Mishnah's casuistic presentation of materials.

The answer to the question of the Mishnah's purpose may lie somewhere in between the traditional polarity between pedagogical collection and normative law code. As with these other legal collections, the Mishnah may well have served both

only makes the ambiguity of the borderline case explicit by presenting two divergent rulings, but it also recreates the legal reasoning that underpins each position. We might think of the different ways of presenting borderline cases as different levels of articulation on the part of the Mishnah. When no dispute is present, the Mishnah provides no articulated evidence of the ambiguity of the case. In these cases, an attentive logical mind must reason out the intellectual interest and legal complexity that compel the Mishnah to preserve and record the case. By way of contrast, when a dispute form is present, the Mishnah provides a clear articulation of the ambiguity of the borderline case. In these cases, however, the legal reasoning behind the two (or more positions) remains unarticulated. The task of teasing out the legal reasoning is left for the students, readers, or listeners. Finally, in a very few cases, the Mishnah is fully explicit about the ambiguity of the borderline case. In these cases, the Mishnah articulates both the nature of the ambiguity with a dispute and spells out the legal reasoning behind each side.[86] I would argue that we can think of the most-articulated cases as developing the full potential of the least-articulated cases. Though only the most articulated cases draw out the plausible resolutions for a given case and spell out the legal reasoning that undergirds them, these tasks can easily be performed with respect to the less-articulated borderline

pedagogical and normative codificatory purposes. The Mishnah could well have communicated normative standards within the legal system at the same time that it taught students how to think within the legal system, that is, how to apply the norms. On the complementarity of the Mishnah's pedagogical and normative functions, see Strack and Stemberger, *Introduction to the Talmud and Midrash,* 154, and Elman, "Order, Sequence and Selection."

86 We might think of the more articulated cases of legal ambiguity as the more "ornamented" cases, following our discussion of ornamentation in Chapter 1. There, we suggested that certain performative versions fill in more of the implicit background concepts. Rather than thinking of such texts as adding something that is missing from the more cryptic version, we proposed using Lord's discussion of ornamentation in performance as a means of making sense of the difference between the more spelled-out and more cryptic versions. Here, too, the idea of ornamentation is a suggestive one for making sense of the difference between the more and less spelled-out versions of borderline cases. The more spelled-out borderline cases result from a certain kind of leisure in the performance that allows for the ambiguity to be expressed more fully.

cases. The fact that in some few cases the activity of legal analysis is explicitly articulated suggests to me that the Mishnah anticipates this level of analysis and engagement in *all* borderline cases. In sum, then, in their many different manifestations, borderline cases sensitize students, readers, and listeners to the complicating factors within a case, and they alert them to the many alternative principles by which any given legal conundrum might be resolved.

When we attend to the diverse ways in which casuistic formulations are presented, we come to recognize that they do more than convey legal norms. The preceding textual analysis suggests four different ways in which mishnaic discourse participates in and engages its students in complex legal analysis. For the ancient student of m. Shevuot, the exercise of studying Mishnah would have entailed retracing the connections between the particular and the general, mastering the matrix of legal principles that undergird the system as a whole through exercises of compare and contrast, observing how legal principles from diverse legal spheres intersect, and teasing out alternative principles by which cases can be resolved. By modeling each of these various activities of legal analysis, m. Shevuot would have trained its students to analyze legal scenarios on their own in much the same manner.[87]

Conclusion

The preceding textual analysis stresses the pedagogical function of mishnaic materials. Throughout the chapter I have described various modes of legal analysis that, I argue, m. Shevuot models for its students.

[87] See the similar reflection by Catherine Heszer: "The internal structure of Mishnah, which presents different and partly contradictory opinions side by side, and the fact that matters are left unresolved would motivate the audience and readers to engage in and continue the discussion themselves"; "The Mishnah and Ancient Book Production," in *The Mishnah in Contemporary Perspective,* ed. Alan J. Avery-Peck and Jacob Neusner (Boston and Leiden: Brill, 2002), 191–92.

The Mishnah – by modeling modes of legal analysis – serves the role of teacher, and its audience – by adopting and appropriating the modes of legal analysis – plays the role of student. The process that I am reconstructing, then, is at its core instructional and pedagogical in nature.

The idea that the Mishnah served a pedagogical function is hardly new. What distinguishes the current analysis, then, is not the conclusions reached but the type of evidence brought to bear on a question that has long occupied mishnaic studies: What was the intended function of the Mishnah as redacted by R. Judah the Patriarch?[88] Typically, scholars who conclude that the Mishnah served a pedagogical function do so on the basis of the redactional choices of the editor: What sources did he choose to include (as opposed to exclude)? What order did he arrange them in?[89] Abraham Goldberg, the primary proponent of the Mishnah-as-pedagogical-textbook theory, argues that the editor's interest in achieving certain pedagogical goals affected the selections he made from among his sources and how he arranged them. According to Goldberg, the editor selected and arranged his sources in such a manner so as to 1) expose students to the most foundational legal opinions and 2) facilitate students' absorption of the material (by presenting simpler issues first and introducing more complex materials thereafter and by organizing material topically).[90] Goldberg's methodological approach to discerning the Mishnah's function, then, is to interrogate

[88] Scholars have been split into two basic camps in trying to answer this question. Frankel, *Methods of the Mishnah* (Hebrew), Vol. 2, 224–27; Jacob Brüll, *Introduction to the Mishnah* (Hebrew), Vol. 2 (Frankfurt-am-Main, 1876); Epstein, *ITL,* 225–26; Guttman, *Rabbinic Judaism in the Making,* 240–44; Elon, *Jewish Law,* 1057–78, and others have argued that Rabbi intended to produce a normative code of law. By way of contrast, Albeck, *Introduction to the Mishnah,* 105–7, 270–83, and Goldberg, "The Mishnah," have argued that the collection contains too many internal contradictions and disputes to have functioned as an authoritative standard of law.

[89] See Goldberg, "The Mishnah," and Goldberg, "Purpose and Method in Rabbi Judah Hannasi's Compilation of the Mishna" (Hebrew), *Tarbiz* 28 (1958–59): 260–69 (Eng. abstract, II–IV).

[90] See Goldberg, "Purpose and Method."

the internal evidence of the Mishnah for what it can tell us about its editor's intentions.

This book, however, has been trying to argue that the mishnaic text as we have it does not necessarily provide a transparent view of the choices made by a final editor. Instead, I have been arguing that the internal evidence of the Mishnah can be subjected to other kinds of inquiries. A different methodological lens can yield additional perspective even while confirming conclusions that have already been reached. The methodology employed here in the analysis of m. Shevuot focuses on what I would call the "performative effect" of mishnaic materials. Such a method tries to imagine what would *result* from performing the materials.[91] That is, it inquires into the "effect" of oral performance. A focus on the performative effect of the materials suggests that the modes of thinking that lie behind the composition of the materials are *also* perpetuated through oral reenactment of the written materials. Though the textually crystalized version of m. Shevuot before us today presents a series of analytic exercises that have already been performed and solved, we can also read the textual artifact as an invitation to reenact the exercises. I argue that the pedagogical value of performing the various types of analytic exercises catalogued in this chapter lies in the extent to which performing such exercises teaches students how to perform such exercises on their own. In short, it teaches them to apply the norms of the legal system judiciously and appropriately.

Though the conclusion that mishnaic materials served a pedagogical function is an old one, as has been noted, the new methodological means by which the conclusion is reached provides credibility to the old position in new ways. One critique to which the theory of the Mishnah-as-pedagogical-handbook has often been vulnerable concerns the extent to which the Mishnah cannot function

[91] On the idea that oral performance of a text can have an effect on its audience, see Handelman, "The 'Torah' of Criticism and the Criticism of Torah," 366, and my discussion in n. 9 of this chapter.

as a freestanding instructional tool.[92] The Mishnah assumes a level of knowledge, of both technical terms and legal norms, that make it daunting for the novice to engage without guidance. If one does not assume, however, that the primary pedagogical aim of the Mishnah was to convey legal content, then the theory of the Mishnah-as-pedagogical-handbook is not so vulnerable to this critique. This chapter has proposed that one important pedagogical function of m. Shevuot was to train students in various modes of legal analysis. In this view, reconstructing the logic by which various cases are resolved and understanding their implications constitutes the primary exercise of "studying Mishnah." There is no reason to assume that a more advanced sage would not have been available to help the less experienced novices by filling in gaps and facilitating the process.[93] Alternatively, one may speculate that training in the kind of legal analysis facilitated by m. Shevuot was not intended for the novice, but rather for disciples who had already been initiated into a program of study.[94] By stressing that the pedagogical benefit of m. Shevuot lies in

92 Elman offers one such critique of Goldberg in "Order, Sequence and Selection," 69. It is an oft-remarked feature of the Mishnah in standard introductions for the student that it takes much information for granted. See, e.g., Goldenberg, "The Talmud," 133–34; Neusner, *Judaism: Evidence of the Mishnah,* note on 269.

93 Jaffee, in *Torah in the Mouth,* discusses the importance of "knowledge gained . . . in the form of a living teacher" (151) within the ancient rabbinic context. As Jaffee imagines ancient rabbinic pedagogy, the sage or teacher plays a prominent role, and so in any event it would make no sense to imagine that the Mishnah functioned as a freestanding instructional tool. As he writes with respect to the philosophical training in Greco-Roman instructional settings (which he sees as similar to rabbinic instructional settings), "the primary goal of such study was not merely to master knowledge discursively. The privileged path to such transformation lay in emulating the living embodiment of that knowledge in the writings and deeds of one's teachers. . . . In the person of the philosophical Sage, the instructional text came alive" (151). In this way of thinking, the teacher is an integral part of the instructional process. See Jaffee, *Torah in the Mouth,* 147–52; Jaffee, "The Oral-Cultural Matrix of the Talmud Yerushalmi: Graeco-Roman Rhetorical Paideia, Discipleship, and the Concept of Oral Torah," in *The Talmud Yerushalmi in Graeco-Roman Culture,* ed. Peter Schfer (Tubingen: J. C. B. Mohr (Paul Siebeck), 1998), 53–60; and Jaffee, "Written and Spoken Word."

94 When speculating about the pedagogic function of legal materials in the Bible, Raymond Westbrook makes a similar proposal. He suggests that legal materials in the

imparting a method of legal analysis, rather than conveying content,[95] the thesis that the Mishnah served in an instructional setting buttresses itself against the critique that it is ineffective as a freestanding instructional aid.

Arguing for the Mishnah's pedagogic function by stressing its performative context strengthens the position in yet another way: The conclusions reached here do not preclude the possibility that the materials *also* served as an authoritative source of normative law. As mentioned earlier, scholars often have been split into two opposing camps, with some arguing that the Mishnah functioned as a law code (i.e., as an official source of normative law) and others arguing that the Mishnah functioned in a more pedagogical capacity. The two positions are generally seen as mutually exclusive, in part because the early proponents of the two positions had radically different visions of what the editor intended to accomplish through his redactorial choices.[96] By grounding their

Bible functioned in a pedagogic capacity for advanced, rather than inexperienced, initiates of the material. He argues that casuistic legal records served as a resource for judges (a highly trained professsional group) when considering particularly difficult cases. See Westbrook, "Biblical and Cuneiform Law Codes," 254. Likewise, the casuistic legal formulations from the ancient Near East have often been linked with the scribal schools. See, e.g., the casuistically formulated Sumerian tablet (Yale Babylonian Collection 2177), which is now understood to be from the scribal schools. See J. J. Finkelstein, "Sumerian Laws, YBC 2177," in *The Ancient Near East: Supplementary Texts and Pictures Relating to the Ancient Near East,* ed. James B. Pritchard (Princeton, NJ: Princeton University Press, 1969), 525–26. For a discussion of this text in its pedagogical context, see Westbrook, *Biblical and Cuneiform Law,* 40. These institutions were not primary schools for novice learners, but rather institutes for advanced training in a specialized profession. The idea that the Mishnah functioned pedagogically for *advanced,* rather than novice, learners stands in sharp contrast to many of the conventional understandings of the pedagogic purposes of the Mishnah. Gerhardsson, e.g., assumes that study of the Mishnah constituted an elementary kind of education, as learning was done through rote memorization, often without understanding. See Gerhardsson, *Memory and Manuscript,* 79–92.

95 Jaffee, in *Torah in the Mouth,* makes a similar point about the value of study in ancient settings: The goal was not to "master knowledge discursively" (147). Rather, it was to bring to life the teachings of the teacher, thereby extending the life of the master into the next generation. See *Torah in the Mouth,* 147–51.

96 As will be recalled, Goldberg (the major proponent of the Mishnah-as-pedagogical-handbook theory) argues that Rabbi intentionally arranged his sources in a manner

respective positions in conclusions about the editor's redactorial intentions, the two positions formulated their arguments in positivistic terms that did not make room for the opposing point of view.

Recently, however, a new set of approaches for resolving the question of the Mishnah's intended function is emerging, a set that does not imply the mutual exclusivity of the two views.[97] I would argue that the approach taken here – that m. Shevuot trains its students in modes of legal analysis – does not necessarily contradict the view that the Mishnah conveys the authoritative norms of the legal system. As a law student at the University of Virginia pointed out to me at the conclusion of his first year, which traditionally exposes students to many of the fundamental principles of the American legal system through a series of classic "borderline" cases: "in order to learn to apply the principles you need to know what the principles are. The very same cases that teach you to think 'like a lawyer' also teach you the substance of the law." Our textual analysis of m. Shevuot bears out the same impression that the cases that teach students to apply the law also convey important information about the standards and norms of

that would facilitate the student's integration of the materials. See Goldberg, "Purpose and Method." Epstein (an early and articulate proponent of the Mishnah-as-law-code theory) develops an argument equally rooted in speculations about the editor's redactorial choices. Epstein discusses a number of editorial strategies that Rabbi employed when compiling his sources (*ITL*, 212–24). Most pointedly, Epstein posits that Rabbi emended the Mishnah to accord with his own legal views (213). He also notes that in other instances, Rabbi endorsed the majority position (even where he disagreed) because of the principle that majority ruling takes priority (214, 225). Many of the editorial policies that Epstein discusses indicate Rabbi's intent to create an authoritative code of normative law, a position he articulates explicitly in the next chapter (225–26). See Epstein, *ITL*, 212–26. Zechariah Frankel also articulates 45 principles that he believes Rabbi used in the selection, arrangement, and ordering of his sources. See Frankel, *Methods of the Mishnah* (Hebrew), 282–321.

97 See Strack and Stemberger, *Introduction to the Talmud and Midrash*, 154, and Elman, "Order, Sequence and Selection." Zlotnick supports the basic view that the Mishnah functioned as a code, but rather than grounding this understanding in an argument about Rabbi's intentions, he grounds his conclusions in information about how the Mishnah was *received and used* by the amoraim. This argument, too, need not exclude the possibility that the Mishnah was *also* received and used pedagogically. See Zlotnick, *The Iron Pillar*, 194–217.

the legal system.[98] As will be recalled, two of the four modes of legal analysis accomplish a task usually associated with law codes: They communicate the basic norms of the legal system.[99] While the foregoing discussion of casuistic form in the Mishnah cannot provide for a comprehensive theory of the Mishnah's function (a comprehensive theory would have to take account of a number of other factors),[100] it does corroborate the conclusions of a growing number of studies that the pedagogical and normative functions of the Mishnah are compatible, rather than mutually exclusive.

In the next chapter, I will explore one final implication of reading m. Shevuot with an eye to its performative effect. When we read mishnaic materials as modeling and teaching several modes of analysis, we are alerted to important continuities between the academic culture of the tannaim and that of the amoraic and post-amoraic sages. The next chapter discusses the persistence of these modes of analysis among those who transmitted and handled m. Shevuot after the tannaitic period had concluded.

98 In that this chapter only considers the significance of the casuistic form in m. Shevuot, the results obtained here should not be seen as endorsing a view of the Mishnah as a whole. As noted earlier in this chapter where, while the casuistic form is a *dominant* literary form in the m. Shevuot, it is not the only literary form. The tractate also includes a few rules. This analysis is intended to shed light on the presence and the dominance of the casuistic form alone. It does not aim to present a comprehensive theory of the Mishnah's function.

99 As noted, the basic casuistic form renders particular circumstances of a specific case into a more general formulation that allows for broad applicability. To the extent that circumstances in future cases are analogous with those of the protasis, the legal resolution found in the apodosis can be applied. The basic case, then, provides a normative standard, according to which future cases are evaluated. Likewise, the process of generating variables of a prototype case helps students detect underlying patterns and principles that run through the legal system as a whole. Working through a prototype and its variables supplies greater familiarity with the norms of the legal system. Both of these features of the casuistic form aid the Mishnah's readership or audience in amalgating the norms of the system.

100 A comprehensive theory of the Mishnah's function would have to take *all* of the Mishnah's literary forms into account: midrashic elements, aggadic elements, rules, disputes, cases, etc. It would also have to account for the choices of redaction by comparing the Mishnah with its tosephtan parallels.

4

The Cultivation of an Analytic Habit and Its Impact on Mishnaic Exegesis

In the years following the Mishnah's compilation, it became a central text in the rabbinic curriculum of sacred study. One manifestation of this curricular centrality is the fact that the Mishnah serves as the skeletal structure around which the two Talmuds are organized.[1] Additionally, the so-called curriculum pericopes indicate that mishnaic traditions consistently occupied a place of honor in rabbinic academic settings.[2] Moshe Halbertal has noted that when texts are canonized in a curricular sense, that is, when they become central pedagogical texts, they determine "how to think, how to see the world and what

1 See discussion of this phenomenon in Martin S. Jaffee, "Oral Torah in Theory and Practice: Aspects of Mishnah-Exegesis in the Palestinian Talmud," *Religion* 15 (1985): 387–410.

2 The subjects of study central to the rabbinic curriculum are discussed in the so-called curriculum pericopes. Mishnah study or halakhah is typically included in the list. See discussions in Louis Finkelstein, "Midrash, Halakhot, and Aggadot" (Hebrew), in *Yitzhak Baer Jubilee Volume on the Occasion of His Seventieth Birthday*, ed. S. W. Baron et al. (Jerusalem: Historical Society of Israel, 1960), 28–46, and Jaffee, *Torah in the Mouth*, 87–92. For other discussions of the centrality of the Mishnah in the rabbinic curriculum, see Lieberman, *HJP*, 82–92, and Zlotnick, *The Iron Pillar*, 221, 226.

objects to meditate upon."[3] Following on Halbertal's observation, in this chapter I am interested in documenting the effect of the Mishnah's canonization as a centerpiece in the rabbinic curriculum on rabbinic habits of thought and analysis. Building on his observation, I wish to argue that study of m. Shevuot conditioned a particular way of thinking about legal problems.

In the previous chapter, I argued that the textual materials of m. Shevuot functioned as a script for ongoing reenactment of the legal exercises it records. By presenting difficult cases along with their legal resolutions, m. Shevuot trained its readers and students in particular methods of analyzing legal cases. It familiarized them with the basic principles that undergird the legal system as a whole, it modeled strategies for balancing the concerns of conflicting legal principles, and it taught students to explore the ambiguity of individual cases. While the previous chapter illustrates the modes of legal analysis embodied by the casuistic form of m. Shevuot, the current chapter aims to expose the persistence of these habits in later literatures.[4]

Moshe Silberg observes that the two Talmuds, like the Mishnah on which they are based, engage law largely in its casuistic form.[5]

[3] Moshe Halbertal, *People of the Book: Canon, Meaning and Authority* (Cambridge, MA: Harvard University Press, 1997), 100. Halbertal discusses the way in which Jewish canonical texts *influence ways of thinking*. The full citation reads: "Once Talmud became the principal formative text in Jewish life, it came to determine not only what people should do but how to think, how to see the world, and what objects to choose to meditate upon." He argues that texts can be canonized in many different ways. Insofar as the Talmud (which he examines) and the Mishnah (which I examine) become central *curricular* texts, they influence "modes of thought and objects of reflection" (124–25).

[4] Though the current chapter is limited to documenting the persistence of these habits in talmudic literature, one can imagine that it would be fruitful and generative to examine the continued cultivation of the same intellectual habits in later talmudic commentary, particularly among the Tosafists and among the Eastern European schools of pilpul from the eighteenth through twentieth centuries.

[5] See Silberg, *Talmudic Law*, 11–21, esp. 19: "Talmudic law generally takes the form, not of abstract principles, but of brief recitations of incidents which appear to be – because of the constellation of details included – summations of cases, decisions

It is reasonable to expect that the very modes of legal analysis that characterize the casuistically formulated Mishnah should also play a prominent role in the casuistically inclined Talmuds.[6] Silberg cites a midrashic dictum in this regard, "the actions of the fathers provide the model for their descendants."[7] My goal in this chapter is to explore the continuities between mishnaic and talmudic habits of analysis. Like the tannaim before them, talmudic sages formulated difficult cases that lay at the intersection of discrete legal principles in order to practice balancing the concerns of competing legal principles.[8] And like the tannaim before them, they juxtaposed laws with a single shifting variable in order to highlight larger patterns and point to underlying principles.[9] Furthermore, the Mishnah's concern with the abstract principles that inform individual cases is perpetuated by the Talmud's tendency toward abstraction and conceptualization.[10] In each of these ways, the two Talmuds participate in, adopt as their own, and further develop the intellectual program modeled by the Mishnah.[11]

or resolutions that had come before the court for adjudication." Though Silberg here links the casuistic form with actual cases, elsewhere he states that the casuistic formulation was used "for the sake of exemplifying the general, abstract principle which could logically be derived from it" (21).

6 It is, however, important to note prominent differences between mishnaic and talmudic form. Whereas the Mishnah takes the form of a code or collection of law, the Talmuds take the form of commentary. Discussion, interpretive give and take, and argumentation all play a prominent role in the Talmuds, though not in the code-like Mishnah. For an in-depth discussion of these differences in form, see Kraemer, *The Mind of the Talmud,* 26–98, and Halivni, *Midrash, Mishnah and Gemara,* 38–92.

7 Silberg, *Talmudic Law,* 16.

8 See discussion in Silberg, *Talmudic Law,* 20–21, and Alexander, "Study Practices That Made the Mishnah," 146–72.

9 See Silberg, *Talmudic Law,* 17–19, and Alexander, "Study Practices That Made the Mishnah," 120–25, 132–72.

10 See Moscovitz, *Talmudic Reasoning,* and Jeffrey L. Rubenstein, "On Some Abstract Concepts in Rabbinic Literature," *Jewish Studies Quarterly* 4 (1997): 33–73.

11 A question emerges here: What kind of causality am I proposing between the existence of these practices among tannaim and their persistence among amoraic and post-amoraic sages? I do not necessarily wish to argue that the presence of these practices among the amoraim and post-amoraic sages is *directly attributable* to their use among

The Talmud is, of course, not code-like in literary form as is the Mishnah. It engages in wide-ranging legal discussions, most notably commenting on the Mishnah, but also recording debates among scholars and ranging off into digressions on related and not-so-related topics. The analytic habits identified in the last chapter are put to service in the accomplishment of each of these diverse tasks. They are employed in the discussion of various legal topics, in the analysis of disputes, and in the work of mishnaic interpretation. The diversity of contexts in which these analytic practices appear suggests that they were pervasive and widespread. Of particular interest for the current project is examining the use of these analytic practices in the context of mishnaic exegesis. In these instances, we see that the intellectual habits that permeate m. Shevuot *are also central for its interpretation.* It appears that the "analytic" hens have come to roost, so to speak. Insofar as performance of m. Shevuot engenders an analytic program that can be detected in the talmudic work of mishnah exegesis, the Mishnah can be said to promote a method and culture of study to which it, itself, eventually becomes subject.

This chapter, then, proposes a new way of thinking about how practices of oral transmission influenced the talmudic project of interpreting m. Shevuot. The dominant scholarly paradigm proposes that practices of oral transmission led to minor losses and corruptions in both the mishnaic text and its interpretive traditions over time. According to this paradigm, the distinctive character of talmudic exegesis flows from the fact that the defective sources did not accurately represent the original relationship between text and commentary. The result was compensatory measures – trying to make a square peg fit in a round hole – and what David Weiss Halivni has called "forced" interpretations

the tannaim. I am not trying to make an argument of causality at all. Rather, I wish to bring indirect evidence of the cultivation of certain habits of inquiry. Each generation is equally responsible for the prominence of these techniques. For each generation, they are equally compelled by the nature of the materials. But irrespective of causality, the persistence of these habits of study forms a cultural and intellectual link between the earlier and later rabbinic periods in terms of their methods of study.

(פירושים דחוקים).[12] This dominant scholarly paradigm is a version of the theory of textual corruption discussed in the Introduction; it notes the impact of oral transmission *only insofar as it affects the verbal content of textual materials.* Halivni's theory is particularly interested in how oral transmission effects a breakdown in the conveyance of the verbal contents of these materials. It is certainly true that transmission of m. Shevuot entailed the passing on of textual materials (both text and interpretive tradition). It is also almost certain that some of the verbal contents of m. Shevuot and its interpretive traditions were altered in the context of transmission. We will fail, however, to appreciate the impact of oral transmission on the character of talmudic interpretation if we do not also recognize how *study practices were transmitted* alongside the traditions of m. Shevuot. The modes of legal analysis modeled by oral performance of m. Shevuot and subsequently adopted by its students attest to strong *nonverbal* continuities between the mishnaic and talmudic sages. The methodological innovation of the current study flows from the insight that oral transmission is a vehicle not only for conveying textual materials but also, and equally as important, for perpetuating an intellectual climate rooted in specific study practices and habits of analysis.

Ideally, this chapter would document in detail the proliferation of each of the four study practices discussed in the last chapter. This task, however, far exceeds the reasonable bounds of a single chapter. Given the constraints, I will limit myself to discussion of a single mode of legal analysis. What I lose in breadth of discussion, I hope to make up for in depth. In a sense, my goal here is a limited one: I wish to illustrate *the relevance of transmitted study practices for understanding the character of talmudic interpretation of Mishnah.* Although I will only be able to document the persistence of a single mode of analysis, I hope my methodological model opens readers to the possibility that each of the analytic modes documented in the last chapter persisted beyond the tannaitic period and eventually influenced the work of

[12] See Halivni, *Seder Nashim*, 7–19, and *Midrash, Mishnah and Gemara*, 76–87.

mishnah exegesis.[13] In the pages that follow, I will document specifically the talmudic tendency *to explore the tensions among competing legal principles by formulating borderline cases.* This practice is attested in both of the talmudic commentaries to m. Shevuot in a wide variety of contexts. It is employed in the discussion of related topics, in the analysis of disputes, and in the work of mishnaic interpretation. The manifold contexts in which the practice is employed attest to the fact that it was a powerful tool for legal analysis among the talmudic sages. As I hope to show, oral performance of m. Shevuot served not only the important function of stabilizing the form and content of tradition, but also – and equally as important – *of shaping the intellectual context* within which the textual materials were handled.

Pedagogical Uses of Borderline Cases

In the previous chapter, I argued that the formulation and resolution of borderline cases serves a pedagogical function, attuning students,

[13] Since the work of this chapter is to offer a methodological model only, I think it is valuable to recognize where the work of other scholars can be adopted to support this model. For example, Jeffrey Rubenstein and Leib Moscovitz have done interesting work that documents trends of increasing levels of abstraction in amoraic and post-amoraic discussions of law. Though closer study is required, it seems plausible to suggest that these trends of increasing abstraction are of a piece with the tannaitic tendency to illustrate general principles on the basis of the concrete details of specific cases. See Rubenstein, "Some Abstract Concepts," and Moscovitz, *Talmudic Reasoning*. See also Urbach, *The Halakhah*, 177–205. We might also conjecture that the post-tannaitic desire to discern a coherent system within diverse and often conflicting tannaitic traditions represents a continuation of the mishnaic tendency to find the general abstract principles implicit within the particular cases. See the discussion of this tendency in the Talmud in Goldenberg, "The Talmud," 150, 153–56. Moshe Silberg discusses, albeit briefly, the talmudic interest in unusual and improbable cases. This phenomenon, too, may be seen as linked to the mishnaic interest in unusual and improbable cases. See Silberg, *Talmudic Law*, 20–21. Elsewhere I have discussed the practice among amoraic and post-amoraic sages of juxtaposing two cases in order to highlight a single variable of difference between them. This phenomenon has much in common with the mishnaic form of two contrasting cases discussed in the last chapter. See Alexander, "Study Practices That Made the Mishnah," 120–25, 132–72.

listeners, and readers to the complex factors one must take into account before making any ruling. The following anecdote from the Yerushalmi illustrates one way in which amoraic sages adopted this practice and formulated borderline cases in instructional settings.

y. Shev. 34d (halakhah 3:7)[14]

אבימי אחוי דחיפה אמר: שמשית בנדרין, שמשית בשבועות.
בעי חיפה מיבדקיניה:
היו לפניו חמש ככרין ואמר: שבועה שאוכל ככר זו
וחזר ואמר שתים אילו; וחזר ואמר שלשה אילו; וחזר ואמר ארבעה אילו; וחזר ואמר חמשה אילו. ואכל הראשונה?
אמר ליה: חייב על כל אחת ואחת.
אמר ליה: אינו חייב אלא אחת. מכווין שהזכיר עליה שבועה עשאה כנבילה; מיכן ואילך, כמיחל שבועות על האיסורין.

Abimai, the brother of Haifa, said: I have attended a scholar[15] on the topic of vows, I attended a scholar on the topic of oaths.
Haifa wished to test him:
[Consider the situation in which] a person had five loaves of bread in front of him, and [pointing to a specific loaf] he said:I swear I will [not][16] eat this loaf. And then he reconsidered and said:

[14] Text according to MS Leiden as transcribed in Sussmann, *Talmud Yerushalmi.*

[15] The Bavli tells a similar tale, though several key details are different. In the Bavli's version it is Haifa, rather than Abimai, who has been studying the topic of oaths. The Bavli explains that Haifa (or Efa, as he is called there) was studying oaths under Rabbah (עיפא תני שבועות בי רבה) (see b. Shev. 28b). The Bavli's statement that the study happened under the tutelage of Rabbah clarifies this awkward usage in the Yerushalmi. The Yerushalmi has Abimai saying that he simply attended a scholar (שמשית) on the topic of oaths. The Bavli's version suggests that he was learning under the tutelage of Rabbah.

[16] Dünner explains that although the text states the oath in positive terms ("I swear I will eat"), it must be understood in negative terms ("I swear I will not eat"). Joseph Hirsch (Tzvi) Dünner, *Hidushe Ha-Ritsad: Hagahot, Perushim, Be'urim`al Ha-Bavli Veha-Yerushalmi,* Vol. 3: *Nezikin* (Jerusalem: Mosad Ha-Rav Kuk, 1981), תקמ"ג.

> [I swear I will not eat] these *two* loaves. And then he reconsidered and said: [I swear I will not eat] these *three* loaves. And then he reconsidered and said: [I swear I will not eat] these *four* loaves. And then he reconsidered and said: [I swear I will not eat] these *five* loaves. And then he *ate the first loaf,* [on how many counts is he liable]?
> He [Abimai] said: He is liable on each and every count.
> He [Haifa] corrected him: He is liable only on a single count. [The reasoning is as follows]: As soon as the loaf was prohibited [by virtue of the first oath], it became like carrion [which may not be eaten according to Jewish law]. From that point forward, the oathtaker is like one who swears concerning a prohibited object [and such an oath is not legitimate].[17]

The setting here is clearly pedagogical. Abimai has been learning about vows and oaths, and his brother Haifa wishes to drill him to see how well he has integrated the more subtle points of the law. In order to test his brother, Haifa constructs a new case that reproduces the exercise of the mishnaic borderline cases. As in the Mishnah, the listener, reader, or student is confronted with a case that can plausibly be resolved according to two different rationales. In this very pedagogically motivated use of the borderline case, the two resolutions (though both plausible) are not equally weighted. The resolution offered by Abimai is more naive, responding only to the most obvious features of the case, whereas the resolution offered by Haifa is more sophisticated, taking more subtle features of the case into account. The test challenges Abimai to pursue the less obvious but more thoughtful approach to

[17] M. Shev. 3:4 establishes that if one swears concerning a prohibited object, the oath is not legitimate. The amoraim formulate the principle implicit in the Mishnah's casuistic form as follows: "Oaths do not operate with respect to prohibited objects" (אין שבועות חלות על האיסורין). See y. Shev. 34c, halakhah 3:4. The amoraic articulation of the principle implicit in the tannaitic case is a well-documented tendency. See Goldberg, "Babylonian Talmud," 330–31; Urbach, *The Halakhah*, 177–205; Rubenstein, "Some Abstract Concepts"; and Moscovitz, *Talmudic Reasoning*, esp. 343–66.

the problem, somewhat like a brainteaser.[18] Sadly, Abimai does not rise to the occasion.

The case involves a person who articulates multiple oaths over the same loaf (or set of loaves), each time including one additional loaf in his prohibition. The question is posed: On how many counts of culpability is the oathtaker liable if he eats only the original loaf? Two resolutions present themselves. *Either* the oathtaker is culpable for each and every time that he prohibited the loaf *or* he is liable only once because he ate only one loaf of bread.

At first blush, the case seems to be similiar to the case discussed immediately prior in the gemara.

y. Shev. 34d

שבועה שבועה שבועה שלא אוכל ככר זו, ואכל. מהו?
. . . חייב על כל אחת ואחת.

> [If a person said:] It is an oath, it is an oath, it is an oath that I will not eat this loaf. And then he ate [it]. What is the ruling?
> . . . He is liable on each and every count.

In this case the oathtaker repeats his prohibition and is liable for each and every repetition of the oath. It is not far-fetched to imagine that the principle operative in this case, presented *just before* Haifa's case, would be operative in our case, too. The naive Abimai reasons in this manner

[18] Louis Jacobs likens the borderline case with two *equally* plausible rulings to riddles, suggesting that they functioned as "semi-humorous intellectual exercises" among the sages. See Jacobs, *Teyku: The Unsolved Problem in the Babylonian Talmud* (New York: Cornwall Books, 1981), 300. The comparison to a brainteaser or riddle is perhaps even more well suited to the borderline case in which one resolution is preferable to the other. As with a riddle, the obvious solution is usually the wrong one and the correct solution usually requires subtle and creative thinking outside of the box. See also Hayes's discussion of puzzles and conundrums in the Bavli in *Between the Babylonian and Palestinian Talmuds,* 119.

and suggests that in our case, too, the oathtaker is liable each and every time he prohibits the loaf. Haifa, however, points out that Abimai's reasoning is faulty. Deeper analysis reveals that the subsequent oaths do not "re-"prohibit the original loaf. As soon as the original oath is in place, the loaf is subject to no further oaths. As the amoraim state elsewhere: One may not make an oath about something that is already prohibited (אין שבועות חלות על האיסורין).[19] Haifa implicitly invokes this principle when he explains the reasoning behind his resolution. The language he uses to express himself – "it is like one who makes an oath over a prohibited object" (כמיחל שבועות על האיסורין) – is drawn directly from the language of this widely attested principle. Since oaths on prohibited objects are not legitimate, only the first oath renders the oathtaker culpable when he finally does eat the loaf. Even though two rationales present themselves in the resolution of this case, one is more naive and the other is more learned as it attends to less obvious considerations and reflects greater powers of discernment.

Haifa's interrogation of his brother continues as he formulates a second borderline case. Again, the naive Abimai is tempted to resolve it according to the most obvious logic. Deeper consideration, however, reveals a more sophisticated and appropriate approach for resolving the case.

y. Shev. 34d

חזר חיפה ובדקיה:
היו לפניו חמש ככרות ואמר: שבועה שאוכל חמש ככרים אילו; וחזר ואמר ארבע;
וחזר ואמר שלש; וחזר ואמר שנים; וחזר ואמר זו. ואכל כולם?

[19] Elsewhere this principle is put into the mouths of R. Yohanan and Resh Lakish (y. Shev. 34c). This principle, which the amoraim state as an abstract rule, is derived from the casuistic formulation of m. Shev. 3:4: "If a person said: I swear I will not eat carrion and torn flesh, creeping and crawling beasts [i.e., forbidden foods], and then he ate them – he is not liable."

אמר ליה: אינו חייב אלא אחת.
אמר ליה: חייב על כל אחת ואחת. אילו מי שאמר שבועה שאוכל חמש ככרים, ואכל ד' שמא אינו פטור?

> Then Haifa tested him again:
> [Consider the case in which] a person had five loaves of bread in front of him. [Pointing to them all he said:] I swear I will [not][20] eat these *five* loaves. Then he reconsidered and said *four*. Then he reconsidered and said *three*. Then he reconsidered and said *two*. Then he reconsidered and said this *single one*. If he then ate *all of them*, [what is the ruling]?
> He [Abimai] said: He is only liable on a single count.
> He [Haifa] corrected him: He is liable on each and every count. If someone swears not to eat five loaves, and then he eats only four, is he not exempt? [In order to be liable for eating four loaves, he must make a separate oath not to eat four. From this we learn that each of the subsequent oaths is considered a separate oath, for which the oathtaker is fully culpable since it does not overlap with the earlier oaths.]

This case is very similar to the first case, in fact deceptively so to poor Abimai that he is again misled to respond with an incorrect answer. Here again the oathtaker stands before five loaves, and again he makes a series of oaths. Instead of *including* an extra loaf in each oath, this time the oathtaker *excludes* a single loaf from each subsequent oath. Again the question emerges: On how many counts is the oathtaker culpable when he eats all five loaves in the end? On the basis of similarities between the first case and the second, Abimai speculates that the same principle must be at work in both in determining liability. In the first case, repeated oaths do not produce multiple counts of culpability because an oath cannot prohibit something that is already

[20] Dünner again explains that the positively stated oath ("I swear I will eat") must be understood in negative terms ("I swear I will not eat"). See Dünner, *Hidushe Ha-Ritsad*, תקמ"ג.

forbidden. Abimai reasons that the repeated oaths in this second case are governed by the same principle. He concludes that the oathtaker is liable on only one count. Once again, however, Haifa catches his brother with lazy thinking. Abimai has opted for the most obvious resolution without thinking through the problem very carefully. Upon more pointed reflection, it appears that the principle operative in the prior case is not appropriate for this case. Haifa demonstrates that each subsequent oath *must be considered a separate oath*, since the oaths do not prohibit the *same* object repeatedly. Haifa explains that when the initial oath concerns *five* loaves, an oath about *four* loaves is considered an entirely different oath. The oathtaker is actually liable for all five oaths, since each of the five oaths is a legitimate oath unto itself.

As before, the pedagogical function of this exercise is clear. Haifa intends to test his brother and see if he can avoid the traps of naive thinking and invoke subtle second-order principles in an unsolicited manner. Unfortunately, in both cases, Abimai does not seem up to the task. At any rate, this is how Haifa would tell the story. The final redactor, however, was not as sure. He concludes the sugya with a final comment by R. Yose, which restores Abimai's credibility.

y. Shev. 34d

אמר ר' יוסי: מסתברא כאחוי דחיפה באחריי׳תא וכחיפה בקדמיתא

> R. Yose said: It is reasonable that the brother of Haifa [was correct] in the latter case, and Haifa [was correct] in the former case.

As if to reinstate the ambiguity of the borderline case, the sugya ends by stating that Abimai's resolution is not as naive as Haifa makes it out to be. In the anecdote, Haifa functions as an authoritative figure whose judgment is highly regarded and presumed to be correct. R. Yose's comment, however, lends credibility to Abimai's position. For the reader of the gemara, then, the sugya ends by affirming the plausibility of *both* resolutions. This move has the effect of inviting the reader to continue engaging the case. The reader must now reconstruct the reasoning that R. Yose uses to resurrect Abimai's opinion.[21] I would argue that the pedagogical import of this exercise lies not in eliciting the "correct" answer from the student (because, as it turns out, no single answer is more correct than any other), but in getting the student to think deeply about the problem.[22]

This riddle-like exercise demonstrates one way in which the habit of formulating borderline cases persisted among amoraic sages in pedagogical contexts. By virtue of their inherent ambiguity, borderline cases encouraged students, readers, and listeners to think deeply about how to apply appropriate legal principles.

The Unsolvable Problem

A number of scholars argue that the unusual and far-fetched circumstances of many talmudic cases suggest they were originally discussed

[21] One such reconstruction can be found in the commentary of Pene Moshe. Pene Moshe attempts to explain R. Yose's thinking under the assumption that he (R. Yose) takes Haifa's reasoning into account when he defends Abimai's conclusions. According to Pene Moshe, the oathtaker did not intend not to eat all five loaves at one time when he said: "I swear I will not eat *precisely these* (חמש אילו) five loaves." By specifying that it was "*precisely these five*" loaves that he did not intend to eat, he indicated that the oath could be violated by eating any number of the loaves at any given time. Thus, the subsequent oaths that prohibit fewer than the original five loaves can be seen as redundant repetitions of the first oath and therefore without standing as independent oaths. For these reasons, according to R. Yose, Abimai was actually correct when he stated that the oathtaker is only liable on a single count (presumably for having violated the first oath only). See Pene Moshe s.v. כאחוי דחיפה באחריתא.

[22] The value that this sugya places on mental agility and thinking deeply calls to mind the oft-quoted sugya from b. Eruv. 13b in which R. Meir demonstrates his mental agility by arguing that the pure is impure and the impure is pure. As here, in the b. Eruv. source, the ability to argue in favor of an unlikely conclusion is pedagogically valued because it indicates extreme mental agility. Jacobs discusses the Bavli's general interest in argumentation because of the mental agility it encourages. See Jacobs, *Talmudic Argument*, 1–17. See also Kraemer, *The Mind of the Talmud*, 99–138. Most recently, Rubenstein offers an illuminating account of the Babylonian valuation of dialectical abilities in his *Culture of the Babylonian Talmud*, 39–53.

in pedagogical, rather than strictly juridical, settings.[23] Louis Jacobs argues that certain amoraic teachers were in the habit of formulating unusual cases and posing challenging questions "as a semi-humourous intellectual exercise to sharpen the minds of their students and make them alert for the more serious business of the lesson."[24] When the Bavli's editors set about the task of capturing the intellectual mood of these lessons in literary form, they fashioned the "unsolvable problem" as a literary device.[25] Jacobs observes that cases introduced in the Bavli with the formula "R. X posed a problem" (בעי ר' פלוני) or "they posed a problem" (איבעי להו) are cases that cannot be resolved on the basis of logic alone. When authoritative sources are available to swing the pendulum in one direction or another, they are invoked. When no authoritative source is available, the case is left to stand as irresolvable and the editors declare: *tekyu*, "let is stand" (תיקו).[26] Like the riddle-like cases on which they are modeled, the literarily crafted *tekyu* cases invite students and readers to consider all sides of a case and think ever more deeply about it. In the literary presentation of *teyku* cases, two different approaches to resolving the *teyku* problem

[23] See Jacobs, *Teyku*, 290–301. Silberg discusses the Talmud's tendency toward unusual and far-fetched cases as a product of its casuistic approach to law in *Talmudic Law*, 20–21. David M. Goodblatt introduces the concept of "apprentice lawyers" among the amoraim, whose engagement with unusual cases derives from both academic and juridical interests. Goodblatt explains that for the apprentice lawyers, exposure to cases was mostly occasioned by real live cases that were presented to their teacher, which the disciples would then debate. They learned by testing and second-guessing the rulings of the master and by having him explain his rationales to them. See Goodblatt, *Rabbinic Instruction in Sasanian Babylonia* (Leiden: E. J. Brill, 1975), 272–82. See also Hayes, *Between the Babylonian and Palestinian Talmuds*, 119, and Jacobs, *Talmudic Argument*, 17.

[24] Jacobs, *Teyku*, 300. Hayes comments in a similar vein, noting that the Bavli frequently constructs cases "that expose the tension between two legal principles or that posit a case . . . that does not seem to be accounted for in the existing construction of an issue"; *Between the Babylonian and Palestinian Talmuds*, 119.

[25] In Jacobs's words: "Later editors, knowing of this material, and, possibly, taking it rather more seriously than the original propounders did used it within the framework of the *sugya* to produce the *ba`yot* as we now have them"; *Teyku*, 300.

[26] See Jacobs, *Teyku*, 293–94.

are presented, though neither is understood to be more compelling than the other. As with the borderline cases discussed in the previous section, it is far less important to solve the *teyku* problem definitively than to experiment creatively with different approaches to the problem.

The following *tekyu* case is discussed in the Bavli.

b. Shev. 22b

אמר רבא: שבועה שלא אוכל ואכל עפר – פטור.
בעי רבא: שבועה שלא אוכל עפר, בכמה?
כיוון דאמר שלא אוכל, דעתיה אכזית או דלמא כיון דלאו מידי דאכלי אינשי הוא, בכל שהוא?
תיקו.

> Rava said: [If a person said:] I swear I will not eat and then he ate dust – he is not liable.
> Rava posed a problem:[27] [If a person said:] I swear I will not eat dust, how much [must he eat in order to be liable]?
> [Perhaps] because he said "I will not eat," his intention was [to prohibit] an olive's bulk, or perhaps because [dust] is not usually eaten by people, his intention was [to prohibit] a trace amount?
> Let it stand [unresolved].

The unsolvable problem arises after consideration of a more straightforward case that is drawn from the Mishnah. M. Shev. 3:4 rules that one who swears not to eat and then consumes an inedible substance (אוכלים שאינן ראוין לאכילה) is not liable for violating the oath. Rava paraphrases this mishnah, substituting the specific example "dust" for the mishnah's more general expression concerning "inedibles"

[27] Literally, "Rava asked." Here I follow Louis Jacobs's translation and suggestion that "the Talmudic *ba`ya* is not simply a 'question,' but a formal problem, even one of a contrived nature." See Jacobs, *Teyku,* 15.

(אוכלים שאינן ראוין לאכילה). Since dust is not normally eaten, Rava concludes that an oathtaker who prohibits *eating* does not intend for his prohibition to extend to the consumption of dust, and is not liable for eating dust.

Consideration of this straightforward case, however, leads to other questions: What if the oathtaker *intended* to prohibit the eating of dust; would he then be liable? We must assume that the answer is yes. The unsolvable problem posed by Rava flows from this second case: When an oathtaker *explicitly prohibits the consumption of dust*, how much does he need to eat in order to be liable? Persuasive arguments can be made in two directions. On the one hand, one can argue that this case is no different from other cases in which the oathtaker swears not to eat. Just as in other cases he is liable for eating an olive's bulk of the prohibited food,[28] here too he should be liable only if he eats an olive's bulk of dust. On the other hand, it is also possible to argue that an oath taken not to eat dust is *wholly unlike* other oaths not to eat. Since one does not usually eat dust, the usual norms and standards regarding eating should not apply. In this case, the oathtaker will be liable for eating even a trace amount of dust. Both rationales are equally plausible. Logic alone cannot decide between them, and so the problem must stand as is, *teyku*, unresolved.[29]

Strictly speaking, Rava's unsolvable problem is not a borderline case. No one doubts that one who swears not to eat dust and then does so is liable. The ambiguity of the case, then, does not involve the basic determination that dust is an appropriate object for an oath taker not to eat. Instead, the ambiguity of the case concerns the *limits* of the oathtaker's

[28] In m. Shev. 3:1 the sages defend the position that one should be liable for eating an olive's worth of a food prohibited by oath. R. Akiba takes the opposite view and holds the oathtaker liable even if he eats only a trace amount.

[29] The editors declare *Teyku*, "let it stand." Debate exists as to who is responsible for the term *Teyku*. Was it a later editor or contemporaries of Rava? Jacobs takes the phrase to be a contribution of the latest redactorial stratum (the *stam*) of the Bavli. See Jacobs, *Teyku*, 290–301.

liability: *How much* must he eat in order to be liable? Essentially, the question is one of quantification – where should the boundary be set?[30] Though Rava's unsolvable problem is not formulated as a borderline case, it exhibits the same interest in exposing and exploring alternative approaches to a single problem that we find in the mishnaic borderline cases. Insofar as two resolutions to the question are proposed, the problem case exhibits a certain kind of ambiguity. I submit that the same intellectual habits – valuing the ability to view a matter from two different and even mutually exclusive perspectives – are cultivated by both the *teyku* problem and the borderline case.

It is interesting to note both what *is* and what *is not* resolved in this case. Though neither proposal definitively determines how much dust the oathtaker needs to consume in order to be liable, both agree that clarifying the oathtaker's original intention holds the key to the answer. The analysis focuses on this question: Did the oathtaker *intend* to prohibit an olive's bulk or a trace amount? A difficulty arises from the fact that the language of the oath – "I swear I will not eat dust" – is ambiguous concerning his intentions. Both points of view find support for their position. On the one hand, the fact that the oathtaker swears not to *eat* dust may imply his intention to view the dust as "that which is eaten," and to submit it to the usual norms and standards regarding food. On the other hand, the fact that the oath prohibits the consumption of *dust* may just as well suggest that the norms associated with eating are not operative in this case. Though determining the oathtaker's intention turns out to be impossible, recognizing the importance of the oathtaker's intention in solving the problem represents an important insight. For a student who is learning to adjudicate, this insight can valuably be applied to other related cases. I

30 See Silberg's discussion of the role of quantification in Jewish law in *Talmudic Law*, 42–54. For a more philosophical and contemplative meditation on the role of quantification in Jewish law, see Joseph B. Soloveitchik, *Halakhic Man* (Philadelphia: The Jewish Publication Society of America, 1983), 56–57, where he writes: "the fundamental method of Halakhah is quantification" (56).

would argue that the pedagogical value of Rava's unsolvable problem lies in the way it pushes readers, students, or listeners to develop a constructive approach to the problem, even though no single answer emerges as correct.

It is also interesting to note that though the Bavli represents the case as unsolvable, it also records several attempts to resolve that case (in favor of כזית).[31] The fact that the case was declared irresolvable, *teyku*, did not stop sages from engaging the problem and putting forward creative solutions. The exercise that was intended to stimulate continued engagement of the complex legal issues appears to work.[32]

Using Borderline Cases to Understand Disagreements

In the previous chapter, I noted the value of the dispute form in highlighting the ambiguity of the borderline cases. Each interlocutor offers a different legal resolution, and the disparity between them stands as a manifest sign of the ambiguity of the case. The form of argumentation, so prolific within the two Talmuds, attests to a continued interest among talmudic sages in differences of opinion.[33] The Talmuds not only record different viewpoints but also thoroughly investigate the implications of each view. They examine where they intersect, which assumptions they share, and where they are irreconcilable.[34] One method for highlighting the stakes of a disagreement

[31] See bottom of page, b. Shev. 21b–22a and b. Shev. 22b, right before the mishnah.

[32] This example seems to contradict the conclusions of Guttmann, who claims that the declaration "*Teyku*" aborted all discussion of the case in the academy. See analysis of Guttmann in Jacobs, *Teyku*, 290–92. See original discussion in Yehiel M. Guttmann, "Academic Questions in the Talmud" (Hebrew), *Devir* 2 (1923): 140–41.

[33] On the Bavli's interest in argumentation, see Kraemer, *The Mind of the Talmud*, 50–138, and Jacobs, *Talmudic Argument*.

[34] Louis Jacobs offers the following characterization of argumentation in the Bavli: "The Babylonian Talmud consists almost entirely of arguments, having as their aim the elucidation of the law, ruling, religious teaching or ethical idea. Theories are

is to formulate a borderline case. In this exercise, the Talmud takes as a given that two different points of view exist. It formulates a case that each of the interlocutors will resolve differently in order to provide a clear illustration of the differences between them. The driving question in such an exercise is *mai nafka mina* (מאי נפקה מינה) or "What goes out from it?" That is, what are the pragmatic repercussions that arise from the difference between these two known points of view? The assumption here is that every disagreement has a practical manifestation: When faced with a particular set of circumstances, the two sages who think differently will also rule differently. The challenge is to identify a set of circumstances that exposes the differences.

Mai nafka mina–type exercises perform a different function in the context of talmudic discourse than do borderline cases in mishnaic discourse. Whereas the mishnaic borderline cases provide a means for examining the influence of competing legal principles, *mai nafka mina*–type exercises clarify the nature and extent of a disagreement. In spite of these functional differences, the mishnaic exercise of formulating a borderline case and the talmudic *mai nafka mina* exercise are structurally similar. At core both are constituted by an ambiguous case that can be resolved in two distinctly different ways. I submit that the existence of *mai nafka mina*–type exercises in the two Talmuds evidences the persistence of certain analytic habits cultivated by the Mishnah. Both the mishnaic sages and their talmudic offspring found it analytically useful to formulate cases for which multiple resolutions exist.

The following discussion calls for the creative invention of a distinctive case to highlight the difference between two very similar points of view.

advanced and then contradicted. They are examined from many points of view and qualified where necessary. One argument leads to another when logic demands it. The claims of conflicting theories are investigated with great thoroughness and much subtlety. Fine distinctions abound between apparently similar concepts." See Jacobs, *Talmudic Argument*, 1.

y. Shev. 34d

שבועה שאוכל ככר זה היום, ועבר היום ואכלה–
ר' יוחנן וריש לקיש תריהון אמרין פטור. לא טעמא דאהן.
טעמ' דר' יוחנן משם שאינו ראוי לקבל התרייה.
טעמ' דריש לקיש משום שהוא בלא תעשה שאין בו מעשה.
מה מפקה מביניהון?
שרפה והשליכה לים
אין תימר משם שאינו ראוי לקבל התרייה, פטור.
ואין תימר משום שהוא בלא מעשה, הרי יש בו מעשה.

[If a person took] an oath, [saying I swear] I will eat this loaf today, and the day passed [and only then] did he eat it[35] –
R. Yohanan and Resh Lakish both agree he is not liable.
But each has a different reason.
R. Yohanan reasons [he is exempt] because he cannot receive appropriate warning.
Resh Lakish reasons [he is exempt] because it is a negative command[36] that is transgressed without a concrete action.
What is the practical difference between them [or: what pragmatic situation highlights this difference in approach]?
If he burned [the loaf] or[37] threw it into the sea:

35 The Bavli emends the text here, adding a negation of the verb so that it reads: "and he did *not* eat it." Wewers notes that such an emendation is not necessary, since he fails to fulfill the terms of the oath by eating the loaf *after* the day passes. See Gerd A. Wewers, trans., *Talmud Yerushalmi Band IV/5 Makkot – Geißelung, Shevuot – Schwüre* (Tübingen: J. C. B. Mohr (Paul Siebeck), 1983), 130, n. 148.

36 The negative command to which the text refers here is the commandment against swearing falsely. The rabbis root this prohibition in both Lev. 19:12 and Ex. 20:7. See, e.g., b. Shev. 20b: "When R. Dimi came from Palestine he said that R. Yohanan said: [If one says: 'I swear] I shall eat' or '[I swear] I shall not eat' [and he transgressses the oath], it is a false oath and its prohibition is derived from this verse: *Ye shall not swear by my name falsely* (Lev. 19:12). [If one says 'I swear] I have eaten' or "I swear I have not eaten" [and it is untrue], it is a vain oath and its prohibition is from this verse: *Thou shalt not take the name of the Lord thy God in vain* (Ex. 20:7)".

37 Following Jacob Neusner, trans., *The Talmud of the Land of Israel: A Preliminary Translation and Explanation*. Vol. 32. *Shebuot* (Chicago: University of Chicago Press, 1983), 272, n. 13, I read the *vav* disjunctively.

> If you say [above that he is exempt] because he cannot receive an appropriate warning, then he is exempt.
> If you say [above that he is exempt] because it is a negative command that is transgressed without a concrete action, behold, then this case involves a concrete action [so he is liable].

This discussion begins by examining a puzzle-like case along the lines of that presented by Haifa. The question is raised concerning an individual who swears that he will eat a given loaf on a specific day. If he fails to meet his obligation by the stated time, is he held accountable? The obvious and unreflective answer – that the oathtaker *is* liable for violating his oath – proves to be wrong. Both R. Yohanan and Resh Lakish recognize the complexity of the case and agree that *even though* the oathtaker broke his word, he is not liable. Unlike Abimai previously, R. Yohanan and Resh Lakish are learned sages and not tricked by the deceptive simplicity of the case. Both are attentive to the subtle features of the case that lead to exemption. In the end, though, each exempts the oathtaker for a different reason. R. Yohanan notes that when someone promises to eat a certain loaf *today*, it is impossible to warn him as is required by rabbinic law. Under ordinary circumstances a witness must warn an errant individual *before* he commits his act of wrongdoing. R. Yohanan notes that it is impossible to warn an individual under the described circumstances because he can always say, "I'm still planning to eat the loaf later today." As commentator Moses Margulies (Pene Moshe) explains, only at the very end of the day is it possible to give him a genuine warning that cannot be thus refuted, and by that point, of course, the day has already passed, and the warning comes too late to be of use.[38] Since there is no way to appropriately warn the wrongdoer in this case, R. Yohanan rules that he is not liable. Resh Lakish has a different reason for exempting the

[38] See Pene Moshe s.v. משם שאינו ראוי לקבל התראה. The situation is one where the witness warns him about something that might or *might not* happen. "This is considered to be a "doubtful warning" (התראת ספק) or warning about something that will only *doubtfully* occur.

errant oathtaker. He notes that the errant individual never commits a concrete act of wrongdoing. On the basis of the principle that one must do a concrete deed in order to be liable for a wrongdoing,[39] Resh Lakish reasons that the oathtaker is not liable. Though both end up with the same legal outcome, they ground their rulings in different observations about the case at hand and draw on different principles.

The second part of the discussion attempts to convey the nature of these differences more precisely. The gemara asks *mai nafka mina*,[40] or "what is the practical difference" between these two positions? It then constructs a case in which R. Yohanan exempts the oathtaker and Resh Lakish considers him liable. In this way, the stakes of their debate are clarified. The case that clarifies the difference builds on the original case.[41] In the event that an oathtaker swears to eat a particular loaf today, *and subsequently burns it or throws it into the sea*, the two sages will rule differently. R. Yohanan will exempt the errant oathtaker because it still remains impossible to give him an appropriate warning. Resh Lakish, however, will hold the oathtaker *liable* because his violation of the oath now involves a concrete act. When the oathtaker burns the loaf or throws it into the sea, he ensures that he will not be able to eat the loaf later in the day. Through these concrete acts, he violates the

39 R. Lakish's ruling seems to be based on the principle as it is appears in t. Mak. 5(4):10 (Zuckermandel, 444): "This is the general rule: Every [instance in which one transgresses by means] of a concrete act, they flog him, and every [instance in which one transgresses] without performing a concrete act, they do not flog him, except in the case of substituting one vowed animal for another (מימר) and using the name of God to curse a friend." It is interesting that y. Shev. 35a cites the same principle, but adds the oathtaker (הנשבע) to the list of exceptions. R. Lakish's position cannot be based on the Yerushalmi's version of the principle because there the oathtaker is explicitly exempted from the rule. One must conjecture that the Yerushalmi's version of the principle represents the position of R. Yohanan, since it is not important to him that the oathtaker be exempt on the basis of the fact that his wrongdoing involves no concrete act.

40 Represented as *"Mah mafkah mi-benehon?"* in the Yerushalmi's idiom.

41 Pene Moshe comments to this effect (s.v. מה מפקה מביניהון). Since the exercise seeks to construct a case that will clarify the difference between the two points of view on *this particular case*, it takes the circumstances of the case at hand as a starting point.

oath. Consequently, the basis for Resh Lakish's earlier exemption is removed, and he holds the oathtaker liable.

In this exercise, the framers of the sugya find it useful to formulate a borderline case that can plausibly be resolved in two different ways. Unlike other borderline cases discussed, the one here is not valued for its inherent ambiguity. The case is not posed in order to force students to probe more deeply into the issues lurking behind a set of circumstances. That is, the case is not posed as part of a pedagogical *inquiry*. Instead, the case is framed as an *answer* to a different kind of question. The inquiry in this sugya attempts to convey the stakes of the disagreement between R. Yohanan and Resh Lakish with greater subtlety.[42] The formulation of the borderline case helps to accomplish this. Though it is put to a different purpose than the classic borderline case, I would argue that the strategy employed in this exercise (and others like it)[43] attests to the fact that the particular habits of analysis and patterns for structuring thought were cultivated by an engagement of law in its casuistic form. Just as casuistic law is explicitly concerned with concrete formulations of cases over and against the implicit principles that

[42] Robert Goldenberg notes that the gemara is often interested in showing the systematic consistency that characterizes the rulings of different sages. See Goldenberg, "The Talmud," 150, 153–56. He writes that for the Talmud, "each man's teachings must be both internally consistent and also in some way distinguishable from every other man's" (156). Insofar as this exercise clarifies the distintiveness of each sage's approach, it also lends clarity to the systematic legal approach that implicitly underlies the ruling of each sage. For a different approach to fleshing out the differences between R. Yohanan's and Resh Lakish's positions, see b. Mak. 15b–16a. There, the significant difference between the two sages is seen to lie in their respective opinions as to whether or not "doubtful warning" (התראת ספק) functions as a legitimate warning.

[43] The *mai nafka mina* exercise is a common one for clarifying the difference between two stated opinions. In Chapter 3 of y. Shev., it is employed at least three times in addition to the present instance. On y. Shev. 34b, the exercise is used to clarify the difference between the positions of R. Akiva and the sages in m. Shev. 3:1; on y. Shev. 34d, it clarifies the difference between positions adopted by R. Yohanan and R. Lazar; and on y. Shev. 35, it clarifies the difference between positions adopted by R. Yohanan and Resh Lakish (though on a different matter than the one discussed here). See also b. Shev. 41a where the strategy is used to clarify the nature of a disagreement between R. Yose and Rav Hisda. The ubiquity of the exercise suggests that it becomes a routinized strategy for clarifying the difference of opinion between two sages.

govern them, the analysis of different opinions strives to uncover the *practical situations* in which differences occur. Disagreements remain abstract insofar as they are merely a matter of holding different *principles.* Only when faced with specific circumstances that cause one sage to rule one way and another to rule another way are the framers of the gemara satisfied that they have truly grasped the extent and nature of the differences between them.[44]

In yet another way, then, the analytic habits associated with the casuistic form, and the borderline case specifically, continued to exert an influence on the study practices of talmudic sages.

Borderline Cases in Mishnaic Exegesis

We have seen that in the gemaras, talmudic sages engaged in a number of different kinds of discussion. They engaged in discussion of topics related to, but not specifically treated in, the mishnaic text. In addition, they also engaged in extensive discussions about differing viewpoints; the nature and extent of disagreements were analyzed in great detail. One of the foremost analytic projects that engaged the talmudic sages, however, was exegesis of the mishnaic text – detailed examination of its linguistic idiosyncrasies, its structure, and its meaning. In the following section, I wish to argue that the habits of analytic thought embodied by the casuistic form of the m. Shevuot and cultivated in the talmudic discussion of related topics and disagreements *also impacted upon how talmudic sages executed the task of Mishnah exegesis.* Though it is not surprising to find that similar analytic tendencies permeated the different domains of study and discussion recorded in the Talmuds, the routine use of these study practices has special significance for the project of Mishnah exegesis. When put in the service of understanding

44 Such analysis of disagreements also assures the student that the two opinions are not in any way redundant and so emphasizes the value of recording both opinions. For a discussion of the increasing interest in reading amoraic statements as exhibiting verbal economy, see Alexander, "Study Practices That Made the Mishnah," 183–90.

the Mishnah, these analytic practices had the distinct effect of drawing attention to the very features of the text that already embodied these analytic practices. In an interesting and almost circular fashion, study of m. Shevuot encouraged its students, practitioners, and performers to submit it to the very analytic tasks encoded within its cases. Sages who were sensitized to the importance of borderline cases and their analytic utility began to read them all the more aggressively into the mishnaic text.

When applied to the task of Mishnah exegesis, the study practice of formulating borderline cases produced interesting and somewhat counterintuitive readings of m. Shevuot. Though many cases in m. Shevuot are legitimately borderline cases, the persistent application of this study practice led interpreters to read ambiguity into mishnaic cases in creative and innovative new ways.

When the Bavli wishes to read a particular mishnaic case as borderline, it follows a standard procedure. As will be recalled, borderline cases are those for which two equally plausible resolutions exist. Since the Mishnah usually presents one ruling per case, the Bavli needs to imaginatively (re)construct a second plausible ruling in order for the case to be understood as borderline. The Bavli often (though not always) signals the reconstruction of this second plausible ruling with the technical phrase *hava amina* (הוה אמינא), literally, "this is what I might have said" or concluded, had not the Mishnah told me otherwise. The presence of the *hava amina* formula indicates that the proposed ruling is plausible on theoretical grounds. But for the Mishnah's commitment to its already recorded position, the proposed ruling could just as easily have been adopted. The Bavli typically executes this interpretive strategy as part of a larger effort to justify the mishnaic text. It will be recalled that in the latter half of the talmudic period, interpreters of m. Shevuot increasingly felt the need to affirm that the text was neither redundant nor self-evident.[45] Exposing the *hava*

[45] In addition to my discussion in Chapter 2, see Hayes, *Between the Babylonian and Palestinian Talmuds,* 92–121.

amina of a mishnaic case justifies its inclusion within the text because it shows how the received text helps prevent wrong-minded legal conclusions.[46]

The major analytic task that faces the interpreter who wishes to justify the mishnaic text by reading it as a borderline case is the construction of a plausible alternative ruling. Since the Mishnah has already presented and legitimated one ruling, creativity is required to rationalize a second, different ruling.[47] One approach to this challenge is to argue by way of analogy with a similar case that has a different ruling: Since the ruling in a similar case contradicts that of the mishnah, one can easily imagine that the law in the mishnaic case might have been different. Once the gemara finds a way to present an alternative ruling as plausible, it asserts that the value of the mishnaic case lies in the fact that it rejects this perfectly reasonable conclusion.

The Bavli's interpretation of the following mishnah seeks to justify its inclusion in the text by showing that an alternative ruling is also plausible. The gemara indicates the plausibility of the alternative ruling by pointing to a seemingly analogous case that is resolved differently. The mishnah reads as follows:

[46] See discussion of *hava amina* in Hayes, *Between the Babylonian and Palestinian Talmuds,* 116 and 232, n. 42.

[47] As I remarked in n. 22 of this chapter, talking about the analytic creativity and agility required to construct a plausible ruling that contradicts the ruling already presented in the Mishnah calls to mind the stories related in b. Eruv. 13b concerning various sages (R. Meir, an anonymous student at Yavneh and Ravina) who could argue concerning the ritually pure that it was impure and/or concerning the ritually pure that it was impure. The importance ascribed by talmudic culture to the ability to construct arguments against established positions also comes through in R. Yohanan's pain at the loss of his study partner Resh Lakish. Though Eleazar b. Pedat is offered to him as a new study partner, R. Yohanan is sorely disappointed. He laments: "when I would put forward a position to Resh Lakish, he would rebuff me with twenty-four objections to my point and I would answer him with twenty-four refutations and the the matter would become clear" (b. BM 84a). Each of these sources corroborate's the sense that talmudic culture valued the mental agility that is present in the *hava amina* argument: the construction and defense of a position that contradicts a position that is already established and authoritative. See the discussion of these two texts in a simliar vein in Jacobs, *Talmudic Argument,* 6–7. See also Rubenstein, *Culture of the Babylonian Talmud,* 39–53.

m. Shev. 3:7

שבועה שלא אוכל ככר זו, שבועה שלא אוכלנה, שבועה שלא אוכלנה, ואכלה – אינו חייב אלא אחת.

> [If a person took] an oath, [saying I swear] I will not eat this loaf, I swear I will not eat it, I swear I will not eat it, and he ate it – he is liable on only one count.

This mishnah examines the case of a person who swears not to eat a certain loaf of bread and then reiterates the same intention under oath several times. Though he repeats his oath several times, he is liable for only one count of culpability.[48] The Bavli's interpretation seeks to justify the inclusion of this case in the Mishnah. In order to do so, the Bavli demonstrates the intrinsic ambiguity of the case by showing that in a comparable case, the oathtaker is liable on *two* counts. Though the Mishnah could have likewise held the oathtaker in the mishnaic case liable on two counts, it did not. The value of the text as we have it in the Mishnah, then, is that it establishes the commitments of the legal system to hold such an oathtaker liable on only one count.

b. Shev. 27b

למה לי למיתני שבועה שלא אוכל שבועה שלא אוכלנה?
הא קמ''ל:
טעמא דאמר שלא אוכל והדר אמר שלא אוכלנה, דלא מיחייב אלא חדא.
אבל אמר שלא אוכלנה והדר אמר שלא אוכל, מיחייב תרתי, כדרבא.
דאמר רבא: שבועה שלא אוכל ככר זו – כיוון שאכל ממנה כזית חייב.
שלא אוכלנה – אינו חייב עד שיאכל את כולה.

[48] See also m. Ned. 2:3, which makes a similar point: "There are vows within vows, but there are not oaths within oaths. . . . [E.g., if a person said:] I swear I will not eat, I swear I will not eat, and [then] he ate – he is only liable on one count."

> Why is it stated in the mishnah: "**[If a person said:] I swear I will not eat [this loaf], I swear I will not eat it, [he is liable on only one count = m. Shev. 3:7**]"?
> This is what it teaches [i.e., the import of the teaching is as follows]: The reason that he is only liable on one count is because he [first] said: "I swear I will not eat," and subsequently he said: "I swear I will not eat it."
> But if he had [first] said: "I swear I will not eat it" and [only] subsequently said: "I swear I will not eat," he would have been liable on two counts, in accordance with [the interpretation of] Rava.
> As Rava said: [When he says:] "I swear I will not eat this loaf" – he becomes liable upon eating an olive's bulk.
> [When he says:] "I swear I will not eat it" – he is only liable when he eats the entire [loaf].

The Bavli begins its analysis by inquiring about the purpose and value of the mishnaic case. From the Bavli's perspective, the Mishnah's conclusion that the oathtaker is only liable on one count appears to be altogether self-evident.[49] In order to justify the inclusion of this case in the Mishnah, the gemara speculates that it is equally reasonable to conclude that the oathtaker is liable on two counts. Since the Mishnah, however, has already ruled that the oathtaker is liable on one count, analytic creativity is required. The gemara skillfully constructs a comparable case in which all agree that the oathtaker is liable on two counts.

The emerging ideology concerning the scriptural character of the mishnaic text plays a large role in how the gemara constructs the

[49] Benovitz suggests that the Bavli's need to justify the inclusion of this mishnah arises from its apparent redundancy with m. Ned. 2:3. Though our sugya makes no explicit mention of m. Ned. 2:3, his suggestion is a plausible and viable one. See Benovitz, "Chapter III of Tractate Shevuot," 487.

comparable case.[50] In the mishnaic case, the oathtaker first states: "I swear I will not eat this loaf." When he reaffirms the same intention under oath a second time, he uses the pronoun "it" to refer to the loaf: "I swear I will not eat *it*." For most readers, the substitution of pronoun ("it") for noun ("loaf") is routine and unremarkable. The gemara, however, attributes great significance to these fine details of language. Drawing on an early interpretive tradition by Rava, the gemara concludes that the two terms are legally significant in different ways.[51] Whereas the explicit expression ("I swear I will not eat this loaf") renders the oathtaker liable upon eating an olive's bulk, the implicit reference to the loaf ("I swear I will not eat *it*") renders the oathtaker liable only upon eating the *whole* loaf. The relationship between noun and pronoun is transformed. No longer does the pronoun ("it") function as a simple allusion to the antecedent noun ("loaf").[52] Instead, each usage is understood to have distinct legal consequences.

In addition to attributing significance to the fine details of language, the gemara also attaches importance to the *order* in which the clauses are arranged. In the mishnah, the oathtaker *first* states his intention

[50] On the emerging ideology concerning the scriptural character of the mishnaic text, see Chapter 2 in this book and Christine Hayes, *Between the Babylonian and Palestinian Talmuds,* 92–121.

[51] Benovitz suggests that Rava's statement had a different meaning in its original context than is implied by the Bavli's manipulation of the tradition. He convincingly argues that Rava's initial intent was to distinguish between the simple oath "I swear I will not eat this loaf," for which one is liable upon eating an olive's worth, and a clarifying oath (שבועה מתפרשת) appended onto a simple oath "I swear I will not eat this loaf, I swear I will not eat it," for which one is liable only upon eating the entire loaf. As Benovitz understands the matter, Rava himself was not responsible for the counterintuitive reading in which the pronoun is not dependent on the antecedent noun for its meaning. See Benovitz, "Chapter III of Tractate Shevuot," 482–87. For other examples of early interpretative traditions that are understood differently by the editors of the Bavli than by the early amoraic sages who pronounced them, see Alexander, "Study Practices That Made the Mishnah," 132–91.

[52] This fact poses a problem for post-talmudic commentators. See Benovitz, "Chapter III of Tractate Shevuot," 483 and 736, n. 7.

"not to eat the loaf" and *then* reiterates the intention "not to eat *it*." In accordance with grammatical norms, the noun precedes the pronoun. The Bavli's use of Rava's interpretive tradition, however, undoes the dependence of the pronoun on the antecdent noun. In the Bavli's understanding of Rava's view, the pronoun signals the oathtaker's intent to be liable only when he eats the whole loaf. Theoretically, then, the clause with the noun need not precede the clause with the pronoun. Since the two formulations communicate different intentions, the order in which they are arranged has legal consequences. If the more severe restriction ("I swear I won't eat even an olive's bulk") is stated first, then the second oath is a legally meaningless repetition of the first. If, however, the more lenient restriction ("I swear I won't eat the whole loaf") is stated first, then the second oath does not overlap with the first.[53] In this event, the oathtaker is liable for *each of the two oaths*. When the gemara wishes to construct a comparable case for which the oathtaker is liable on two counts, it does so by manipulating the order of the clauses. If the oath with the pronoun ("I swear I will not eat *it*") is stated first, then the oathtaker is liable on two counts. This case is the comparable one for which an alternate ruling exists. Though one might be tempted to understand the mishnaic case in similar terms, the force of the mishnaic ruling is to preclude this faulty reasoning. For the Bavli, the mishnaic case is needed to prevent the compelling, but ultimately inappropriate, analogy between the two cases.

The resulting interpretation attributes much significance to the fine details of language and word order. Elsewhere I have noted how the emerging ideology concerning the text's scriptural quality affected how the materials were manipulated and interpreted. In this context, however, I wish to highlight the analytic moves served by the detailed

53 The same principle appears to be functioning here as in the second "test" case of Haifa. The oathtaker is liable for reiterations of the same prohibition only when the first oath prohibits *less* than the second oath. See y. Shev. 34d and discussion earlier in this chapter.

textual observations. When the gemara wishes to justify the text of m. Shev. 3:7, it does so by constructing it as a borderline case.[54] The significance of the mishnaic ruling emerges precisely because a rationale exists for resolving a comparable case otherwise. As in the mishnaic case, the comparable case has the oathtaker swear twice, prohibiting both "the loaf" and "it." Since the comparable case contains the same elements as the mishnaic case, it is reasonable to conclude that the two cases should be resolved in the same manner. Constructing a *comparable* case with a *different* ruling, then, indicates an ambiguity inherent within the mishnaic case. The analytic genius of the gemara's interpretation consists in its construction of a plausible basis for ruling against the Mishnah.[55]

Having noted how the Bavli's use of an inherited analytic practice contributes to its exegetical manipulations, I wish to consider how the current description of the Bavli's exegetical work differs from one that is more closely associated with the theory of textual corruption. As will be recalled from the brief discussion at the beginning of this chapter, the dominant paradigm of scholarship argues that oral transmission impacts the Bavli's interpretation of Mishnah insofar as various different sources get corrupted in the course of transmission. According to this scholarly model, interpretive traditions that originally illuminated the mishnaic text with great perspicuity often became corrupt in the course of transmission. Though corruption had occurred, either to the interpretive sources or even sometimes to the mishnaic text itself, the received sources remained authoritative. As a result, corrupt sources were made to relate to each other in a forced manner that did not reflect the originally intended meanings. Although the compilers

[54] As discussed in the previous chapter, Raymond Westbrook makes an observation that echoes the Bavli's intuition that if a case is borderline, the law has been expressed in an economical and efficient manner. He notes that one advantage of the borderline case is its economical expression. He writes that casuistic codes have a preference for borderline cases "since the law in the ordinary case could be learned from it by implication." See Westbrook, *Biblical and Cuneiform Law*, 4.

[55] Again, I am compelled to highlight the kinship between this practice and the rabbinic love of argument. See the discussion of sources in nn. 22 and 47 of this chapter.

of the Bavli working with these inherited sources might have liked to explain the mishnaic text in a straightforward and literal-minded manner, the authoritative sources before them simply did not permit it. The result was what David Weiss Halivni calls "forced" interpretations (פירושים דחוקים) of the mishnaic text.[56]

Moshe Benovitz draws on the theory of textual corruption and offers one such analysis of the Bavli's interpretation of m. Shev. 3:7 that we have just reviewed. Benovitz describes the Bavli's interpretation as "puzzling" and "forced."[57] Notably, he is puzzled by the Bavli's decision to undo the relationship between noun and pronoun, and read the oath "I swear I will not eat it" as an independent oath. In order to account for the strange turn of events, Benovitz reconstructs the transmissional journey of m. Shev. 3:7 and the interpretive tradition of Rava, attempting to recover the "original" unadulterated meaning of his interpretive gloss. He argues (convincingly, I believe) that when Rava originally formulated his interpretive gloss on the mishnah, he did not intend to disengage the pronoun from the noun. Apparently, Rava understood his statement differently than did the later editors of the Bavli's sugya. According to Benovitz, Rava originally meant to say something like this:

> If the oathtaker takes a single oath not to eat a certain loaf, then he is liable upon eating an olive's bulk. If, however, he adds an addendum to the initial oath, stating his intention not to eat *it* also, then he is only liable upon eating the entire loaf.[58]

56 See Halivni, *Seder Nashim,* 7–19, esp. 10–13.

57 See Benovitz, "Chapter III of Tractate Shevuot," 483: אולם פירוש זה לדברי רבא ומהלך הסוגייה תמוהים. See also p. 485, where he adopts Halivni's descriptive term and speaks of a פירוש דחוק. In adopting Halivni's vocabulary of "forced interpretations" and attempting to explain their genesis, Benowitz would seem to be accepting the challenge that Halivni puts forward in his writings when he states that the greatest challenge facing rabbinic scholars today is accounting for the "forced" interpretations. See Halivni, *Seder Nashim,* 13. Here, Benovitz tries to understand from whence comes this forced interpretation.

58 Benovitz, "Chapter III of Tractate Shevuot," 482–87.

According to this understanding, the second oath with the pronoun *functions not as an independent prohibition but as an addendum to the original oath.* In this reconstruction, the pronoun will *always* follow the antecedent noun, and so the possibility that the Bavli raises – that the oath with the pronoun would *precede* the oath with the antecedent noun – could never occur.

Benovitz subsequently inquires "why the editors of the sugya took Rava's words out of their original context and constructed such a forced interpretation" (485), and he uses a version of the theory of textual corruption to account for what appears to him as the Bavli's odd disregard for the plain-sense meaning of the mishnah. He explains that by the time Rava's tradition reached the editors of the sugya, the concept that an oath can serve as an addendum to an earlier oath was a foreign one. In other words, an important principle, necessary for a proper understanding of the inherited sources had been lost in transmission.[59] Though the editors of the sugya had no access to this illuminating principle, they still had to make sense of their inherited sources. In Benovitz's view, the Bavli's suggestion that the pronoun functions independently of the noun was a good-faith attempt to make sense of a cryptic and difficult tradition. His reconstruction of the original meaning of Rava's statement is creative and insightful. What his analysis fails to account for, however, is why the original understanding of the tradition was lost and why the editors of the sugya compensated for the loss in the manner that they did. The theory of textual corruption simply fails to take into account how the intellectual climate into which the sources were received affected how they were handled and manipulated.

The loss of certain traditional ways of understanding a source was only one result of rabbinic practices of transmission. Another equally important effect involved the perpetuation of a prevailing set of study

[59] See also David Weiss Halivni, who likewise accounts for the presence of forced interpretations with a theory of textual corruption. He argues that even though the sages had a genuine sensitivity to the literal meaning of their sources, they had no choice but to abandon literal interpretations when the received sources did not preserve their original form and meaning. See Halivni, *Seder Nashim,* 7–19, esp. 10–13.

practices and analytic habits. The inherited strategy of formulating borderline cases shaped the analytic approach pursued by the framers of the sugya. Their interpretive work is marked by a deep commitment to probing the ambiguity of the mishnaic case. The odd reading that divorces the pronoun from the antecedent noun results from the ideological commitment to reading every word of the mishnaic text as scripturally significant and from the analytic habit that juxtaposed the mishnaic case to an analogous one with different legal consequences. The advantage of the proposed analysis is that it explains the interpretive choices that *were made*, rather than only illuminating the difficulties that faced interpreters.

Although m. Shev. 3:7 is already a borderline case, the counterintuitivity of the Bavli's interpretation comes from the fact that the Bavli identifies a *new source of ambiguity* in the mishnah. In its tannaitic context, m. Shev. 3:7 expresses the principle that repeating an oath does not make the oathtaker doubly liable.[60] In the tannaitic setting, the ambiguity of the borderline case lies in the question of whether or not repetitions of the same oath result in multiple counts of liability. For the Bavli, the ambiguity of the case concerns a different, more subtle principle.[61] As the Bavli understands the mishnah, it is significant because it conveys the principle that repeated oaths take effect only when the first prohibition is more lenient than the

60 A similar point is made in parallels in t. Shev. 2:1–2 and m. Ned. 2:3. Even though the text of the three different formulations differs in minor ways, I would argue that the variants are a function of different degrees of ornamentation. Building on the argument in Chapter 1, I attribute significance to the fact that the parallels share an underlying structural framework, a fixed phrase, and an underlying concept. When a fluid conception of the traditions of m. Shevuot prevailed, the different versions would have been understood as different performative versions of the same tradition.

61 The fact that the Bavli is not satisfied with reading the point of the mishnaic ruling in a straightforward manner (according to a so-called literal interpretation) speaks to the success of exercises like the one executed by Haifa. The riddle-like cases that he formulated pushed his brother to attend to less obvious details of the case. This interpretation of the mishnaic case by the Bavli attests to the ultimate success of the pedagogical program. Here, the interpreter points to the relevance of a principle that is not at all immediately obvious. Haifa would be pleased.

later prohibitions.[62] I would argue that the Bavli's interpretation feels counterintuitive because the borderline case is read to be borderline in a new way. On the one hand, the reader senses that it is appropriate to read ambiguity into the mishnaic case as if it were a borderline case. This analytic move is justified by the fact that m. Shev. 3:7 is itself a borderline case and engagement with borderline cases is generally encouraged within the casuistic framework of the Mishnah. On the other hand, the ambiguity that the Bavli attributes to the case differs from the ambiguity that interested tannaitic framers of the case. A jarring sense of counterintuitivity arises for the reader because of the cognitive dissonance between these two positions.

An Extended Exercise in Probing Mishnaic Ambiguity

In this final section, I wish to discuss a textual example in which the cultivated practice of probing ambiguity influences the Bavli's interpretation of the Mishnah on multiple levels. The mishnah that is the subject of the Bavli's interpretation contains a debate between R. Akiba and the sages. The tannaitic dispute attests to an inherent ambiguity within the case. The Bavli's discussion, however, attempts to clarify the exact nature of the case's ambiguity. Much like the *mai nafka mina* exercises, the Bavli's strategy for articulating the case's ambiguity involves defining the nature and extent of the disagreement. Unlike the *mai nafka mina* exercises discussed earlier, however, two different but equally plausible ways to understand the disagreement are proposed. To the extent that two different interpretations of the dispute are explored, the exercise is structurally similiar to a *teyku* problem in which two equally plausible resolutions are proposed. Furthermore, one of the interpretations of the dispute involves justifying the mishnaic case by reading it as borderline. In each of these different ways, the transmitted practice of formulating borderline cases as a means of

[62] This is also the principle that Haifa invokes in the second half of his test.

exploring legal ambiguity influences the manner in which the Bavli executes its interpretation.

The Bavli's discussion aims to clarify the following disagreement between R. Akiba and the sages:

m. Shev. 3:1

שבועה שלא אוכל ואכל כל שהוא – חייב, דברי ר' עקיבא.
אמרו לו לר' עקיבא: היכן מצינו באוכל כל שהוא חייב, שזה חייב?
אמר להם ר' עקיבא: וכי היכן מצינו במדבר ומביא קרבן, שזה מדבר ומביא קרבן?

> [If a person took] an oath, [saying I swear] I will not eat, and [then] he ate a trace amount – he is liable. These are the words of R. Akiba.
> The sages said to R. Akiba: Where else have we found a case in which a person who eats a trace amount is liable, such that this one should be liable?
> R. Akiba said to them: Where else have we found a case in which a person [merely] speaks and then must bring an offering, such that this one [who merely] speaks should bring an offering?

The debate in this mishnah concerns an individual who transgresses his oath by eating only a minimal amount. Under most circumstances, one must consume an olive's bulk of food in order for the act to have legal significance.[63] Rejecting the usual standards, R. Akiba declares the oathtaker liable, even when he consumes less than an olive's bulk. The sages are perplexed by R. Akiba's ruling. They point out that Jewish law has no precedent for regarding the consumption of less than an olive's bulk as a legally significant act. Though the mishnah does not say so explicitly, the reader must assume that the sages render the oathtaker

[63] For example, one is liable for eating on the Day of Atonement at the point at which one eats an olive's bulk. Likewise, the mitzvah of "eating" matzah is fulfilled only when one has consumed an olive's bulk.

liable only upon eating an olive's bulk. R. Akiba responds to the sages' challenge by noting that oaths are a unique legal phenomenon. An oathtaker is bound on the basis of his own speech. R. Akiba reminds the sages that in no other area of law does the mere act of speech produce legal culpability. As he reasons, the difference between oaths and other areas of law is so fundamental that the standards operative in other areas of law concerning eating simply do not apply to oaths.[64]

The Bavli frames its discussion of this mishnah as an inquiry concerning the nature and the extent of the disagreement. Does R. Akiba always think that eating a trace amount is legally significant, or is his position on the legal significance of eating a trace amount limited to the matter of oaths?

b. Shev. 21b

איבעיא להו: ר''ע, בכל התורה כר''ש ס''ל, דמחייב במשהו?
דתניא: ר''ש אומר:
כל שהוא למכות, ולא אמרו כזית אלא לענין קרבן.

> The [sages] raised a problem:[65] In all [other] matters of Torah [law] does R. Akiba hold like R. Shimon who imposes liability for [eating] a trace amount?

64 Benovitz reconstructs Akiba's reasoning in the following manner. Since all other obligations are established at Sinai, a single, consistent set of norms regulates them. By way of contrast, the obligation incurred by an oath is independently determined by the oathtaker, and so the norms associated with other Sinaitic laws are irrelevant. What is noteworthy is that the oathtaker states and defines the prohibition himself. It does not come from an outside source. Since the source of the obligation is his own invocation, it is subject to his own standards. According to Benovitz, R. Akiba assumes that most people consider the consumption of even a trace amount to be eating. See Benovitz, "Chapter III of Tractate Shevuot," 156.

65 Translation of the phrase איבעיא להו follows Jacobs, *Teyku*, 13.

> As it is taught: R. Shimon says:
> A trace amount [imposes liability] for lashes. The [sages] stated the minimum amount of an olive's bulk [to impose liability] only for sacrifices.

The Bavli's discussion opens with an open-ended question. Noting that R. Akiba in this mishnah rules in accordance with R. Shimon (who elsewhere considers eating a trace amount legally significant),[66] the Bavli wonders whether or not Akiba's sympathies consistently lie with R. Shimon. In other words, the Bavli wants to know if the disagreement between the sages and R. Akiba is a global or a local one. Do they usually disagree regarding the legal significance of consuming a trace amount of food? Or do they usually agree that eating a trace amount is not legally significant, save in this one exceptional instance? The academic nature of the inquiry is highlighted by the fact that the phrase that introduces the discussion ("the sages raised a problem," איבעיא להו) also frequently introduces *teyku* problems.[67] As with *teyku* problems, the perplexing nature of the question will be revealed by showing that two different resolutions are theoretically possible. The key difference between the discussion that follows and the discussion of a *teyku* problem is the fact that authoritative tannaitic sources are later invoked to resolve the question definitively.[68] In the final analysis, the Bavli concludes that R. Akiba usually agrees with the sages; only the exceptional nature of oaths leads him to rule differently in this case.

Before presenting any evidence in favor of one position or the other, however, the Bavli establishes the *logical viability of both positions.*

66 See m. Mak. 3:2, which states: "How much must an individual eat in order to be liable for eating untithed produce? R. Shimon says: a trace amount; the sages say: an olive's worth" (כמה יאכל מן הטבל ויהא חייב? רבי שמעון אומר: כל שהוא, וחכמים אומרים: כזית).

67 According to Jacobs, the *ba'aya* type problem can either be framed anonymously or atrributed to a particular sage. See Jacobs, *Teyku,* 13.

68 According to Jacobs, there is no substantive difference in nature between *teyku* problems and other *ba'aya* type problems, save the fact that authoritative sources are presented to resolve the latter, whereas no sources are available to resolve the former. See Jacobs, *Teyku,* 13–14, 290.

b. Shev. 21b

ובדין הוא דבעי איפלוגי בעלמא,
והאי דקא מיפלגי הכא להודיעך כוחן דרבנן,
דאף ע"ג דאיכא למימר הואיל ומפרש חייב, סתם נמי חייב, קא משמע לן דפטרי.
או דלמא בעלמא כרבנן סבירא ליה,
והכא היינו טעמא הואיל ומפרש חייב, סתם נמי חייב.

A. It stands to reason that they always disagree, and the reason the disagreement is repeated here is to convey the force of the sages' position:
Even though [the sages] could have used the following analogy to conclude [that the oathtaker is liable],
Since one who explicitly prohibits [a trace amount] is liable [for eating a trace amount], the one who makes a general prohibition [against eating] should also be liable [for eating a trace amount] – they nonetheless exempt him.
B. Or alternatively, perhaps [R. Akiba] always holds like the sages, and the reason [he disagrees here that consumption of a trace amount is legally binding is because of the following analogy]: Since one who explicitly prohibits a [trace amount] is liable [for eating a trace amount], the one who makes a general prohibition [against eating] should also be liable [for eating a trace amount].

In this complicated logical exercise, both positions are shown to be theoretically possible. A offers a rationale for understanding the tannaitic disagreement in global terms, and B indicates it is just as reasonable to assume that the two parties disagree only on the matter of oaths. Introducing the first interpretation of the debate, the Bavli states, "it is *reasonable*" (ובדין הוא) to assume that the two parties always disagree. This expression is conventionally used to introduce a position that, though logically sound, will eventually be rejected.[69] Indeed, in

[69] See Yitzhak Frank, *The Practical Talmud Dictionary* (Jerusalem: Ariel United Israel Institutes, 1992), 71.

the continuation of its discussion, the Bavli does ultimately arrive at the *opposite* conclusion (that they usually agree). The Bavli's rhetorical promotion of the "wrong" position first is especially significant when one considers the fact that a plain-sense reading of the mishnah also supports the position that the two parties usually agree. As Benovitz notes, the sages' argument takes for granted that Akiba concedes in other areas of law that eating has legal significance only when an olive's bulk is consumed. Likewise, Akiba's response to the sages, which points out the distinction of oaths from other areas of law, argues that oaths are exceptional within the law.[70] If literary evidence in the mishnah itself and the evidence of other sources ultimately support one view, why does the Bavli lead with the opposing view?

I would argue that the Bavli here presents the less obvious interpretation of the mishnah first as part of an intellectual exercise. As with the *teyku* problem discussed earlier, this exercise hones a set of analytical skills. By articulating, and even defending, a counterintuitive position, the Bavli demonstrates competence in probing ambiguity.[71] The fact that the Bavli leads with what later turns out to be the "wrong" answer is pedagogically significant. Certain similarities with Haifa's test of

70 See Benovitz, "Chapter III of Tractate Shevuot," 150.

71 It is worth noting that Benovitz argues that the Yerushalmi arrives at the opposite conclusion. As he understands the Yerushalmi, it concludes that the disagreement is a global one. If that is the case, then the ambiguity that the Bavli is probing here is genuine, insofar as other ancient readers reached the opposite conclusion in good faith. See Benovitz, "Chapter III of Tractate Shevuot," 150–51, 154–55. I, however, am not fully convinced by Benovitz's argument that the Yerushalmi reaches the opposite conclusion from the Bavli. The Yerushalmi's discussion of the debate never explicitly draws a connection between Akiba's position in the matter of oaths and other laws concerning eating. All examples that are discussed are drawn from the domain of oaths. This fact leads me to believe that the conclusions reached there concern the differences between Akiba and sages in the domain of oaths alone. Thus, when the phrase "eating a trace amount is considered eating" (כל שהוא אכילה) is attributed to Akiba's position, I would argue that the generalization is relevant to the domain of oaths alone. See y. Shev. 34b. It is important to be open to reading the Yerushalmi without superimposing the intellectual framework or agenda of the Bavli. While Benovitz generally does a good job of reading early sources in their own right, I think that in this case, by following traditional commentators he has fallen into an old trap.

brother Abimai come to mind. The reader will recall that Haifa's test was deceptive to a certain extent. Though certain approaches to the problem are more obvious, they are ultimately rejected in favor of more sophisticated and subtle approaches. Part of the challenge that Abimai faces is learning to defer his first impressions of the problem. A similar challenge may face the intended student of the Bavli here. When the Bavli leads with what ultimately turns out to be an unsatisfying answer, it may also be testing its students. The challenge for readers of the argument is likewise to learn to defer the first impressions of logic, and instead probe the problem deeply.[72]

Turning back to the specific argumentational strategies employed, how does the Bavli defend the first position? On what basis does the Bavli claim that it is reasonable to assume that R. Akiba and the sages usually disagree? The Bavli's argument is rooted in and dependent upon the emerging ideology concerning the scriptural character of the mishnaic text. From the Bavli's perspective, an acceptable position is one that shows the mishnaic text to be neither self-evident nor redundant, but necessary.[73] The assumption that the disagreement between the two parties is universal and global makes it *seem as if* m. Shev. 3:1 is redundant and self-evident. If the two parties always disagree on the matter of the legal significance of eating a trace amount,

[72] It may be helpful to view the strategic positioning of the incorrect answer first as a kind of "re-oralization" of the very practices that lie behind the text. In the previous chapter, I noted in n. 6 that Fraade offers a useful metaphor for understanding the process of re-oralization of study practices that lie behind the composition of m. Shevuot. He speaks of an oral circulatory process that involves the interfacing of literary texts in an oral circulatory system. See Fraade, *From Tradition to Commentary*, 19, and "Literary Composition and Oral Performance," 35–36, 46. As I understand the metaphor, Fraade proposes that certain oral rhetorical practices (in this case, study practices of formulating borderline cases to explore legal ambiguities) lie behind literary texts (in this case, the Bavli), but are also perpetuated by the text (in this case, projected students of the sugya). Here I see myself answering Fraade's call, at the end of his book, to explore the pedagogical interfacing of oral and literary media in talmudic literature, after he so fruitfully explored how it works in midrashic literature. See Fraade, *From Tradition to Commentary*, 160.

[73] See Hayes, *Between the Babylonian and Palestinian Talmuds*, 92–121, and discussion in Chapter 2 of this book.

why restate the disagreement as it pertains to the matter of oaths specifically? Insofar as the Bavli can show that it is necessary to restate the disagreement in this particular case, it establishes both the merit of the mishnaic text and the viability of the position that the two parties usually disagree.

In order to account for the apparent redundancy, the Bavli explains that even though the two parties take the same positions elsewhere, their positions here are not inevitable. The Bavli focuses on the sages' position specifically. Here and elsewhere, the sages rule that one must eat a full olive's bulk in order for the act to have legal significance. Their position is worthy of restatement, however, if there is a compelling reason to think that they might have ruled *otherwise* in the case of oaths. Though "one might have thought" (איכא למימר) that the sages agreed with R. Akiba in the specific case of oaths, they do not. Restating the disagreement is worthwhile because it shows the force of their position. Under *absolutely no circumstances* do the sages agree with Akiba, even when there is a compelling basis for doing so.

Given the fact that the sages consistently rule that consuming an olive's bulk is necessary for the act to have legal significance, it is difficult to imagine why they would hold differently in the case of oaths. As in the previous example discussed, the *ḥava amina* position ("what I might have thought") is constructed by drawing an analogy with a comparable case. The comparable case concerns one who *explicitly prohibits a trace amount*. All agree that one who says "I swear I will not eat even a trace amount" is liable when he eats a trace amount.[74] The Bavli then argues by way of analogy. Since the one who *explicitly prohibits a trace amount* is liable for eating a trace amount, it is reasonable to conclude that one who makes a general prohibition ("I swear I will not eat") should also

[74] See y. Shev. 34b: "If we are talking about a person who says, 'I swear I will not eat a trace amount,' even the sages acknowledge [the worthiness of Akiba's position and rule that one who eats a trace amount is liable]." See also b. Shev. 22a: "The dispute concerns generally stated oaths, but when [the oathtaker] explicitly [prohibits a trace amount], all agree he is liable for [eating] a trace amount" (אמר רבא: מחלוקת בסתם, אבל במפרש דברי הכל בכל שהוא).

be liable for eating a trace amount. The merit of the analogy may be debated on its own terms,[75] but functionally it opens up a new way of thinking about the sages' position. Instead of seeing their rejection of the significance of eating a trace amount of food in violation of an oath as inevitable, their position on the matter of oaths appears deliberate, intentional, and worthy of inclusion in the Mishnah. As we found in the previous example, the Bavli here justifies the mishnaic text by reading it as borderline. Even though the sages had a plausible basis for agreeing with R. Akiba that eating a trace amount is legally significant in the case of oaths, they did not adopt that position. While the overarching framework of the discussion stresses the ambiguous nature of the disagreement, this particular move stresses the ambiguous nature of the question facing the sages.[76]

Having vigorously defended the view that the disagreement is global, the Bavli next shows that it is equally reasonable to reach the opposite conclusion. The next part of the argument offers a rationale for assuming that the two parties agree in all other matters and disagree only as regards oaths.

b. Shev. 21b

או דלמא בעלמא כרבנן סבירא ליה,
והכא היינו טעמא הואיל ומפרש חייב, סתם נמי חייב.

> Or alternatively, perhaps [R. Akiba] always holds like the sages, and the reason [he disagrees] here [that consumption of a trace amount is legally binding is because of the following analogy]:

75 See discussion in Benovitz, "Chapter III of Tractate Shevuot," 156–57, 645, n. 25.

76 With so many sources of ambiguity being stressed simultaneously, it is not surprising that a student of the Bavli's interpretation might find it to be disorienting or counter-intuitive. The challenge for such students is to understand each proposal on its own terms, while still allowing for the other possibilitities.

> Since one who explicitly prohibits [a trace amount] is liable [for eating a trace amount], the one who makes a general prohibition [against eating] should also be liable [for eating a trace amount].

Here, the Bavli defends the position that elsewhere R. Akiba agrees with the sages. In this way of interpreting the disagreement, it is limited to the domain of oaths. The argument seeks to explain why R. Akiba abandons his usual stance requiring that an olive's bulk of food be consumed in order for the act to be legally significant. If in all other cases R. Akiba agrees with the sages, why does he disagree in the case of oaths? The Bavli's reconstruction of Akiba's reasoning draws on the analogy that figures prominently in the argument just prior: Since explicitly prohibiting a trace amount makes one liable for eating a trace amount, one may argue by way of analogy that even generally stated oaths produce liability for eating a trace amount (הואיל ומפרש חייב, סתם נמי חייב). The Bavli speculates that the logic of this analogy could be the reason that Akiba parts ways with his colleagues.

Several features of the argument in favor of the second position are noteworthy. First, in attempting to establish the plausibility of this position, the Bavli does not rely on the literary evidence of the mishnah that readily supports its position. Instead, the Bavli argues on the basis of logical premises: If the two parties agree in all other instances, then there must be a compelling reason for Akiba to part ways. The Bavli establishes the *viability* of the position on logical grounds alone. By way of contrast, the *merits* of the case are still to be determined on the basis of literary evidence, which is examined later in the sugya. Second, it is also notable that the *same* analogy is artfully manipulated to support two *diametrically opposed* positions. It is possible that the analogy circulated as an independent source before being incorporated into this argument.[77] If this is so, then

[77] I have not been able to confirm this by source-critical means. The phrase is attested only here and later in the same sugya. Benovitz proposes that the formulation of the analogy is drawn from Rava's language on b. Shev. 22a.

the Bavli artfully manipulates a single preexisting source to serve *two* mutually exclusive ends. Apparently, having certain sources at one's disposal does not make any single conclusion inevitable. At its core, this exercise demonstrates (and promotes among its readers) analytic versatility. By manipulating both logical premises and a single analogy in different ways, the Bavli argues two completely different positions. The intellectual habit of probing ambiguity cultivated throughout the talmudic period led the Bavli to read ambiguity quite actively into the mishnaic text at hand. While it is true that the mishnaic dispute testifies to an ambiguity about the matter in a tannaitic context, talmudic readers trained to probe ambiguity with high degrees of sophistication and subtlety perceived within m. Shev. 3:1 an even more intense degree of ambiguity.

Conclusion

The mishnaic practice of exploring legal ambiguities through the device of a borderline case remained an influential study practice well beyond the tannaitic period. Throughout the talmudic period, sages recreated the structure of the borderline case as a means of exploring legal ambiguities. Talmudic sages formulated problem cases like that of Abimai in order to promote sophisticated analytic thinking. As with *teyku* problems, one measure of a case's ambiguity came to be the existence of two equally plausible resolutions. Proposing two different resolutions was a common strategy for exploring legal ambiguities. Even when the different resolutions were not equally appealing, both were argued for vigorously as a means of instilling intellectual versatility. Since the presence of a dispute was a mark of ambiguity, disputes were analyzed in great detail. Determining the exact nature and extent of a disagreement was yet another means of probing legal ambiguities. The proliferation of these practices *generally* had a distinctive influence *on how the work of mishnaic interpretation was conducted, in specific.* When put in the service of mishnaic exegesis, these practices had the effect of calling attention to the very features of mishnaic discourse that are rooted in these practices. The aggressive application of these practices to the mishnaic text often resulted in the perception of new elements of ambiguity in the mishnaic text. As part of the ambient intellectual environment, these practices nurtured a spirit of intense and vigorous intellectual inquiry, a spirit that often led to emphatic readings of ambiguity within the mishnaic text.

Rabbinic practices of transmission, then, provided not only for the conveyance of textual materials, but equally as important, for the cultivation of particular intellectual habits. As much as anything else, the prevalence of these intellectual habits impacted how the text of m. Shevuot was received, understood, and interpreted by the talmudic sages.

Conclusion

This book has explored what is at stake and what is gained when we use an oral conceptual lens to frame the encounter with and interpretation of the literary artifacts of the Mishnah. The primary insights that we have drawn from research in the field of orality studies concern 1) the fact that orally transmitted texts should not be reflexively conceptualized as fixed and discrete textual entities, and 2) the fact that those who pass on texts play an active role in constructing what they transmit. These insights have allowed us to reimagine ancient processes of transmitting mishnaic texts in profound new ways.

The work of Chapter 1 offered us new ways to think about continuity among performative renditions of mishnaic materials that are not grounded in the presence of identical linear sequences of words. Quite importantly, different performative versions of mishnaic tradition also have structural frameworks, fixed phrases, and underlying conceptual concerns in common. These common elements, which I called compositional building blocks, allowed for mishnaic traditions to be reproduced with a high degree of similitude without requiring that the texts in question be fixed. The greater the number of compositional building blocks in common, the greater the correspondence between them. These findings were important because they helped us see that though the Mishnah was orally transmitted, it was not necessarily fixed, or equally as important, viewed as fixed, from the moment of its promulgation. The recognition that the Mishnah could have been conceptualized as fluid in the earliest stages of its transmission is valuable because it points out the contrast between early stages of transmission and later stages, when it certainly was viewed as fixed.

In Chapter 2, we observed incremental shifts that took place over a fairly lengthy period of time in which the mishnaic text *did* come to be viewed as fixed, and also authoritative. We observed how talmudic sages who studied and transmitted mishnaic texts ascribed importance to what they *perceived* to be editorial intentions. Thus, though mishnaic authority has often been seen to be a function of its literary form, which itself is seen to be a product of the editor who crafted a final and definitive version of the text, we came to recognize that the authority of mishnaic texts is largely a product of the repeated attentions of a devoted reading community. Those who lovingly studied mishnaic traditions as a centerpiece of the early rabbinic curriculum did not inherit a fixed and authoritative text; *they made it into one.* Unlike publication today, where the text achieves a final form before it is distributed among a reading audience, the publication of the Mishnah seems to have joined both those who formulated the traditions and those who repeated them in a collaborative process of making the Mishnah what it became.

In Chapter 3, we returned to the earliest stages of the Mishnah's transmission and exposed the analytic activities that would have been central to the construction of the Mishnah's legal cases. Recognizing that the literary artifacts before us today were not conceptualized as fixed in the earliest stages of transmission led us to the valuable insight that the very modes of analysis that would have been required for composition also would have been perpetuated through performance of Mishnah. Although it has often been acknowledged among scholars of oral transmission that the texts before us today represent a synopsis of material that was already performed, it is less often recognized that the texts before us today *also* served as a springboard for *future* performative events. A focus on the performative effect of mishnaic texts exposed the possibility that alongside the verbal content, study practices or ways of thinking about the texts were also transmitted.

We tested this hypothesis in Chapter 4, where we documented the persistence of one of the analytic modes discussed in Chapter 3, among later students and handlers of the Mishnah. We noted that like their tannaitic predecessors, talmudic sages also used the literary construct of borderline cases to explore legal ambiguities. The value of this exercise lay in exposing the continuity between analytic practices in early and later rabbinic study culture. Whereas many scholars have previously read the literary forms of the Mishnah and the Talmuds as evidence for profound intellectual discontinuities between the two genres, attention to the oral performative life embodied and perpetuated by these texts allowed us to perceive the commonalities between them.

Recognizing that transmission of mishnaic tradition entailed *both* the conveyance of verbal content *and* perpetuation of a set of analytic practices through which to view the text also offered new insight into how some of the Bavli's counterintuitive interpretations of the Mishnah were produced. Rather than seeing the role of oral transmission in terms of breakdowns and losses that required corrupt sources and interpretations to be reconciled in a forced manner, we recognized that oral transmission conveyed a set of analytic practices that emphatically drew attention to the very features of the text that give rise to them in the first place. The work of Chapter 4, in conjunction with the conclusions of Chapter 2, helped us recognize that the ambient intellectual environment that was created and perpetuated by Mishnah study played an enormous role in shaping how the text was received and understood. When we reflect on it, it may seem to be a bit of a paradox. The mishnaic text served as a springboard and helped create the intellectual character of an animated world of study. The particular ways of thinking about legal issues that were cultivated in this environment in turn influenced how the text of the Mishnah was interpreted. In an ironic way, the mishnaic text helped create the social performative culture and ultimately the intellectual lens through which it was, in turn, viewed.

As I hope to have shown, then, transmitting Mishnah was hardly a passive exercise in rote memorization or mindless regurgitation. Rather, those who transmitted Mishnah played an active role in shaping not only the vagaries of its concrete formulation but also, and equally importantly, the intellectual environs within which it was received.

Bibliography

Albeck, Chanoch. *Introduction to the Mishnah* (Hebrew). Jerusalem, Tel Aviv: Dvir, 1959.

Alexander, Elizabeth Shanks. "Study Practices That Made the Mishnah: Evolution of a Tradition of Exegesis." Ph.D. diss., Yale University, 1999.

"Art, Argument and Ambiguity in the Talmud: Conflicting Representations of the Evil Impulse." *Hebrew Union College Annual* 73 (2002): 97–132.

"Casuistic Elements in Mishnaic Law: Examples from Tractate Shevuot." *Jewish Studies Quarterly* 10, no. 3 (November 2003): 189–243.

"The Orality of Rabbinic Writing." In *Cambridge Companion to Rabbinic Literature*, edited by Charlotte Fonrobert and Martin Jaffee. Forthcoming.

Alt, Albrecht. "The Origins of Israelite Law." In *Essays on Old Testament History and Religion*, 103–71. Garden City, NY: Anchor, 1966.

Benovitz, Moshe. "A Critical Commentary on Chapter III of Tractate Shevuot in the Babylonian Talmud." Ph.D. diss., Jewish Theological Seminary of America, 1993.

Bokser, Baruch. "Jacob N. Epstein's *Introduction to the Text of the Mishnah*." In *The Modern Study of the Mishnah*, edited by Jacob Neusner, 13–36. Leiden: E. J. Brill, 1973.

Bottéro, Jean. *Mesopotamia: Writing, Reasoning and the Gods*. Chicago: University of Chicago Press, 1992.

Brody, Robert. *The Geonim of Babylonia and the Shaping of Medieval Jewish Culture*. New Haven, CT: Yale University Press, 1998.

Brüll, Jacob. *Introduction to the Mishnah* (Hebrew). Vol 2. Frankfurt-am-Main, 1876.

Calinescu, Matei. "Orality in Literacy: Some Historical Paradoxes of Reading." *Yale Journal of Criticism* 6, no. 2 (1993): 175–90.

Carruthers, Mary. *The Book of Memory: A Study of Memory in Medieval Culture.* New York: Cambridge University Press, 1990.

The Craft of Thought: Meditation, Rhetoric and the Making of Images, 400–1200. New York: Cambridge University Press, 1998.

Cassuto, U. *A Commentary on the Book of Exodus.* Translated by Israel Abrahams. Jerusalem: Magnes Press, 1967.

Clements, Ronald E. *Exodus.* The Cambridge Bible Commentary. Cambridge: Cambridge University Press, 1972.

Cohen, Aryeh. *Rereading Talmud: Gender, Law and the Poetics of* Sugyot. Atlanta: Scholars Press, 1998.

Cohen, Shaye J. D. "The Significance of Yavneh: Pharisees, Rabbis and the End of Jewish Sectarianism." *Hebrew Union College Annual* 55 (1984): 27–53.

Dünner, Joseph Hirsch (Tzvi). *Hidushe Ha-Ritsad: Hagahot, Perushim, Be'urim àl Ha-Bavli Veha-Yerushalmi,* Vol. 3: *Nezikin.* Jerusalem: Mosad Ha-Rav Kuk, 1981.

Elman, Yaakov. "It Is No Empty Thing: Nahmanides and the Search for Omnisignificance." *Torah U-Madda Journal* 4 (1993), 1–83.

Authority and Tradition: Toseftan Baraitot in Talmudic Babylonia. Hoboken, NJ: Ktav Publishing House, 1994.

"Order, Sequence and Selection: The Mishnah's Anthological Choices." In *The Anthology in Jewish Literature,* edited by David Stern, 53–80. New York: Oxford University Press, 2004.

Elon, Menachem. *Jewish Law: History, Sources, Principles* (Ha-Mishpat Ha-Ivri). Vol. 3. Translated by Bernard Auerbach and Melvin J. Sykes. Philadelphia: Jewish Publication Society, 1994.

Epstein, J. N. *Introduction to Tannaitic Literature: Mishnah, Tosephta, and Halakhic Midrashim* (Hebrew). Edited by E. Z. Melamed. Jerusalem: Magnus Press, 1957.

Introduction to Amoraitic Literature: Babylonian Talmud and Yerushalmi (Hebrew). Edited by E. Z. Melamed. Jerusalem: Magnus Press, 1962.

Introduction to the Text of the Mishnah (Hebrew), 3d ed. Jerusalem and Tel Aviv: Magnes Press and Dvir, 2000.

Faur, Jose. *Golden Doves with Silver Dots: Semiotics and Textuality in Rabbinic Tradition.* Bloomington: Indiana University Press, 1986.

Finkelstein, J. J. "Sumerian Laws, YBC 2177." In *The Ancient Near East: Supplementary Texts and Pictures Relating to the Ancient Near East,* edited by James B. Pritchard, 525–26. Princeton, NJ: Princeton University Press, 1969.

The Ox That Gored. Philadelphia: The American Philosophical Society, 1981.

Finkelstein, Louis. "Midrash, Halakhot, and Aggadot" (Hebrew). In *Yitzhak Baer Jubilee Volume on the Occasion of His Seventieth Birthday,* edited by S. W. Baron et al., 28–46. Jerusalem: Historical Society of Israel, 1960.

Finnegan, Ruth. "Literacy vs. Non-Literacy: The Great Divide?" In *Modes of Thought: Essays on Thinking in Western and Non-Western Societies,* edited by Robin Horton and Ruth Finnegan, 112–44. London: Faber and Faber, 1973.

Oral Poetry: Its Nature, Significance and Social Context. Bloomington: Indiana University Press, 1977.

Literacy and Orality: Studies in the Technology of Communication. Oxford: Basil Blackwell, 1988.

Fitzpatrick-McKinley, Anne. *The Transformation of the Torah from Scribal Advice to Law.* Journal for the Study of the Old Testament Supplement Series. Sheffield, Eng.: Sheffield Academic Press, 1999.

Foley, John Miles. *The Theory of Oral Composition: History and Methodology.* Bloomington and Indianapolis: Indiana University Press, 1988.

Immanent Art: From Structure to Meaning in Traditional Oral Epic. Bloomington: Indiana University Press, 1991.

The Singer of Tales in Performance. Bloomington: Indiana University Press, 1995.

"Oral Tradition and Its Implications." In *A New Companion to Homer,* edited by Ian Morris and Barry Powell, 146–73. New York: Brill, 1997.

Fraade, Steven D. *From Tradition to Commentary: Torah and Its Interpretation in the Midrash Sifre to Deuteronomy.* Albany: State University of New York, 1991.

"Literary Composition and Oral Performance in Early Midrashim." *Oral Tradition* 14, no. 1 (March 1999): 33–51.

Frank, Yitzhak. *The Practical Talmud Dictionary.* Jerusalem: Ariel United Israel Institutes, 1992.

Frankel, Zacharias. *Methods of the Mishnah* (Hebrew). Tel Aviv: Sinai, 1959 (repr.).

Friedman, Shamma. "A Critical Study of Yevamot X with a Methodological Introduction" (Hebrew). *Texts and Studies: Analecta Judaica.* Vol. 1, edited by H. Z. Dimitrovsky, 275–441. New York, 1977.

"Historical Aggadah in the Babylonian Talmud" (Hebrew). In *Memorial Volume for R. Saul Lieberman,* edited by Shamma Friedman, 119–64. New York and Jerusalem: Jewish Theological Seminary, 1993.

"An Ancient Tosefta: On the Relationship of Parallels in the Mishnah and Tosefta (1): All Holy Writings (Shabbat 16:1)" (Hebrew). *Tarbiz* 62, no. 3 (1993): 313–38.

"An Ancient Tosefta: On the Relationship of Parallels in the Mishnah and Tosefta (2): The Story of Rabban Gamaliel and the Elders" (Hebrew). *Bar Ilan Sefer Ha-Shanah* 26–27 (1995): 277–88.

"The Primacy of Tosefta to Mishna in Synoptic Parallels." In *Introducing Tosefta: Textual, Intratexual, and Intertextual Studies,* edited by Tirzah Meacham, Harry Fox, and Diane Kriger, 99–121. N.P.: Ktav Publishing House, 1999.

"Uncovering Literary Dependencies in the Talmudic Corpus." In *The Synoptic Problem in Rabbinic Literature,* edited by Shaye J. D. Cohen, 35–57. Providence, RI: Brown Judaic Studies, 2000.

Tosefta Atiqta. Pesah Rishon: Synoptic Parallels of Mishna and Tosefta Analyzed with a Methodological Introduction (Hebrew). Ramat-Gan: Bar Ilan University Press, 2002.

Gerhardsson, Birger. *Memory and Manuscript: Oral Tradition and Written Transmission in Rabbinic Judaism and Early Christianity.* Grand Rapids, MI: William B. Eerdmans Publishing, 1961, repr. 1998.

Goldberg, Abraham. "Purpose and Method in Rabbi Judah Hannasi's Compilation of the Mishnah" (Hebrew). *Tarbiz* 28 (1958–59): 260–69 (English abstract, II–IV).

"Everyone According to the System of R. Akiva" (Hebrew). *Tarbiz* 38 (1969): 231–54.

"The Babylonian Talmud." In *The Literature of the Sages: First Part: Oral Torah, Halakha, Mishna, Tosefta, Talmud, External Tractates,* edited by Shmuel Safrai, 323–45. Philadelphia: Fortress Press, 1987.

"The Mishnah – A Study Book of Halakha." In *The Literature of the Sages,* edited by Shmuel Safrai, 211–51. Philadelphia: Fortress Press, 1987.

"The Tosefta: Companion to the Mishna." In *The Literature of the Sages,* edited by Shmuel Safrai, 283–301. Philadelphia: Fortress Press, 1987.

Goldenberg, Robert. "The Talmud." In *Back to the Sources: Reading the Classic Jewish Texts,* edited by Barry Holtz, 129–75. New York: Simon and Schuster, 1984.
Goodblatt, David M. *Rabbinic Instruction in Sasanian Babylonia.* Leiden: E. J. Brill, 1975.
Gray, Alyssa. "A Talmud in Exile: The Influence of PT Avodah Zarah on the Formation of BT Avodah Zarah." Ph.D. diss., Graduate School of the Jewish Theological Seminary, 2001.
Guttman, Alexander. *Rabbinic Judaism in the Making.* Detroit: Wayne State University Press, 1970.
Guttmann, Yehiel M. "Academic Questions in the Talmud" (Hebrew). *Devir* 2 (1923): 101–64.
Halbertal, Moshe. *People of the Book: Canon, Meaning and Authority.* Cambridge, MA: Harvard University Press, 1997.
Halivni, David Weiss. *Sources and Traditions: A Source Critical Commentary on Seder Nashim* (Hebrew). Tel Aviv: Dvir Publishing House, 1968.
Sources and Traditions: A Source Critical Commentary on Seder Moed (Hebrew). New York: Jewish Theological Seminary, 1975.
"The Reception Accorded to Rabbi Judah's Mishnah." In *Jewish and Christian Self-Definition,* Vol. 2, *Aspects of Judasim in the Graeco-Roman Period,* edited by E. P. Sanders with A. I. Baumgarten and Alan Mendelson, 204–12. London: SCM Press, 1981.
Midrash, Mishnah and Gemara: The Jewish Predilection for Justifed Law. Cambridge, MA: Harvard University Press, 1986.
Sources and Traditions: A Source Critical Commentary on Tractate Baba Kamma (Hebrew). Jerusalem: Magnus Press, 1993.
Handelman, Susan. "The 'Torah' of Criticism and the Criticism of Torah: Recuperating the Pedagogical Moment." In *Interpreting Judaism in a Postmodern Age,* edited by Steven Kepnes, 221–39. New York: New York University Press, 1996.
Harrington, Hannah. *The Impurity Systems of Qumran and the Rabbis.* Atlanta: Scholars Press, 1993.
"The Halakhah and Religion at Qumran." In *Religion in the Dead Sea Scrolls,* edited by John Collins and Robert Kugler. Grand Rapids, MI: Eerdmans, 2000.
"The Relationship Between Scripture and Mishnah." Paper presented at the American Academy of Religion/Society of Biblical Literature. Denver, November 2001.

"The Rabbinic Reception of Leviticus." In *The Book of Leviticus: Composition and Reception*, vol. 93, edited by Rolf Rendtorff and Robert A. Kugler, Supplements to Vetus Testamentum, 383–401. Leiden: Brill, 2003.

Harris, Jay M. *How Do We Know This?: Midrash and the Fragmentation of Modern Judaism.* Albany: State University of New York Press, 1986.

Hauptman, Judith. "Mishnah as a Response to 'Tosefta.'" In *The Synoptic Problem in Rabbinic Literature,* edited by Shaye J. D. Cohen. Providence, RI: Brown Judaic Studies, 2000.

Hayes, Christine. *Between the Babylonian and Palestinian Talmuds: Accounting for Halakhic Differences in Selected Sugyot from Tractate Avodah Zarah.* New York: Oxford University Press, 1997.

Heszer, Catherine. "The Codification of Legal Knowledge in Late Antiquity: The Talmud Yerushalmi and Roman Law Codes." In *The Talmud Yerushalmi in Graeco-Roman Culture,* edited by Peter Schafer, 581–642. Tubingen: J. C. B. Mohr (Paul Siebeck), 1998.

"The Mishnah and Ancient Book Production." In *The Mishnah in Contemporary Perspective,* edited by Alan J. Avery-Peck and Jacob Neusner, 167–92. Boston and Leiden: Brill, 2002.

Houtman, Alberdina. *Mishnah and Tosefta: A Synoptic Comparison of the Tractates Berakhot and Shebiit.* Texte und Studien Zum Antiken Judentum. Tubingen: J. C. B. Mohr (Paul Siebeck), 1996.

Huss, Boaz. "*Sefer Ha-Zohar* as a Canonical, Sacred and Holy Text: Changing Perspectives of the Book of Splendor Between the Thirteenth and Eighteenth Centuries." *Journal of Jewish Thought and Philosophy* 7 (1998): 257–307.

Jacobs, Louis. *Teyku: The Unsolved Problem in the Babylonian Talmud.* New York: Cornwall Books, 1981.

The Talmudic Argument: A Study in Talmudic Reasoning and Methodology. Cambridge: Cambridge University Press, 1984.

Jaffee, Martin S. "Oral Torah in Theory and Practice: Aspects of Mishnah-Exegesis in the Palestinian Talmud." *Religion* 15 (1985): 387–410.

"Writing and Rabbinic Oral Tradition: On Mishnaic Narrative, Lists and Mnemonics." *Journal of Jewish Philosophy and Thought* 4 (1994): 123–46.

"A Rabbinic Ontology of the Written and Spoken Word: On Discipleship, Transformative Knowledge and the Living Texts of Oral Torah." *Journal of the American Academy of Religion* 65, no. 3 (Fall 1997): 27–61.

"The Oral-Cultural Matrix of the Talmud Yerushalmi: Greco-Roman Rhetorical Paideia, Discipleship, and the Concept of Oral Torah." In *The*

Talmud Yerushalmi in Graeco-Roman Culture, edited by Peter Schäfer, 27–61. Tubingden: J. C. B. Mohr (Paul Siebeck), 1998.

"Oral Tradition in the Writings of Rabbinic Oral Torah: On Theorizing Rabbinic Orality." *Oral Tradition* 14, no. 1 (March 1999): 3–32.

Torah in the Mouth: Writing and Oral Tradition in Palestinian Judaism, 200 BCE–400 CE. New York: Oxford University Press, 2001.

Jastrow, Marcus. *A Dictionary of the Targumim, the Talmud Babli, and Yerushalmi, and the Midrashaic Literature.* New York: Judaica Press, 1989.

Kalmin, Richard. *The Redaction of the Babylonian Talmud: Amoraic or Saboraic?* Monographs of the Hebrew Union College. Cincinnati, OH: Hebrew Union College Press, 1989.

Kaplan, Julius. *The Redaction of the Babylonian Talmud.* New York: Bloch Publishing Company, 1933.

Kehati, Pinchas. *Seder Nezikin, Pt. 2.* Vol. 8 of *Mishnah with Commentary* (Hebrew). Jerusalem: Hekhal Shlomo, 1977.

Klein, Hyman. "Gemara and Sebara." *Jewish Quarterly Review* 38 (1947): 67–91.

"Gemara Quotations in Sebara." *Jewish Quarterly Review* 43 (1953): 341–63.

"Some Methods of Sebara." *Jewish Quarterly Review* 50 (1959): 124–46.

Kraemer, David. *The Mind of the Talmud: An Intellectual History of the Bavli.* New York and Oxford: Oxford University Press, 1990.

Reading the Rabbis: The Talmud as Literature. New York and Oxford: Oxford University Press, 1996.

Kraus, Fritz. "Ein Zentrales Problem Des Altmesopotamischen Rechtes: Was ist der Codex Hammurabi?" *Genava* 8 (1960): 283–96.

Kugel, James L. *The Idea of Biblical Poetry: Parallelism and Its History.* New Haven, CT: Yale University Press, 1981.

"Two Introductions to Midrash." In *Midrash and Literature,* edited by Geoffrey H. Hartman and Sandford Budick, 77–103. New Haven, CT: Yale University Press, 1986.

In Potiphar's House: The Interpretive Life of Biblical Texts. Cambridge, MA: Harvard University Press, 1990.

The Bible as It Was. Cambridge, MA: Belknap Press of Harvard University Press, 1997.

Lapin, Hayim. *Early Rabbinic Civil Law and the Social History of Roman Galilee: A Study of Mishnah Tractate Baba' Mesi'a.'* Atlanta: Scholars Press, 1995.

Lauterbach, Jacob Z. "Midrash and Mishnah." In *Rabbinic Essays,* 163–256. Cincinnati, OH: Hebrew Union College Press, 1915, repr. 1951.

Leighty, Erle. *The Omen Series Šumma Izbu.* Locust Valley, NY: J. J. Augustin, 1970.

Lewin, B. M., ed. *Iggeret Rav Sherira Gaon: The Spanish Text and the French Text* (Hebrew). Haifa: Itzokofsky, 1921.

Lieberman, Saul. *Hellenism in Jewish Palestine.* New York: Jewish Theological Seminary of America, 1994.

Lord, Albert B. *The Singer of Tales.* 2nd ed. Edited by Stephen Mitchell and Gregory Nagy. Cambridge, MA, and London: Harvard University Press, 2000.

MacKenzie, R.A.F., S. J. "The Formal Aspect of Ancient Near Eastern Law." In *The Seed of Wisdom: Essays in Honor of T. J. Meek,* edited by W. S. McCullough, 31–44. Toronto: University of Toronto Press, 1964.

McLuhan, Marshall. *The Gutenberg Galaxy: The Making of Typographic Man.* London: Routledge and Kegan Paul, 1962.

Menahem ben Shlomo (Hameiri). *Perushei Hamishnah l' Hameiri.* Vol.5, edited by Menachem Mendel Meshi Zahur. Jerusalem: Dvar, 1974.

Milgrom, Jacob. *Leviticus 1–16: A New Translation with Introduction and Commentary.* The Anchor Bible. New York: Doubleday, 1991.

Moscovitz, Leib. *Talmudic Reasoning: From Casuistics to Conceptualization.* Tübingen: Mohr Siebeck, 2002.

Nahum Sarna. *Exodus.* The JPS Torah Commentary. Philadelphia: The Jewish Publication Society, 1991.

Najman, Hindy. *Seconding Sinai: The Development of Mosaic Discourse in Second Temple Judasim.* Leiden: E. J. Brill, 2002.

Neusner, Jacob. *The Modern Study of the Mishnah.* Leiden: E. J. Brill, 1973.

A History of the Mishnaic Law of Purities: The Redaction and Formulation of the Order of Purities in Mishnah and Tosefta. Studies in Judaism in Late Antiquity. Leiden: E. J. Brill, 1977.

A History of the Mishnaic Law of Damages, Part 5: The Mishnaic System of Damages. Studies in Judaism in Late Antiquity. Leiden: E. J. Brill, 1985.

Oral Tradition in Judaism: The Case of the Mishnah. New York: Garland Publishing, 1987.

Judaism: The Evidence of the Mishnah. Atlanta: Scholars Press, 1988.

The Mishnah: An Introduction. Northvale, NJ: Jason Aronson, 1989.

The Tosefta: An Introduction. Atlanta: Scholars Press, 1992.

Neusner, Jacob, trans. *The Talmud of the Land of Israel: A Preliminary Translation and Explanation.* Vol. 32. *Shebuot.* Chicago: University of Chicago Press, 1983.

The Mishnah: A New Translation. New Haven, CT: Yale University Press, 1988.
Ong, Walter J. *Orality and Literacy: The Technologizing of the Word.* London and New York: Methuen, 1982.
Parry, Milman. "L'epithète traditionelle dans Homère." In *The Making of Homeric Verse: The Collected Papers of Milman Parry,* edited by Adam Parry, 1–190. Oxford: Clarendon Press, 1928, repr. 1971.
The Making of Homeric Verse: The Collected Papers of Milman Parry. Edited by Adam Parry. New York and Oxford: Oxford University Press, 1987.
Paul, Shalom. "Cuneiform and Biblical Legal Formulations." In *Studies in the Book of the Covenant in Light of Cuneiform and Biblical Law,* 112–24. Leiden: E. J. Brill, 1970.
Pease, Donald E. "Author." In *Critical Terms for Literary Study,* edited by Frank Lentricchia and Thomas McLaughlin, 105–17. Chicago: University of Chicago Press, 1990.
Rabinowich, Rabbi Nosson Dovid, trans. and annotation. *The Iggeres of Rav Sherira Gaon.* Jerusalem: Rabbi Jacob Joseph School Press – Ahavath Torah Institute, 1988.
Rovner, Jay. "Rhetorical Strategy and Dialectical Necessity in the Babylonian Talmud: The Case of Kiddushin 34a-35a." *Hebrew Union College Annual* 65 (1994): 177–223.
Rubenstein, Jeffrey L. "On Some Abstract Concepts in Rabbinic Literature." *Jewish Studies Quarterly* 4 (1997): 33–73.
Talmudic Stories: Narrative Art, Composition, and Culture. Baltimore and London: The Johns Hopkins University Press, 1999.
The Culture of the Babylonian Talmud. Baltimore and London: The Johns Hopkins University Press, 2003.
Safrai, Shmuel. "Oral Tora." In *The Literature of the Sages,* edited by Shmuel Safrai, 35–120. Philadelphia: Fortress Press, 1987.
Sanders, E. P. "Jacob Neusner and the Philosophy of the Mishnah." In *Jewish Law from Jesus to the Mishnah: Five Studies,* 304–31. Philadephia: Trinity Press International, 1990.
Schäfer, Peter. "Research into Rabbinic Literature: An Attempt to Define the Status Quaestionis." *Journal of Jewish Studies* 37, no. 2 (1986): 139–52.
Schiffman, Lawrence. *From Text to Tradition: A History of Second Temple Judaism and Rabbinic Judaism.* Hoboken, NJ: Ktav Publishing House, 1991.

Shemesh, Aharon. *Punishments and Sins: From the Bible to Rabbinic Literature* (Hebrew). Jerusalem: Magnes Press, 2003.
Silberg, Moshe. *Talmudic Law and the Modern State.* Translated by Ben Zion Bokser. New York: Burning Bush Press, 1973.
Smith, Jonathan Z. "Sacred Persistence: Towards a Redescription of Canon." In *Approaches to Ancient Judaism,* edited by William Scott Green, 19–27. Missoula, MO: Scholars Press, 1978.
Soloveitchik, Joseph B. *Halakhic Man.* Philadelphia: The Jewish Publication Society of America, 1983.
Steinsaltz, Adin. *The Talmud: The Steinsaltz Edition: A Reference Guide.* New York: Random House, 1989.
Stock, Brian. *The Implications of Literacy: Written Language and Models of Interpretation in the Eleventh and Twelfth Centuries.* Princeton, NJ: Princeton University Press, 1983.
Strack, H. L., and G. Stemberger. *Introduction to the Talmud and Midrash.* Translated by Markus Bockmuehl. Minneapolis, MN: Fortress Press, 1992.
Sunstein, Cass. *Legal Reasoning and Political Conflict.* New York: Oxford University Press, 1996.
Sussmann, Yaacov. "Once More on y. Nezikin" (Hebrew). In *Mehqerei Talmud,* edited by Yaacov Sussmann and David Rosenthal, 55–133. Jerusalem: Magnes Press, 1990.
Talmud Yerushalmi According to Ms. Or 4720 (Scal.3) of the Leiden University Library with Restorations and Corrections. Jerusalem: The Academy of Hebrew Language, 2001.
Thomas, Rosalind. *Literacy and Orality in Ancient Greece.* Key Themes in Ancient History. Cambridge: Cambridge University Press, 1992.
Ulrich, Eugene. *The Dead Sea Scrolls and the Origins of the Bible.* Grand Rapids, MI: Eerdmans, 1999.
"From Literature to Scripture: Reflections on the Growth of a Text's Authoritativeness." *Dead Sea Discoveries* 10, no. 1 (2003): 3–25.
Urbach, Ephraim E. *The Halakhah: Its Sources and Development.* Translated by Raphael Posner. Tel Aviv: Modan Publishing House, 1996.
Westbrook, Raymond. "Biblical and Cuneifrom Law Codes." *Revue Biblique* 92, no. 2 (April 1985): 247–64.
Studies in Biblical and Cuneiform Law. Paris: J. Gabalda et Cie., Editeurs, 1988.
Property and Family in Biblical Law. Journal for the Study of the Old Testament Supplement Series. Sheffield, Eng.: JSOT Press, 1991.

“What is the Covenant Code?” In *Theory and Method in Biblical and Cuneiform Law: Revision, Interpolation and Development,* edited by Bernard Levinson. JSOT Supplement Series 181. Sheffield, Eng.: Sheffield Academic Press, 1994.

Wewers, Gerd A., trans. *Talmud Yerushalmi Band IV/5 Makkot – Geißelung, Shevuot – Schwüre.* Tübingen: J. C. B. Mohr (Paul Siebeck), 1983.

Yaron, Reuven. “Forms in the Laws of Eshnuna.” *Revue Internationale des droits de l'antiquite, 3e Série* 9 (1962): 137–53.

Laws of Eshnuna. Jerusalem: Magnes Press, 1969.

Zaiman, Joel H. “The Traditional Study of the Mishnah.” In *The Modern Study of the Mishnah,* edited by Jacob Neusner, 1–12. Leiden: E. J. Brill, 1973.

Zlotnick, Dov. *The Iron Pillar – Mishnah: Redaction, Form, and Intent.* Jerusalem: Ktav Publishing House, 1988.

Index

Lightning Source UK Ltd.
Milton Keynes UK
UKHW01f2146080918
328580UK00001B/28/P

9 780521 104623